LYING-IN

LYING-IN

A History of Childbirth in America

Richard W. Wertz
and
Dorothy C. Wertz

SCHOCKEN BOOKS · NEW YORK

First published by Schocken Books 1979
10 9 8 7 6 5 4 3 2 1   79 80 81 82

Published by arrangement with The Free Press

Library of Congress Cataloging in Publication Data

Wertz, Richard W.
  Lying-in.

  Bibliography: p.
  Includes index.
  1. Obstetrics—United States—History. 2. Childbirth—United States—History. 3. Obstetrics—Social
aspects—United States—History. 4. Maternal health
services—United States—History. I. Wertz, Dorothy C.,
joint author. II. Title.
RG518.U5W47 1979   618.2'00973   78-26045

Manufactured in the United States of America

Acknowledgments

GEORGE J. ENGELMANN, *Labor Among Primitive Peoples*, St. Louis, 1882. See pages 14 and 15.

HENDRIK VAN DEVENTER, *Operationum Chirurgicarum Novum Lumen Exhibentium Obstetricantibus*, Pars Primum, Leyden, 1733. See page 14.

EUCHARIUS ROESSLIN, *Der Swangern Frauwen und hebammen Rosegarten*, Strassburg, 1513. See page 14.

THOMAS RAYNALDE, *The Byrth of Mankinde*, London, 1598. See page 16.

JACQUES-PIERRE MAYGRIER, *Nouvelles Demonstrations D'Accouchemens*, Paris, 1822. See pages 31, 36, 38, 78, 84, and 88.

FRANÇOIS MAURICEAU, *Des Malades des Femmes Grossés et Accouchées*, Paris, 1668. See pages 32, 35, and 102

ANDRÉ LEVRET, *L'art des Accouchemens*, Paris, 1761. See page 33.

J. C. ULLERY and M. A. CASTALLO, *Obstetric Mechanisms and Their Management*, Philadelphia, F. A. Davis, 1957. Reproduced with permission. See page 36.

WILLIAM SMELLIE, *An Abridgement of the Practice of Midwifery and a Set of Anatomical Tables*, Boston, 1786. See page 37.

JOHN BLUNT, *Man-Midwifery Dissected*, London, 1793. See page 41.

Seventeenth-century French print. See page 43.

WOOSTER BEACH, *An Improved System of Midwifery*, New York, 1847. See pages 45 and 111.

Frank Leslie's Illustrated Weekly Newspaper, New York, April 16, 1870. See page 53.

BARTON COOKE HIRST, *A Textbook of Obstetrics*, Philadelphia, W. B. Saunders Co., 1918. See page 90.

Dr. McIntosh Natural Uterine Supporter Co., Chicago, ca. 1881, advertising circular. See page 103.

JAMES ASHTON, M.D., *The Book of Nature: Containing Information for young people Who Think of Getting Married, On the Philosophy of Procreation and Sexual Intercourse showing How to Prevent Conception and To Avoid Child-bearing*, New York, 1861. See page 104.

BENJAMIN GRANT JEFFERIS and J. L. NICHOLS, *Search Light on Health: Light on Dark Corners*, Parkersburg, W. Va., 1904. See page 111.

ROBERTO MARGOTTA, *An Illustrated History of Medicine*, Feltham, Middlesex: Hamlyn Publishing Group, 1968. Reproduced with permission. See page 116.

HAROLD SPEERT, *Iconographia Gyniatrica*, Philadelphia: F. A. Davis, 1973. See page 134.

EDWARD F. STEVENS, *The American Hospital of the Twentieth Century*, New York, 1918. See page 134.

Courtesy of Lane Bryant, Inc. See page 149.

Archives of the Schlesinger Library, Radcliffe College, Cambridge, Mass. See pages 151 and 153.

The Roosevelt Hospital, 1871–1957, New York, Roosevelt Hospital, 1957. Reproduced with permission. See page 154.

NICHOLSON J. EASTMAN, *Williams Obstetrics*, 11th Edition, New York: Appleton-Century-Crofts, 1956. See page 166. Twelfth edition, 1961. See page 171. Reproduced with permission.

JIM HARRISON. See pages 184 and 238. Reproduced with permission.

THOMAS WASHINGTON SHANNON, *Nature's Secrets Revealed,* Marietta Ohio, 1920. See page 207.

Mississippi State Board of Health, *Manual for Midwives, 1927.* See page 214.

CHARLES E. TERRY, "Save the Seventh Baby," *Delineator* 92, October 1917. See page 216.

Contents

Introduction

For ye shall heare some women in tyme of theyr trauayle, meued through great payne and intollerable anguyshe, forswere and vowe them selfe, neuer to companye with a man agayne; yet after that the panges be passed, within short whyle, for entyre loue to theyr husbandes, and singular naturall delyte betwene man and woman, they forget both the sorow passed and that is to come. Such be the privie works of God, and such be the prickes of nature, which neuer createth no special pleasure unaccompanied with some sorrow.

Thomas Raynalde, The Byrth of Mankynd, *1545*

Thomas Raynalde observed in 1545 that women forget the great pain and intolerable anguish of birth and, out of love for their husbands and because of "singular naturall delyte" between man and woman, "companye with a man agayne." Pleasure in procreation and sorrow in birth resulted from the purposes of God and Nature, Raynalde thought, but he also believed it entirely appropriate to introduce more pleasure to birth. *The Byrth of Mankynd* was the first English manual of childbirth advice, the first of many attempts to tell people what birth was, how they should accomplish it successfully, and how they should relate to one another while doing so.

Most later writers on childbirth have shared Raynalde's conviction that between Providence and biology, between "the privie works of God and . . . the prickes of nature," there is room for the intentions of third parties. Birth has thus been a social event; a gathering of people with comfort, skills, and knowledge to offer; a kind of social construction that looks with awe upon fate and grapples with nature. Because people have understood and shaped birth in changing ways, both the means and the meaning of childbirth have a history, an extraordinary one because childbirth is at once a creative act, a biological happening, and a social event.

The aim of this book is to describe how Americans have understood and accomplished birth during the past 350 years or so. In part it is a story of changes in the settings, participants, understandings, and feelings of birth. The scene of birth shifts, for example, from bedroom or kitchen in the family home to the hospital, from a place with family and friends to a place with hired workers and machines. The midwife gives way to the family doctor, who in turn yields to the obstetrical specialist as the one who "stands before" the expectant and laboring woman with technical aids. The character of the aids themselves alters markedly: Oil of lilies to "sople the privie parts" becomes the pudendal block, opium becomes scopolamine. The woman who faces the fear of death comforted by friends and by religion becomes the woman who may elect to feel nothing, neither pain nor fear, under the technical comforts of medicine. Childbirth as a social event aided by the cunning of women becomes a medical event aided by the tools and skills of men. Childbirth as an act of God becomes a medical indicator of the health of the whole society.

These fascinating transformations do not explain themselves. Nor do they explain why rituals of birth in America developed along different lines from those in other countries. A history of birth must look beyond the event of birth itself. Doctors replaced midwives during the nineteenth century to a markedly greater extent in America than in other countries, for example; to learn why, one must know something about the historical processes in American medicine and in the roles of women. Along with the story of birth there must be analysis of the reasons for change.

We see the central and unique aspect of American birth in its being viewed as a potentially diseased condition that *routinely* requires the arts of medicine to overcome the processes of nature. Our object is to ask how this view originated. Certainly it did not result simply from medical conspiracy or villainy; certainly also it benefited birth enormously. Yet it is still important to ask what the reification of birth as pathogenesis has meant for patients, for health, and for medical practice. Birth is, after all, not like cancer or diseases of the heart. How, then, did it come to be regarded as a recurrent illness?

We believe a history of how Americans have accomplished delivery will interest many people, not the least because it is a ritual that people are still recreating in response to new medical knowledge and new styles of life.

We have titled this history *Lying-In* rather than, say, *Childbirth* to emphasize that birth is more than biology and that our concern lies with its social and cultural as well as its purely medical aspects. "Lying-in" was the name early Americans gave to the event of birth and recuperation. Later, they applied the term to the first maternity hospitals to describe the multiple dimensions of birth hospitals encompassed.

The research for this book began in 1972 after an advocate of home birth, speaking in one of our classes, led us to wonder what had caused earlier alterations in birth practices. Since that time many books on the history of women, of the family, and of health have appeared, including some on birth. For that reason, we think it right to alert readers to what this book is and is not.

This is not a history of obstetrics as a science or as a profession; it does not detail doctors' lives or progress in knowledge and practice. Such histories have been written before and have their value. Rather, this book explores how attitudes and practices of birth have come about, how they have changed, and what they mean for patients and for health. It does not see the history of birth in terms of medical discovery alone, for that aspect, while important, is too narrow to explain the transformations and significance of birth rituals. Birth is always the product of interacting cultural, social, and medical preferences. Beliefs about proper roles for men and women, for example, have continually shaped birth rituals. This is the history, then, of a complex and changing social construction, the results of intentions as well as techniques, of disease as well as perceptions of it, of mistakes as well as successes.

Since birth has been elemental in the behavior of women and families, its character and practice have been deeply influenced by many matters: changing sex roles, abortion, family planning, feminism, work, and other behavioral changes. We soon realized that a history of birth had broad social scope and thus had to have limits. We discuss such social matters only as we have judged them important to the shaping of birth practices. Therefore readers who are interested in a thorough history of abortion, for example, should look elsewhere.

We have mentioned that we do not think transformations in birth resulted solely from medical developments. We also do not believe that such developments have been invariably progressive. This will not be a whiggish history in which everything becomes better and better because of enlightened practical science. On the other hand, however, we do not share the view that what is wrong with birth is the simple result of doctors' greed, power hunger, insensitivity, or inordinate fondness for technique. Perhaps it is best to say this is not advocacy or ideology but an attempt at a critical and analytic history. In the Epilogue we do offer some judgments about appropriate actions and perspectives.

Also, we want to comment about our method, especially about the difficulty of writing in the absence of conclusive empirical evidence. Up to the twentieth century no nationwide records exist to illuminate birth in regard to its sickness and death, its attendants, its costs, or even its frequencies. Although demographic historians have assembled data from scattered early communities as well as later towns and localities, one cannot form a statistical profile of birth during the 350 years of American life. There results an inevitable tentativeness in discussions about the effectiveness of midwives or comparisons of their practice with the practice of trained physicians before the twentieth century, when, for the first time, statistics about morbidity and mortality unmistakenly improve. But of course there are other records about birth in earlier periods and we have drawn from the whole variety, hoping to portray, if not the statistics of birth, at least its character, its organization and its meaning. In this we believe we have come close to accuracy, and although we fully expect that new manuscript evidence will emerge, we believe new evidence will not disestablish the evidence we have used. The judgments we have made about this evidence are subject to review, but that of course is the nature of historical study, and we welcome renewed attention to this aspect of American social history.

Because we conceived this book to interest the general reader, we have included a bibliography of the most significant sources for those who wish to pursue aspects of childbirth. It is not exhaustive since we think most readers would not have access to a reference library. On the other hand, most of the important scholarly works are cited in footnotes.

Finally, we must express our indebtedness for many acts of assistance and suggestive criticism to Richard Wolfe and his staff in the rare book library at Harvard Medical School, to the staff of the Yale Medical Library, and to James Reed, Mary Roth Walsh, Mary Howell, Joan E. Mulligan and Peter Reich.

Midwives and Social Childbirth in Colonial America

All things within this fading world hath end,
Adversity doth still our joys attend;
No ties so strong, no friends so dear and sweet,
But with death's parting blow is sure to meet.
The sentence past is most irrevocable,
A common thing, yet oh inevitable.
How soon, my Dear, death may my steps attend,
How soon't may be thy lot to lose thy friend,
We both are ignorant, yet love bids me
These farewell lines to recommend to thee,
That when that knot's untied that made us one,
I may seem thine, who in effect am none.

Anne Bradstreet (1612–1672), *"Before the Birth*
of One of Her Children"

WHEN the English settled in America they brought the traditional English customs and practices of childbirth to the New World. Most notably, the practices made birth the exclusive province of women, and this was to be true during most of the colonial period. Women attended and aided each other during birth itself and during the several weeks of "lying-in" that followed. Not until the revolutionary period did educated doctors seek to attend births. For more than 150 years, therefore, old birth customs prevailed in America: Expectant women looked to female friends and kin for aid and comfort—to a social childbirth—and turned to midwives for skillful attendance.

Birth in colonial America was much as it was in England at the time, but not exactly. More plentiful food and less crowding in the New World environment promoted health and thus, it appears, permitted childbirth to be more successful. Women and children died less often for reasons of birth in some American towns than in English towns of the same period. Also, it seems that the religious culture of some colonies eliminated more effectively than in England the magical practices long associated with birth. American women continued to manage birth, but they began to perceive its religious and natural dimensions differently.

The primary aim here is to reconstruct social childbirth and the work of the midwife, which are inherently interesting practices and which established important continuities in American women's lives. Social childbirth continued into the nineteenth century to be the primary occasion on which women expressed their love and care for one another and their mutual experience of life. Another aim is to examine New World women's perceptions of birth to learn why they were more disposed to accept doctors' care than were women in England and in European countries at the same time. Finally, a history of colonial childbirth should consider two persistent ideas about what birth was in the time before medical men appeared with new science and new medical arts. Many people think of midwives stereotypically as having been ignorant and dangerous women, so the quality of care American midwives provided merits attention. On the other hand, some have idealized colonial childbirth for having been an experience within the province of women, and have seen it as similar or even superior to today's natural childbirth for having been without medical (and male) interference. This idea also needs consideration.

～～～

In the colonies, English-born women continued long-standing rituals of birth; female friends and relatives came to the expectant woman to provide comfort and practical aid. The importance of those female rites—which we call social childbirth—becomes evident when one considers the exhausting demands of frequent childbearing and continued childrearing. For colonial women the practice of social childbirth acted as a palliative, a respite from incessant child care over a period of twenty to twenty-five years of their lives.

The pattern of prolonged childbearing meant that most of a woman's adult life was spent rearing children. The average age of women at marriage was usually around twenty-two, and the first child was born about sixteen months later. The last child, however, was not born until the woman was about forty, which meant that her last child might still be at home when she was sixty years of age, if she were still alive.[1] Such extended childbearing meant that most marriages were actually of shorter duration than the period of childrearing. In the eighteenth century, 69 percent of Quaker marriages were ended by the death of one of the spouses before the last child left home.[2] A woman's last child and first grandchild might be of the same age; she and her daughter might give birth in the same year. There was no lengthy period of a woman's life without the presence of children in the home.

Births usually occurred about fifteen to twenty months apart, because conception was biologically unlikely as long as a woman was still nursing an infant. The practice of breast-feeding to the age of at least one year was almost universal in the colonies, because hiring a wet-nurse was too expensive. (However, mothers who produced no milk had a wet-nurse, and Southern women often gave new babies to slave wet-nurses.) Where births occurred at shorter intervals than fifteen months, examination of the family records usually shows that the first baby died before the period of nursing would normally have ended. Some women nursed for two years, and some were aware that longer nursing postponed another pregnancy, though it is not known how often that was a reason for prolonged nursing.[3]

In some rural communities there was a seasonal periodicity to the arrival of children. Conceptions were lowest in September and October, when people worked around the clock gathering the harvest. In November, December, and January conceptions reached a secondary peak, then declined in February and March, ascended to a major peak in April, May, and June, and fell off rapidly in July and August. The same pattern appeared in rural France and may correlate not only with work demands and consequent exhaustion but also with nutritional variations. By the eighteenth century the seasonal pattern became less noticeable, though it persisted in rural areas until the early nineteenth century.[4]

Women were well aware of how such frequent childbearing taxed their energies and made performing household chores immediately before and after birth nearly impossible. Managing a household with children was simply so difficult and exhausting that the last stage of pregnancy, delivery itself, and the postpartum period would weaken and even kill a woman if she also had to continue her chores without help. The practices of social childbirth permitted the mother to "lie-in," to keep to her bed for three or four weeks, sometimes longer, while others took over the responsibility of the household. The mother was able to rest, to regain her strength, and to initiate her nursing and care for the new child without interruption.

Social childbirth included women who were not members of the family and who were not paid to attend. Many of them acted on the basis of reciprocity, in the expectation that others would care for them in their turn. Childbirth depended for its success upon more than the medical transaction between a woman and a midwife; it required the practical aid of kin and friends who not only attended the birth, to provide emotional support, but took over the household chores during the lying-in period. Ebenezer Parkman recorded in his diary for December 26, 1738:

> A little after 4 in the morning my Wife called Me up by her extreme pain prevailing upon her and changing into signs of Travail. I rode over to Deacon Forbush's and brought her [Mrs. Forbush] over as our midwife. Sister Hicks, old Mrs. Knowlton, Mrs. Whipple, Mrs. Hephzibath Maynard, Mrs. Byles and Mrs. Rogers were call'd and brought and stay'd all Day and Night.[5]

Mrs. Parkman's labor ceased and the women went home, except for the midwife, who remained until the following night, when, the pains having returned, Parkman rode about the neighborhood hastily reassembling the women.

In rare instances women who gave birth suddenly or who lived at some distance from neighbors delivered alone, without assistance of neighbor or midwife, but the normal practice was to make birth itself a social event for a coterie of women, whom the husband often assembled. In many instances the new mother had the assistance of her own mother, who might travel some distance to spend a month or two with her daughter and new grandchild. Older women, past childbearing age and perhaps friends of the grandmother, sometimes attended the birth and even aided during the lying-in period.[6]

The event of birth presented an important, perhaps the primary, occasion for female solidarity. Women could help in practical ways at birth, but they attended also, it may be supposed, because they sought to hearten the expectant woman, to share their own knowledge and experiences of birth, and to prepare themselves for their own future deliveries. The laboring woman must have gained confidence from being surrounded by women who had themselves suffered and survived, often to old age. The potential medical value of the psychological support these female friends offered should not be undervalued; the presence of women provided particular reassurance during a woman's first birth, helping her to relax and thus to ease her pain.

In New England, the new mother often reciprocated at the end of the lying-in period by giving a "groaning party" for all her women helpers. The term referred facetiously both to the groans of labor and to the groaning of the table and the women under the weight of food. The wife of Judge Sewall of Boston served "Boil'd Pork, Beef, Fowls: very Good Rost Beef, Turkey Pye, Tarts" to her seventeen helpers.[7] Such parties restored the woman to her neighbors' company, expressed her appreciation, and gave them a jolly and comradely compensation for their various efforts.

Some aspects of social childbirth endured long after the colonial period even though doctors largely replaced midwives, though many upper-class families had nurses and servants to do the chores of birth care and housekeeping, and though many family members lived at some distance from one another. Mothers, kinswomen, and some friends still made attendance at birth an important ritual, expressing their emotional support and care. When the daughters of Elizabeth Drinker, upper-class Philadelphians of the 1790s, delivered their children, they were attended by their mother, an aunt, and a neighbor, as well as by a midwife and a hired nurse. The family also called the doctor as a precautionary measure, for all its women had a tendency to have complicated deliveries.[8] Yet the female relatives and friends oversaw the births and exercised control over the physical aspects of the lying-in room and over care before and after delivery, although they did not necessarily perform the many tasks themselves. Indeed, nineteenth-century doctors, possibly feeling ill at ease under the watchful eyes of many women, were inclined to urge the removal of all from the delivery room except one, a hired nurse or a friend who would obey the doctor's orders.

There is reason to believe that social childbirth continued throughout much of the nineteenth century, long after middle-class families began to hire doctors to perform deliveries and other attendants to care for the mother. As long as it remained in the home, birth remained to large extent the province of women. Women selected the attendants, including the doctor, and were present to give support to the mother. Birth continued to be a fundamental occasion for the expression of care and love among women. Where hired help was unavailable or too expensive, female friends and kin also did the chores in the nineteenth century.

The second notable characteristic of birth in colonial America, besides the female rituals that made birth a social event, was the employment of the midwife. The name literally means "with-woman," a woman who is with a mother at birth. Sometimes her simple presence may have been considered contribution enough, for she could offer the laboring woman the reassurance of having witnessed many births. The first men of this period to attend births in England also kept the same linguistic form, calling themselves "male midwives" and their medical art "midwifery." In fact, medical historians have called the years before 1750 "the age of the midwife," for doctors were few.[9]

Since the colonial midwives came initially from England, English traditions prevailed in the colonies. Before and during the colonial period English society did not consider midwives to be part of the medical establishment or professions but saw them as performing a special social and quasi-religious function. That is, midwives did not formally train for their work, did not organize a guild to license midwives, and did not transmit skills by formal apprenticeships. Rather, midwives succeeded one another by selecting themselves, or being selected by other women, to attend births. The fund of knowledge about birth practices was widely shared among women who had given birth themselves and aided others to do so. A midwife had to satisfy the expectations of such groups of women. Many midwives probably came from networks of women who had aided one another in birth and were distinguished by such intangibles as manual dexterity, sensitivity, and luck. Many may have been older women, themselves past the childbearing age, who were available for the sometimes time-consuming work and possessed of certain admired moral qualities as well as physical abilities.

In the seventeenth century and before, English bishops were the only public authorities overseeing midwifery. The bishops had desired to prevent witchcraft associated with birth and to ensure that midwives were loyal to decrees of the church and state regarding birth, since midwives could baptize infants in emergencies. The bishops required that before beginning practice a midwife receive an episcopal license, which prohibited her from coercing fees, giving abortifacients, practicing magic, or concealing information about birth events or parentages from civil or religious authorities. The license also prohibited her from refusing to attend poor women. The bishops were concerned primarily with moral and civil order, yet they required a prospective midwife to show several affidavits from women that she had a "gentle touch." Historians of English midwifery say, however, that most midwives practiced without licenses and were not punished unless found to have committed irreligious or illegal acts.[10]

In the American colonies where the Anglican influence was most strongly felt, such as New York and Virginia, civil licensing of midwives was required. In 1716 New York City required licensing for midwives in an ordinance that echoed the episcopal licenses of England:

It is ordained that no woman within this corporation shall exercise the employment of midwife until she have taken oath before the mayor, recorder or an alderman to the following effect: That she shall be diligent and ready to help any woman in labor, whether poor or rich; that in time of necessity she will not forsake the poor woman and go to the rich; that she will not cause or suffer any woman to name or put any other father to the child, but only him which is the very true father thereof, indeed according to the utmost of her power; that she will not suffer any woman to pretend to be delivered of a child who is not, indeed, neither to claim any other woman's child for her own; that she will not suffer any woman's child to be murdered or hurt; and as often as she shall see any peril or jeopardy, either in the mother or child, she will call in other midwives for counsel; that she will not administer any medicine to produce miscarriage; that she will not force any woman to give more for her services than is right; that she will not collude to keep secret the birth of a child; will be of good behavior; will not conceal the birth of bastards.[11]

Such licenses in effect placed the midwife in the role of servant of the state, a keeper of social and civil order. There is considerable evidence that civil authorites counted on the reliable testimony of midwives. In court cases about bastardy, for instance, the court often assumed that the mother might have revealed the father's name to the midwife while in labor. In cases of infanticide, the court would summon a midwife to examine the accused woman to determine whether or not she had recently borne a child. Midwives were regularly included in the special "juries of matrons," whose function it was to report on the physical condition of a woman accused of crime (if pregnant, she could not be executed) or on a suspicious death of a woman. Church authorities in American colonies asked midwives to testify on the "age" of a newborn baby, if there were suspicion of its having resulted from fornication.

Many of the existing fragments of information about colonial midwives consist of church and court records. If they tell little about the midwives themselves, they do imply that the colonists accorded midwives considerable authority about women's physical condition, trusted them to speak knowledgeably and reliably, and treated midwives as if they were servants of the moral and civil order of the state.[12]

The importance of midwives to the social order is shown in the fact that several New England towns provided a house or lot rent-free to a midwife on condition that "she doth not refuse when called to it."[13] Non-English colonies often kept midwives on the colonial payroll. In New Amsterdam they were called Ziecken-troosters, or comforters of the sick, and received liberal salaries and special privileges. The Dutch West India Company salaried midwives and gave others free houses in the city on the explicit condition that they attend the poor upon request. The French colony in Louisiana paid midwives until 1756 and provided physicians regularly to examine the quality of their practice. Midwives in the South were usually slaves from large plantations who delivered both blacks and whites and whose services were used by smaller plantations and independent farmers.[14]

Midwives performed invaluable services in colonial communities, and, whether salaried or fee-charging, they often earned high honor for competent and lengthy service. The names of some midwives have come down through history because their communities memorialized their years of service. Mrs. Rebecca Fuller, wife of Dr. Samuel Fuller, practiced in Boston from 1630 to 1663. When she retired, her services were immediately sought by the town of Rehoboth in southeastern Massachusetts. Ruth Barnaby of Boston began to deliver babies in 1724 at the age of sixty and continued to do so for forty years. Elizabeth Phillips came to Boston in 1719 with a license from the Bishop of London and practiced for forty years. Her tombstone in Charlestown noted that she brought more than 3,000 children into the world. A Long Island midwife who practiced from 1745 to 1774 was reported to have delivered 1,300 children "and of that number, lost but two." Other colonies had equally revered midwives.[15]

Little is known about any midwife's life in the colonial years, but the diary of Mrs. Martha Moore Ballard gives the flavor of a rural midwife's life in Hallowell, Maine, during a thirty-four-year period immediately after the American Revolution, 1778 to 1812. Edited, abridged, and printed in 1904, the diary was not written for publication.[16] Like many diaries of farm women, it is filled with trivia about domestic chores and pastimes and was begun only after the author's childbearing and childrearing had ended, presumably because there was little time before for writing. The diary appears to be a trustworthy account of Mrs. Ballard's life and may reflect the work of other rural midwives in earlier years.

Mrs. Ballard became a midwife and "doctoress" in 1778 at the age of forty-three and continued until she died in 1812, aged seventy-seven.* Two things are notable about her activity. She was untrained as a midwife or doctoress, and her activities seem to have had a loosely associated religious function. Mrs. Ballard was very active in her local church, found many of her patients there, and gave all credit to God for her successful work. She, like other midwives, may have done her "good work" as a Christian duty, almost a charity, following New Testament prescriptions. Her fee for attending a birth was small, nine shillings, regardless of distance traveled or treatment, and often went unpaid. Much of her treatment as a doctoress consisted primarily of visiting the sick and offering comfort or sitting up with the dying.

She delivered 996 women, with only four maternal deaths recorded in the printed portion of her diary. She practiced for nine years before she had her first maternal death and in describing the event indicates clearly how exceptional it was. Her phraseology about birth is often suggestive of the attitudes held by

---

*Until the middle of the nineteenth century, anyone who treated illnesses could claim to be a "doctor" or "doctoress"; formal training was not a social requirement for the title, and licensing laws were not enforced even where they existed. Many people who "doctored" were women like Mrs. Ballard, who had knowledge of herbal remedies and whose practical experience in treating a wide variety of illnesses in both men and women had gained them the respect of their communities.

male doctors. She describes women in the last stages of pregnancy or labor as "unwell" or "ill," even though the condition is proceeding normally. She speaks of her own efforts in the active voice even when she refers to a normal and uncomplicated delivery: "I extracted the child," or "I performed the operation," or "the mother was safe delivered." She gives few hints of other practices and does not mention giving medicines, but in a few instances she tells that she had to remove an "obstruction" or to extract the placenta with her hands. This active approach contrasts with the advice given by the manuals for midwives, who were instructed to be passive and to let nature take its course.*

Mrs. Ballard's diary gives the impression that she usually simply offered reassurance to the laboring women, just as she tended the sick by sitting up with them. She occasionally visited a woman before labor commenced to prepare her, often remained with a woman during a slow or intermittent labor but left soon after delivery, for other women attendants were present. The reality of social childbirth is everywhere confirmed in her diary. She speaks of the women's being "called together," tells of mothers' being present, of the "elegant supper" enjoyed by the women while the men gathered outside to "fire the field pieces" and occasionally to drink too much.

Mrs. Ballard attended women of all social classes, the wives of the wealthy as well as the wives of those too poor to pay. Often the women lived at considerable distance, requiring Mrs. Ballard to anticipate the onset of labor. Perhaps because families were sometimes uncertain whether she would be available, some also called a doctor. There seems to have been little competition or animus between Mrs. Ballard and doctors. Whoever reached the house first attended the woman, even if both were there before the birth. Doctors sometimes asked her to attend a birth for one of their patients; she sent for a doctor when a complication appeared, such as a perineal tear. She remarks of both doctors and other midwives that they were occasionally clumsy or unfortunate in their efforts, but she clearly felt that doctors were better able than she to aid in certain complicated births.

At the end of each year of her practice, Mrs. Ballard totaled up

*It may be that the interventionist attitude displayed by many doctors in the eighteenth and nineteenth centuries was not so much a unique aspect of male medicine as a reflection of the general belief of the culture that it was proper to take active measures in the face of illness or death.

the number of children she had brought into the world. The overwhelming impression on reading her accounts is that birth was a routinely successful event. There were occasional dangerous occurrences and some abnormalities such as "fitts," but usually the mother survived. Most births provoked no comment from Mrs. Ballard beyond the length of labor and the sex of the child.

In view of the success of birth in Mrs. Ballard's account, it is appropriate to ask about the quality of care American midwives provided in the colonial period, to inquire if they fitted the stereotyped image of dangerously incompetent birth attendants. It must be said at once that no conclusive historical judgment about midwives of that period is possible in the absence of solid quantitative data about causes of mortality. Yet it is important to make whatever inferences one can about midwives, because it may clarify what childbirth meant to colonial people.

Any stereotyped image of the midwife—whether as blessing or curse—is unlikely to be historically true. The folk practice of midwifery was not a formal, unvarying body of belief and practice after the seventeenth century. New knowledge of birth processes began to affect the practices of midwifery. Some midwives in England studied medicine, apprenticed themselves to doctors, and wrote respected books on practice. A midwife, moreover, performed her work within a culture that was also changing, so that the experiences and expectations of women about birth were not always the same.

There are several reasons for believing that American midwives were not a persistent peril to women. In the first place, there are few recorded instances of incompetence. In 1642 the Reverend John Eliot of Roxbury, Massachusetts, complained of the deaths of two infants through the "unskilfullnesse of midwife."[17] And in 1739 there is an account of an infant who "bled to death at the navel."[18] The colonists appear to have criticized their midwives much less than did the English people at the same time.[19] The absence of criticism is, of course, ambiguous and inconclusive. The fact that there were fewer educated doctors in the colonies than in England could mean that bungled births were less often recognized. The absence of criticism could imply that Americans had a lower level of knowledge about birth and lower expectations for its success, and thus were more tolerant of malpracticing midwives.

On the other hand, the absence of criticism of midwives' incompetence may reflect the reality of their care. One reason is that available demographic comparisons of colonial and English women's mortality indicate that American women were generally healthier and less likely to die in birth, and produced more children. American midwives may have needed to intervene less to help exhausted and unhealthy women than did English midwives and thus may have had less occasion to appear officious and dangerous. Like Mrs. Ballard, American midwives may have been able to be simply present, offering psychological comfort, while natural processes produced healthy delivery.

In addition, one must consider the place American midwives occupied in colonial society in comparison to English society. In England, surveillance of midwives was episodic, centering in episcopal authorities at some remove from birth scenes. Medical doctors had no authority over midwives' practices. In many American colonies, on the other hand, the civil and religious authorities were closer at hand and more watchful.[20] They were deeply concerned with "increase" as a sign of God's favor and as a prospect for prosperity; it seems unlikely that these authorities would tolerate any midwife who consistently failed their expectations. Some colonies, as we have noted, treated midwives as servants of the state, giving them privileges in return for their carrying out certain acts for the moral order. In addition, American clergymen believed themselves knowledgeable about medicine and often treated sick people. That there were fewer doctors in the colonies and that colonial doctors had considerably less authority than English doctors—in short, the fact that medical institutions did not come to the colonies at the same time as institutions of the family, school, and church—may arise from the tendency of clergymen to keep medical authority to themselves. It is not entirely fanciful to imagine early American midwives as exercising a quasi-religious function on the allowance of the clergy. Thus American midwives may have been in a position to receive more rather than less criticism. Whether they were also held to objectively higher standards of practice cannot, unfortunately, be known. It is relevant to recall, however, that colonists memoralized midwives who delivered hundreds of children without fatality.

In addition, we know that midwives caused no recorded epidemics of puerperal fever among their patients. In one instance a midwife and doctoress employed by the French government for its colonists in Louisiana refused to attend scurvy patients lest she spread the "infection" of scurvy (then sometimes thought to be contagious) to her lying-in women.[21] A distinguished medical historian of Virginia has calculated that the illiterate black midwives in that state spread less infection than did doctors until the end of the nineteenth century.[22]

Historians cannot determine with finality the quality of care American midwives offered, for the data are largely absent. It seems likely, however, that a combination of environmental, cultural, and social circumstances both eliminated the need for interventions in birth, which might have proved dangerous, and removed the chances that clumsy or harmful midwives were unknown and unreported. The stereotype of the midwife as a curse upon women seems unfitting for colonial midwives.

If a network of women and the midwife provided the social structure of birth, what they did in the event of birth represented a variety of folklore, some of it moderately useful, some of it neutral or even potentially harmful. It is useful to reconstruct a typical birth scene, even though various aspects of it may not have occurred in every birth.

The family prepared for the birth by purchasing "childbed linen," if they could afford it. This was a layette, often so valuable that women bequeathed it in their wills or gave it as wedding presents. It was, of course, used for successive births within the same family. In early colonial days the birth took place in the "borning room," which was often a small room behind the central chimney, partitioned off from the living areas and shielded from drafts. In larger homes the master bedroom served this purpose. The borning room was also where the mother and child stayed during the lying-in period, away from the household bustle.[23]

Women probably labored in the posture and place most comfortable for them. For some this was perhaps their beds. Judge Samuel Sewall mentions in his diary that the midwife brought a collapsible "birth stool," a chair, in use since medieval times, designed to support the laboring woman's back while encouraging the force of gravity to expedite birth. The device also featured a cut-out seat to provide the midwife with access to the birth canal. She knelt down to receive the baby from below, under the long skirts that kept the mother warm and preserved her modesty. The stool was probably a rather common aid to birth. An adjustable version, called the "portable ladies' solace," was used in Philadelphia as late as 1799. In some instances women attendants took its

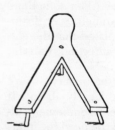

Three versions of the obstetrical stool. The simpler versions date to the mid-sixteenth century. The more elaborate one at right was developed by Hendrik van Deventer in 1701. It has an adjustable seat, hand grips, and a warming pot for the baby.

place, supporting the mother's back and legs during labor. There is even one reference to a husband's acting as a substitute for the birth stool by holding his wife in a sitting position on his lap and pressing down on her abdomen, but this occurred in the nineteenth century on the Midwest frontier and may have been

This sixteenth-century woodcut shows a German midwife delivering a woman on a birth stool.

uncommon earlier. Colonial women were able to move about and assume a variety of positions to help their labors along.[24]

The female attendants provided food and drink for the laboring woman to keep up her strength, offering such things as toast, buckwheat gruel, mutton, broth, and eggs. Cordials and red wine produced relaxation and eased pain. Too many cordials could make the woman drunk, and some English midwives were accused of administering an excess.[25] Warm cloths on the stomach or an enema served to dilate the birth passage.[26] The midwife might put a quill full of "sneezing power" (snuff or white hellebore) up the woman's nose to make her sneeze and so dislodge a difficult birth. A child born as a result of this practice was known as a "quilled baby."[27]

Women also employed a great variety of traditional folk medicines to ease a difficult birth. Cotton Mather, in his medical treatise *The Angel of Bethesda,* included many such prescriptions, such as the following:

> In *Child-Bed Fevers*—Take of *Laudanum* [tincture of opium], a Grain; and of the Powder of *Saffron* half a scruple; Mix, and give it in a spoonful of *Treacle-Water.*

> To prevent *Miscarrying,* Wear a *Load-Stone* about, or above, the Navel. When any Danger of this appears, the Common Practice is, Only to *Keep Quiet,* and Take a Tea of *Double Tansey.*

Mather also described a "Labour Powder" consisting of "Date-stones, Amber, Saffron, and Cummin-Seeds." None of these

An adaptation of the birth chair, in use in rural southern Ohio in the early nineteenth century (left). The husband's lap was also used as a substitute for the birth stool. Note the man-midwife in the illustration at the right.

medicines would have alleviated the listed ailments; tansy, in fact, was commonly used later to produce, rather than to prevent, abortion. The lodestone represented a survival of ancient sympathetic magic; Mather, however, considered it to be a medicine. Acting like a magnet, it was supposed to hold the fetus within the womb. Some medicines in the midwife's bag were valuable, though, and continued to be used by doctors. Opium relieved pain and, with belladonna, served as an antispasmodic before the discovery of ether.[28] Some European midwives knew that ergot was a drug to induce labor and to stop postpartum bleeding, but no evidence exists that American midwives used it.

A numer of "birth manuals," written by men to instruct English midwives, were published from the sixteenth through the eighteenth century. The earliest was *The Byrth of Mankind,* printed in several revised editions from 1545 to 1626. It contained anatomical illustrations of the womb and ovaries and woodcuts of athletic fetuses in strange positions within the womb, illustrating the common belief that babies actively kicked their way into the world. Nicholas Culpeper's *Directory for Midwives* (London, 1653–

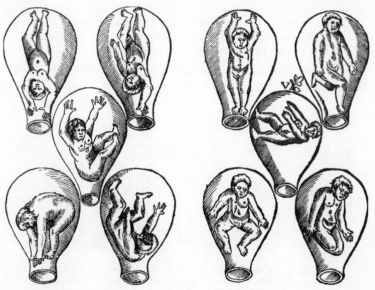

The athletic positions of the fetuses in these sixteenth-century woodcuts reflect the belief that babies actively fought their way into the world.

1777) was very popular. It included sections on astrology and a considerable admixture of other superstitions connected with birth. These books were intended for laypeople rather than physicians, who at that time were only slowly beginning to attend births and who had their own books relating to birth; the lay books blended some anatomical knowledge with folkloric practice, traditional herbals, and remnants of sympathetic magic; they took an empirical and practical approach to managing birth. Later they would be replaced by lay manuals on family medicine, such as Buchan's *Domestic Medicine* (1774), and by books for women of the "Married Ladies' Companion" type, describing practical hygiene for pregnancy and birth.

American women and midwives thus could draw from a considerable reservoir of empirical wisdom and practice if they felt it necessary to aid a lingering or difficult birth. That the midwife should cut her fingernails was useful advice. That she should grease the birth canal with goose fat or lubricate it with "oil of white lilies" was probably less useful. Participants in social childbirth made herbal potions and other medicines if the birth seemed to require such aid. Most were harmless and medically ineffective, but they may have had a positive psychological effect for the laboring woman. The placebo effect, the positive reassurance an inactive medicine gives patients who trust their attendants, can be considerable.

Psychological support for the laboring woman was a matter the manuals stressed. According to *The Byrth of Mankind:*

> Also the midwife must instruct and comfort the party, not only refreshing her with good meat and drink, but also with sweet words, giving her good hope of a speedy deliverance, encouraging and admonishing her to patience and tolerance, bidding her to hold in her breath so much as she may, also stroking gently with her hands her belly above the navel, for that helps to depress the birth downward.[29]

When the woman's labor and delivery were proceeding normally, her attendants and the midwife sought only to sustain her strength, to reassure her, and did not intervene with medicines or with manual aid. Thus the healthful natural processes carried birth along, and the rituals and practices of social childbirth appeared adequate. When, however, the birth was abnormal, the pain excessive, the labor very extended, or the position of the

child resistant to delivery, the women and the midwife were likely
to draw upon their reservoir of special aids. Colonial midwives
apparently turned breech births to normal positions and removed
"obstructions," but how they did so is unknown. It is likely that
American midwives were often inventive interventionists when
faced with an impacted baby (one stuck in the birth canal). Even
so, however, there must have been some instances of abnormality
that they could not treat.

After 1750 English doctors found new ways to deal with impaction, often saving the baby's life, whereas before surgeons had
had to kill the fetus in order to remove it to save the mother. It is
unknown if such surgery was done in America. Birth manuals said
little about other potentially fatal complications of birth, such as
infection, hemorrhage, convulsions, or "milk leg" (phlebitis). In
comparison to the successful births, these were probably rare in
the colonies. If Mrs. Ballard's recorded experience was at all typical, the average midwife encountered such conditions only three
or four times in a career of thirty years.

While empirical practices of childbirth were adequate for
normal labor and delivery, the fact remains that they could not
handle the occasionally complicated birth. Birth was not so
matter-of-fact that women did not fear its pain and the threat of
death. How dangerous was colonial childbirth for the life of
mother and child? How successful were colonial practices? The
measures of success and failure tell us about the value of
childbirth practices, but they also reflect the general health of
women. Indeed, since healthy women were likely to have normal
deliveries, midwives found it necessary to interfere very little, unless they were unduly officious. One can imagine, in fact, an in-
verse relation between health and the absence of interference,
such that each multiplied the other. Better health meant more
normal deliveries that required midwives to do nothing but wait
patiently. Hence there were fewer chances for clumsy or mistaken
interferences to harm health. On the other hand, poor health resulted in more difficult deliveries that needed more assistance,
which increased the chances for damage to health. American
midwives appear to have been more skillful and less damaging
than English midwives of the same period, and this may have been
because American women were healthier than English women.
American midwives and American births were more successful
because they interacted less.

Recent demographic studies of colonial New England indicate that childbearing, while a danger, has been overestimated as a cause of death. Fewer American women died in birth than their English contemporaries, probably because the conditions of American life were more healthful. Americans enjoyed a better and more dependable supply of food and were generally free from the unsanitary effects of urban congestion. They were also spared demographic crises stemming from failure of the harvest, famine, or epidemics that sometimes destroyed one-third of the population of English and French towns and weakened the survivors. The death rate in American towns was between 66 and 80 percent of the death rate in comparable English and French towns.[30]

Colonists infrequently recorded the exact causes of death, so rates of maternal mortality must be inferred from gross statistics. A summary of the evidence, at least from New England, indicates that the popular picture of the colonial cemetery, where the gravestones of many wives surround that of one husband, seriously distorts the dangers of childbirth. In the seventeenth century men did live longer than women, but in the eighteenth century women began to live longer than men. One historian has estimated that even if all the women in seventeenth-century Plymouth who died during childbearing years died because of birth complications, birth was still successful 95 percent of the time. Since many of these women must have died of infections or other diseases, colonial birth, while dangerous and fearful, was still not quite the calamity moderns picture it to have been.[31]

In Southern colonies women's health may have been poorer than in Northern colonies for environmental and nutritional reasons. When families had wet-nurses for the infants, the parents generated more children, a practice not conducive to the mother's good health. Little is known about the health of slave women in the colonial period.[32]

The success of childbirth in terms of the survival and health of newborn infants is more perplexing, for people often did not record the deaths of stillborn, miscarried, and short-lived infants. The greater concern in the colonial period was for the life of the mother. Some historians have estimated infants' deaths in early months to be as high as 10 percent. Many infants died, however, because of infectious diseases rather than birth damage.[33]

The American child in some communities had a much higher

chance of surviving infancy than its English counterpart, a fact
that is reflected in part in the success of birth. A child in Plymouth
had a 75 percent chance of living to the age of twenty-one, and in
Andover an 83 percent chance, but in London before 1660 one-
third of all recorded deaths were those of children younger than
age six.[34] Children in American seaport towns, however, had less
chance for longevity than children in American farming communities, for infections were more prevalent along the coasts.[35]
Although longevity in rural communities such as Andover was
greater than in comparable English villages, mortality rates in
Boston, New York, and Philadelphia were probably as high as
those in English towns of the same size. To the colonists, as to
their English counterparts, death was an ever present menace.
Puritan culture gave death an additional grim emphasis, perhaps
an overemphasis, for it was the gateway to the judgment with
which the religion was preoccupied.[36]

In the course of the eighteenth century, the death of a woman
in childbirth seemed to become a rarer event. Like the diary of
Mrs. Ballard, the diary of the Reverend Ezra Stiles, President of
Yale College, gives the impression that death in childbed was an
occurrence deserving special mention, like death at sea. In his
account of all deaths in Newport, Rhode Island, between 1760
and 1764, where approximately 900 women bore nearly 1,600
children, he listed ten deaths in childbed.[37] Women's diaries of
the same time imply that childbirth had become a routine, rather
than a deadly, event. Actually, however, the percentage of successful births in Newport was similar to the estimated success in
Plymouth in the previous century. But women's (and men's) perception of the dangers of birth may have altered, a matter that
deserves some reflection.[38]

References to feelings of joy and ecstasy in giving birth are
absent from women's diaries throughout the colonial period. A
woman who bore and reared seven or eight children, several of
whom were likely to die, while carrying on the tasks of farm life,
perhaps found the word "joy" inappropriate even for an easy
birth. Esther Burr offered one of the few cheerful comments on
birth in 1755 when, after visiting a new mother, she said that the
woman appeared "hearty" and no longer so "vapory," adding that
"this having children does good some times."[39] Although men like
Ezra Stiles welcomed "increase" as God's blessing, women did not
record this sentiment. Whether they shared the belief or wished to

limit births is simply unknown. The earliest instance of purposeful family limitation occurred among some Quaker families at the time of the Revolution.[40]

Seventeenth-century women approached birth not with joy but with dread; some found pregnancy the proper occasion for meditation upon their impending death.

> How soon, my Dear, death may my steps attend,
> How soon't may be thy lot to lose thy friend

wrote the poet Anne Bradstreet to her husband in a poem entitled "Before the Birth of One of Her Children." Although she gave the lie to her fears by living to the age of sixty, her attitude of potential sorrow is typical. The influential Puritan minister Cotton Mather, in a widely distributed printed sermon, counseled women to repent before their "Hour of Travail and Trouble." He said:

> For ought you know, your Death has entered into you, and you may have conceived that which determines but about nine months at the most, for you to live in the world. Preparation for death is that most reasonable and most seasonable thing, to which you must now apply yourself.

As a kind of Job's comforter, Mather suggested that, since it was reasonable to expect to die in giving birth, it was seasonable to prepare for it. The woman should let the thought of her death—"the wrath of God, the place of torment, the place of dragons"—mightily hasten her flight from sin and her readiness to pray: "Take up resolutions of universal and perpetual piety. Thus you will have gone through the work that will disarm death of all terror." In face of birth's inherent uncertainties, the woman should throw herself on God's mercy, for no medicine could ensure her safety: "No *Midwives* can do what Angels can!"[41]

Mather's remarks are grim, but they are typical of Puritan belief and preaching style. The threat of death was a chance to exhort to salvation, and childbearing women were regularly threatened and hence exhorted. Women may have dreaded birth more because of this cultural emphasis on birth as potential death than because of high rates of mortality.

If religious culture conditioned women to dread birth, it likewise taught them to regard it, like other events, as the direct expression of God's will or the Devil's power, an event symboli-

cally expressive of the spiritual state of man and wife. If a man
and woman generated a child who, when born, was abnormal, the
parents and other people sought the cause not in the failure of
natural processes of fetal development but in the spiritual condition of the parents. The abnormal child was a "sign" from God
before the whole community, indicating the parents' spiritual
status.

When Mary Dyer bore a "monster," actually a headless child,
the civil and religious authorities of early Massachusetts read it as
a sign of God's condemnation of Mary for being a follower of
Anne Hutchinson, a dissenting religious leader who, incidentally,
had assisted at the birth. The authorities suspected the midwife,
not a follower of Hutchinson, of having used witchcraft in the
birth, enjoined her from practicing, and eventually expelled her
from the colony, along with Dyer and Hutchinson. When Hutchinson herself, exiled in Rhode Island, later gave birth to a
grapelike cluster of tissue, probably a hydatiform mole, which is a
benign neoplastic growth in the placenta, the Massachusetts authorities ordered a count of the lumps to see if they equaled the
number of the heresies for which she had been convicted—some
twenty-seven. They did, and thus further confirmed her status as
one displeasing to God.

The idea that abnormal children were "signs" persisted into
the nineteenth century, although the social consequences became
less severe.[42] Mrs. Ballard, for instance, noted in her diary, when a
child was born with a harelip, "May the parents take suitable
notice of the dealings of God toward them."

"Marking the child" became a cause for apprehension among
parents, particularly the mother, for colonists believed that a woman's emotions, environment, and especially chance experiences
during pregnancy affected her child's form at birth or its spiritual
character during its life.[43]

Another cause for fear and dread of birth among
seventeenth-century American women was the Puritan prohibition of the magical practices that for centuries had been associated
with birth. Before the Protestant Reformation midwives regularly
used magic to call spiritual powers to aid the birth. The midwife
might employ special charms, potions, incantations, and even gir-
dles of Mary Magdalene or of Our Lady. Protestant reformers
and churches disparaged these magical means as both useless and

impious. When Mather said midwives cannot do what angels can, he meant that midwives cannot save women from eternal damnation. The deliverance that really mattered was salvation, not warding off evil spirits in childbirth. To use magic was impious, for it was to compete with the church's spiritual function in salvation and to cast doubt upon God's ultimate control of worldly events.

Protestants wanted birth to be a religious occasion, a time for salvation; expectant women were not to avoid this by seeking to avert bad luck or misfortune through magical practices. But magical healing was an ancient form of comfort, a proletarian form of cunning that depended not upon wealth or instituted authority but upon simple rituals that propitiated the complex spiritual powers ruling one's destiny. By claiming that the spiritual powers were actually the devil's, Protestantism not only removed this means to control destiny but also made magic a dangerous social practice. In childbirth the laboring woman could only throw herself on the mercy of God, and the midwife dared do nothing that might appear magical. According to Aveling, in fact, English doctors before 1700 feared to attend births lest they be judged to be magicians.[44]

Such major transitions in belief and practice never occur with unanimous assent. In England magic continued to be an aspect of birth for centuries. In the Protestant colonies of America, however, authorities were more effective in eliminating it and prosecuting its practitioners. It seems very likely that the attack on magic undermined and altered women's mysteries and rituals for childbirth. The midwife no longer had a direct charismatic function; she was only to be an effective instrument of God's will. The expectant woman and her attendants could do nothing to seek and offer comfort except to pray to God. For true believers, this may have been enough in the face of death; for those less faithful, it may have made birth an even more dreadful expectation.

It is not surprising that seventeenth-century American women faced birth not with joy and ecstasy but with fear of death and eternal judgment. Their culture had educated women to feel a great sense of awe about the event of birth, and the culture had disapproved half-measures of propitiation and comfort. Yet it is important to recognize that such dread of birth had little to do with the actual number of deaths in childbirth or with the decrease in birth mortality. American women might have been becoming more healthy and successful in delivery, more so than English women, and still have continued to dread birth as the possible occasion for their death and eternal judgment.

In the eighteenth century, however, women's perceptions and experiences of birth appear to have changed. Their diaries do not mention dread; rather, they report instances of birth matter-of-factly, stating without elaboration that they themselves or other women were "brought to bed." What concerned them was managing a household of many children. Esther Burr, Aaron Burr's mother, wrote that she was "tied hand and foot" after the birth of her second child and wondered "how I shall get along when I have got ½ dozen or 10 children I can't devise."[45]

Women's changed perception of the birth event may have reflected an awareness that they were healthier than their grandmothers and were surviving the rigors of birth more often, as indeed there is some evidence they were. The changed perception may, however, have come primarily from the decline of the Puritan religious view and the growing influence of new scientific views of nature and religious views of God. Nature appeared to follow regular laws that people might understand and act upon. God appeared more distant and more benevolent, willing to share control of events with mankind. Human bodies were part of nature, open to understanding and intervention by people, while human souls remained mysterious and sacred to God.

Where American women were healthy and having largely normal births, their cumulative experience contributed to a new sense of the regularity and reliability of natural processes in birth. Birth was perhaps even a kind of unexpected confirmation of new mechanical views of nature. Perhaps women and midwives did not understand the process of birth more adequately than before or have better means to manage it, but they saw it from a new cultural context.

The degree and effects of health improvement and cultural change should not be exaggerated. Women dreaded birth less than their mothers and grandmothers had, but they still did not fully understand the natural processes, nor could they intervene to overcome imperfect mechanisms. Pain and death remained realities in birth, whether or not they were the result of God's direct judgmental action. Eighteenth-century women were not in the position of women today who seek "natural childbirth," for the earlier women had very limited resources for emergencies and for pain. The degree of trust in nature varies; it is greatest when one is shielded from nature's mistakes, when one has learned to outwit its pain.

The changes in women's perception of birth may help to explain, however, a persistent historical question: Why did doctors, who had been scarce and without much prestige in colonial America, displace midwives after 1800 more rapidly and completely than in Great Britain? There are, of course, several important reasons for that difference, two of which are related to colonial women's cultural and health experiences.

The first reason relates to magic. It may be that where magical birth practices continued, as in many outlying parts of Britain, midwives and women's rituals satisfied pregnant women and kept doctors away. Doctors hesitated to practice where magic abounded, where the distinction between natural and spiritual causes was unclear and unaccepted, because doctors did not want to be thought of as magicians. In America, however, the matter of magic was settled early by more effectively applied Protestant sanctions, and the comforts of magic did not exist to resist or offend doctors. Also, historians have said that Protestantism bred a cultural acceptance of new science and a particular willingness to intervene technically in nature. Many American women, whether urban or rural, were more ready than the majority of English-women to look positively on doctors' new knowledge and technical skills. Doctors therefore inherited a cultural process that had demystified birth and rationalized it before doctors appeared. One can imagine American women saying, in a paraphrase of Mather, "Midwives cannot do what *doctors* can."

In addition, where American women were healthy and were spared demographic crises, bearing children appeared to be a regular process that did not need magical cunning. When difficulty appeared in birth, on the other hand, it seemed to be a fault in nature that should be corrected by manipulating nature, not through magical cunning but through instrumental skills.

Women gradually gave to doctors the medical control of birth, the manipulation of their bodies, but they did not give over the rituals of birth. In a compromise that mirrors earlier accommodations between religion and science, women allowed men to treat them as natural machines that might go wrong, but they kept the spiritual meaning of birth for themselves. Social childbirth continued as a divided affair: the body in the hands of men, the spirit in the company of women.

Notes

1. Daniel Scott Smith, "The Demographic History of Colonial New England," *Journal of Economic History* 32 (1972):177; Kenneth A. Lockridge, "The Population of Dedham, Mass., 1636–1736," *Economic History Review*, 2d series, 19 (1966):331; Philip J. Greven, *Four Generations: Population, Land and Family in Colonial Andover, Massachusetts* (Ithaca, N.Y.: Cornell University Press, 1970), p. 331; John Demos, *A Little Commonwealth: Family Life in the Plymouth Colony* (New York: Oxford University Press, 1970), p. 151.

2. Robert V. Wells, "Demographic Change and the Life Cycle of American Families," *Journal of Interdisciplinary History* 2 (1971):277; idem, "Family Size and Fertility Control in Eighteenth-Century America: A Study in Quaker Families," *Population Studies* 25 (1971): 73–82.

3. Demos, *Little Commonwealth*, p. 68; James Axtell, *The School upon a Hill: Education and Society in Colonial New England* (New Haven: Yale University Press, 1974), pp. 61, 75, 86–87; Ezra Stiles, *The Literary Diary of Ezra Stiles*, 2 vols. (New York, 1901), 1:489.

4. Lockridge, "Population of Dedham," p. 339.

5. "Diary of Ebenezer Parkman," *Proceedings of the American Antiquarian Society*, 1961, pp. 447–448: quoted in Axtell, *School upon a Hill*, p. 65.

6. Axtell, *School upon a Hill*, p. 66n. See also "Journal of Esther Burr," pp. 102–103, 154–155, quoted in Axtell, p. 63.

7. "The Diary of Samuel Sewall, 1674–1729," *Collections of the Massachusetts Historical Society* 5:394. For other births, see pp. 166, 233, 328.

8. Cecil Drinker, *Not So Long Ago: A Chronicle of Medicine and Doctors in Philadelphia* (New York, 1937), pp. 51–61.

9. Richard H. Shryock, *Medicine in America* (Baltimore: Johns Hopkins Press, 1966), p. 180.

10. James Hitchcock, "A Sixteenth-Century Midwife's License," *Bulletin of the History of Medicine* 41 (1967):75.

11. Quoted by Francis R. Packard, *History of Medicine in the United States*, 2 vols. (New York, 1931), 1:43.

12. Wyndham B. Blanton, *Medicine in Virginia in the Seventeenth Century* (1930; reprint ed., New York: Arno Press, 1972), p. 167; Packard, *History of Medicine*, 1:52; Julia C. Spruill, *Women's Life and Work in*

the Southern Colonies (New York: Norton, 1972), p. 273; Emil Oberholzer, Jr., *Delinquent Saints* (New York: AMS Press, 1956), p. 133; Samuel Eliot Morison, ed., "Records of the Suffolk County Court, 1671–1680," *Publications of the Colonial Society of Massachusetts* 29 (Boston, 1933):185.

13. Franklin B. Dexter, ed., *New Haven Town Records* 1 (1649–1662) (New Haven, 1917):265; Stiles, *Literary Diary*, 1:489.

14. James J. Walsh, *History of Medicine in New York* (New York, 1919, pp. 10–30; John Duffy, ed., *The Randolph Matos History of Medicine in Louisiana*, 2 vols. (New Orleans: Louisiana State University Press, 1958), 1:14–16, 62–63; Blanton, *Medicine in Virginia*, pp. 164–168.

15. Spruill, *Women's Life and Work*, p. 273; Packard, *History of Medicine*, 1:51–52; Page Smith, *Daughters of the Promised Land* (Boston: Little, Brown, 1970), p. 55.

16. Charles Eventon Nash, *The History of Augusta, Including the Diary of Mrs. Martha Moore Ballard, 1785–1812* (Augusta, 1904), pp. 229–464.

17. Report of the (Boston) Record Commissioners, 2d ed. (Boston, 1884), 6:170.

18. *Proceedings of the American Antiquarian Society*, n.s. 72 (1962):36.

19. J. H. Aveling, *English Midwives, Their History and Prospects* (London, 1872), pp. 38, 44–45, 100–102.

20. *The Charter and General Laws of the Colony and Province of Massachusetts Bay* (Boston, 1894), pp. 76–77; Nathaniel B. Shurtleff, *Records of the Governor and Company of the Massachusetts Bay in New England* 3 (1644–1657) (Boston, 1854):209. These show laws respecting midwives.

21. Duffy, *Randolph Matos History*, 1:62–63.

22. Blanton, *Medicine in Virginia*, p. 164.

23. Spruill, *Women's Life and Work* p. 50; Alice Morse Earle, ed., *Diary of Anna Green Winslow, a Boston Schoolgirl of 1771* (1894; reprinted, Detroit: Singing Tree Press, 1970), p. 12; Demos, *Little Commonwealth*, p. 13; Alice Morse Earle, *Customs and Fashions in Old New England* (New York, 1916), pp. 8–9.

24. Sewall, "Diary of S. Sewall" 5:394; Drinker, *Not So Long Ago*, p. 61; Julius Jarcho, *Postures and Practices During Labor Among Primitive Peoples* (New York, 1934), pp. 33, 41–45. Aristotle (pseud.), *Aristotle's Masterpiece*, First New England Edition (1809), p. 69 (orig. London, 1684), describes many postures.

25. William Buchan, *Domestic Medicine* (Fairhaven, Vt., 1798), p. 353.

26. Aristotle, *Aristotle's Masterpiece* (1684 ed.), p. 137.

27. Madge Packard and R. Carlyle Buley, *The Midwest Pioneer* (Crawfordsville, Ind., 1945), p. 32.

28. Gordon Jones, ed., Cotton Mather's *The Angel of Bethesda: An Essay*

Upon the Common Maladies of Mankind (Barre, Vt.: American Antiquarian Society, 1972), pp. 246–247.

29. Thomas Raynalde, *The Byrth of Mankind* (London, 1626 ed.), p. 97; Aristotle, *Aristotle's Masterpiece* (1684 ed.), pp. 99–100.

30. Lockridge, "Population of Dedham," p. 331.

31. Demos, *Little Commonwealth*, pp. 66, 131–132.

32. Martha C. Mitchell, "Health and the Medical Profession in the Lower South, 1845–1860," *Journal of Southern History* 10 (1944):424–446; Spruill, *Women's Life and Work*, pp. 46–49, 57.

33. Demos, *Little Commonwealth*, pp. 131–132; Spruill, *Woman's Life and Work*, p. 53; Axtell, *School upon a Hill*, pp. 73–74; Ernest Caulfield, "Some Common Diseases of Colonial Children," *Proceedings of the Colonial Society of New England* 35 (April, 1942):4–65.

34. Axtell, *School upon a Hill*, p. 71; Demos, *Little Commonwealth*, pp. 66, 131–183; Greven, *Four Generations*, pp. 25–26.

35. Maris A. Vinovskis, "Mortality Rates and Trends in Massachusetts Before 1860," *Journal of Economic History* 32 (1972):200.

36. David E. Stannard, "Death and the Puritan Child," in Stannard, ed., *Death in America* (Philadelphia: University of Pennsylvania Press, 1975), pp. 16–17.

37. Ezra Stiles, "Death in Newport, R.I., 1760–1764," *New England Historical and Genealogical Register* 62 (1908):283–291, 352–363; 63 (1909):51–58.

38. "Diary of Mrs. Mary Vial Holyoke," in *The Holyoke Diaries, 1709–1856* (Salem, Mass., 1911), pp. 47–139.

39. "Journal of Esther Burr," p. 132, quoted in Axtell, *School upon a Hill*, p. 63.

40. Wells, "Family Size," pp. 73–82.

41. Cotton Mather, *Elizabeth in Her Holy Retirement* (Boston, 1710), pp. 7, 13.

42. J. Savage, ed., *John Winthrop's History of New England* (Boston, 1853), 1:271; Packard, *History of Medicine*, pp. 48–49.

43. Mather, *Elizabeth*, p. 21; Spruill, *Women's Life and Work*, pp. 50–51.

44. Aveling, *English Midwives*, p. 11. See also Thomas Forbes, *The Midwife and the Witch* (New Haven: Yale University Press, 1966), and Keith Thomas, *Religion and the Decline of Magic* (New York: Charles Scribner's Sons, 1971).

45. "Journal of Esther Burr," p. 108; See also "Diary of Mrs. Mary Vial Holyoke," in *Holyoke Diaries*.

2

The New Midwifery

[The young doctor] will probably fail at first, for want of judgment, to discriminate accurately between one case and another, as well as for want of skill and dexterity in the application of his instruments; and finding himself foiled in the use of the safer lever and forceps, he will become alarmed, confused and apprehensive for his patient's safety, as well as for his own reputation. And now, deeming a speedy delivery essential to both, and that, having taken the case into his own hands, and began his work, he thinks he must not desist before he has accomplished it, he flies to the crotchet [an instrument for killing, cutting and extracting a fetus lodged in the birth canal] as more easy in its application, and more certain in its effect—with this he probably succeeds; and although the poor infant is sacrificed, yet he persuades himself, perhaps honestly believes, this was necessary.

Dr. Samuel Bard, Compendium of the
Theory and Practice of Midwifery,
New York, 1815

AFTER 1750 American men began to return from medical education abroad to practice in colonial towns and cities. Perhaps the most notable medical attainment they brought, in terms of potentially widespread and concrete medical benefit, was new knowledge and skills to aid women in birth in ways that uneducated American midwives could not match. The doctors called their science and arts relative to birth by the traditional term "midwifery," but they realized that it constituted medical science's first major practical advance. They were eager to practice the new midwifery in order to establish their professional value in a society that did not yet accord them much status and thereby to set themselves apart from and above the many and various uneducated medical empirics whose practice proceeded from trial-and-error methods rather than theory. Fortunately for doctors, American women chose them increasingly to attend deliveries, thus beginning an important transformation in birth: its inclusion within the medical practice of men.

Before the first doctors returned from training, Americans had been relatively isolated from medicine and its developments for more than a century. In 1750 they had no medical schools, hospitals, or organized medical profession such as existed abroad. Unlike the family, the church, the college, and the law, medicine had still to find institutional shape and place in American society; it had to organize and validate itself. These problems of professional structure and status existed concurrently with the emergence of the new midwifery in practice, a coincidence which meant that practicing midwifery was not only a humanitarian activity but also medicine's avenue to wide social acceptance and to professional consensus. Births became, therefore, occasions of mutual need, events that initiated the enduring symbiosis of women and doctors. For if it was true that expectant women sought doctors in the belief that they were the most knowledgeable and able attendants, it was also true that doctors sought out expectant and laboring women in the belief that women's approbation would give doctors enduring responsibility and prestige in society. Midwifery was medicine's first professional gambit in America.

The new midwifery was not yet, however, a coherent regimen of practice, for it was too new. Doctors were still deliberating some of its serious medical and social aspects, and doctors were, obviously, not the only interested parties. There were four essential matters. Most parties agreed about the new theory of birth, the doctors' explanation of its natural processes, but were not in accord about when and how to use new techniques when natural processes failed. Nor had the interested parties determined what training was needed to practice the new midwifery—a full medical education or only a short course in midwifery. Finally, there was the unresolved matter of what part women would play in the new midwifery, of how or whether doctors were to share responsibility.

The purpose of this chapter is to examine briefly the medical and social origins of the new midwifery abroad and then to look more carefully at its development in American society.

~~~~~~~

During medieval times women took care of birth except when they called on men to perform surgery to save the life of mother or child. Perhaps because surgeons saw the difficult and dangerous births, they kept custody of medical knowledge about birth and sought answers to perplexing questions about it. They asked, for example, what was natural and normal in birth—its patterned regularity—and what caused or constituted the natural. They inquired if there were signs that a birth would be easy or difficult, and they sought means to ease difficult or protracted labor. Until surgeons could observe many births and, equally important, find an organizing principle for what they saw, their curiosity and concern bore little fruit.

The first advances in understanding birth resulted from opportunities to observe and attend births in the hospital-schools established in Paris to train midwives in the early sixteenth century. In the maternity wards for poor women, surgeons and midwives developed a new rational view of birth processes and a number of techniques to aid them. The surgeons and midwives were helped in their work by anatomical studies of the uterus and birth canal. Knowing better the organs involved, they studied how the fetus moved from the uterus through the canal and devised manual manipulations to ease the passage. They also perfected a

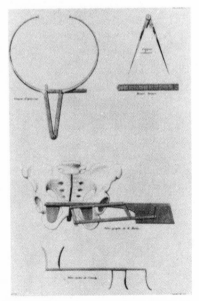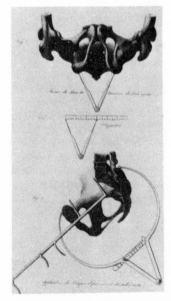

French tools and techniques for measuring the pelvis to determine whether birth was possible.

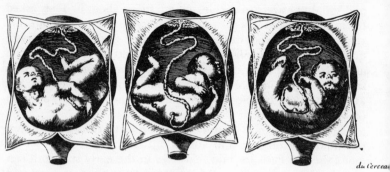

du Cerceau

These sophisticated French birth figures from a seventeenth-century manual show fetuses in various "unnatural" positions.

simple way to measure the size of the birth passage so that they could estimate *in advance* how difficult the passage of the fetus would be. That technique of measuring the bony structure gave a medical function to the traditional "touch" of the attendant, who now sought not only to ascertain the degree of dilatation of the cervix or to lubricate the passage but also to foresee the actual mechanical adequacy of the structure to perform its function.[1]

In a scientific sense, the French had achieved much, largely because they had organized their many observations of birth around the idea that natural processes were machine-like. Just as some doctors were speaking of the function of the stomach as if it were a machine with knives and scissors to pulverize food, so the surgeons and midwives spoke of the womb and birth canal as though they formed a mechanical pump that in particular instances was more or less adequate to expel the fetus.[2]

Much was remarkable in this new view of birth, as the French were well aware. The rationalizing of birth processes led them to call their new midwifery a science. Indeed, in a number of ways, the new midwifery *was* a science. For one, its explanation of the birth event freed the practitioners themselves from the fears and constrictions of traditional magical and religious explanations of birth. They laughed at those older views of birth; they did not have to fear involving themselves in holy or mysterious doings. They derided the ancient superstitious aids to birth, the mumbled prayers, the sympathetic magical practices; they knew that direct physical manipulation alone aided birth. They celebrated their liberating insight in an endless stream of books during the seventeenth and eighteenth centuries, among them François Mauriceau, *Traité des malades des femmes grosses et accouchées* (1668); André Levret, *L'art des accouchemens* (1761); and Jean-Louis Baudeloque, *L'art des accouchemens* (1789).

By defining birth as a natural process that followed its own laws, as a machine with shapes and movements of its own, the French reduced its potentially awesome aspects and removed its emotional and spiritual associations from their consideration. They could then look intently at what determined the success or failure of birth, and that would be their arena for further scientific study and medical art.

They could have done this and have been wrong. It was common practice at that time to sever the sacred and the natural and to posit mechanical models for natural processes. But the mechanical model of birth was fortuituously accurate and adequate to describe many of the normal and abnormal events of birth.

The French achievement consisted primarily in finding a better understanding of birth rather than in discovering new techniques to aid it. Even their mechanistic view did not explain many

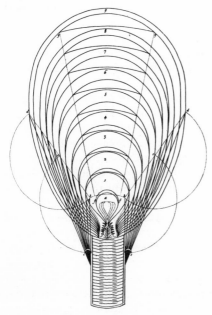

French physicians regarded the uterus as a complex mechanism to be measured precisely. This eighteenth-century drawing shows the volumetric progression of the uterus at different months of gestation.

of the pathologies of birth. It led some surgeons to make deep
cuts to expand the birth canal or to open the abdomen, but, since
the women usually died, they had to abandon such attempts to
reshape or circumvent the birth machine. The French did develop some manual skills, based upon their greater understanding
of anatomy, to ease the passage of the fetus through the canal, but
those arts had limited utility in many difficult births. Measuring
the size and shape of the birth canal indicated their concern with
the machine-like nature of birth more than a new ability to ease
birth. Often knowing that the canal was misshapen or inadequate
only enabled them to announce that a woman would die. The
French dispelled many traditional and useless practices, but they
had found few new arts to aid birth.

The new midwifery had a different beginning in England.
There it was not associated with medical institutions in which
generations of birth attendants accumulated experience and formulated a new view of birth's processes. Rather, it began in the
often desperate struggles of poorly educated medical empirics,
the barber-surgeons, to save the life of the mother by extracting
the child with whatever tools they could devise. Midwives called
these men, in accord with ancient practice, when it seemed
surgery alone could complete delivery.

These empirical operators had a wide range of instruments—
in fact, a real armamentarium—to extract the fetus, living or
dead. They had blunt hooks to bring down the thighs in a breech
delivery, sharp hooks (crotchets) and knives and perforators to
puncture the fetus's head when it was completely impacted or
dead, and the ancient device of the *speculum matricis* to dilate the
vagina and make it easier to cut out obstructions or reach the
fetus. Often they used the fillet, a strip of flexible but firm material, to slip into the uterus and loop around the child to pull it out.
Most often the surgeons had to kill the impacted child in order to
save the mother's life. Their efforts were not those of scientific
observers but of desperate practical technicians, experimenting
with various tools to aid delivery, rushing to save life often by
killing life.

In the early seventeenth century one such man, Peter Chamberlen, invented the forceps, which was an improvement over
other instruments in that it freed the fetus without killing it. Because it was the custom of the surgeons to regard their tools, often
of their own design and fabrication, as their own property,

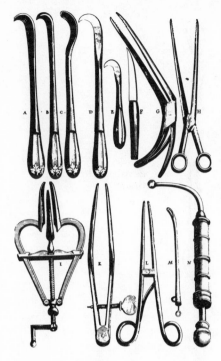

Seventeenth-century obstetrical instruments. A, B, C: Crotchets for extracting a dead fetus; D, E: Sharp hooks for piercing the head or dismembering a fetus; F: Scalpel for performing a Caesarean section on a dead mother; G, H: Grippers for removing obstructions from the birth canal; I, K, L: Cervical dilators; M: Catheter; N: Syringe for uterine injections and for baptism *in utero*.

Chamberlen and his family kept the forceps a family secret for more than a century. The device consisted of two enlarged spoons with handles that could be inserted separately into the birth canal and then joined and locked together so that the spoons cupped the baby's head to draw it out. By the early eighteenth century the forceps had become widely known to English doctors, who experimented with various shapes that would fit both the angles of the birth canal and the baby's head. The forceps was able to do what other tools and manual skills could not, but it was a dangerous instrument when used hastily or clumsily, for it could damage the mother or crush the child. Early forceps were far from being perfected instruments for their purpose. There were to be hundreds of modifications in design in following centuries; not until the late nineteenth century were their mechanical problems fully resolved.[3]

After 1700 French theories and practices of birth became

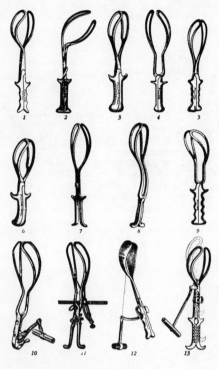

Various styles of forceps in
modern use.

known to and widely accepted by English doctors, and educated
English physicians contributed to the anatomical knowledge of
the female reproductive system.[4] On the other hand, there was
growing use of forceps among the empirical surgeons, who often
had little knowledge of birth science. As the two traditions—

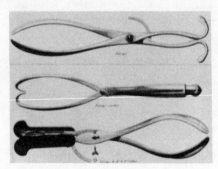

French versions of the forceps
and crotchet used in the late
nineteenth century.

French science and English forceps—began to fuse in England, the question arose among both male and female birth attendants about how much and what kind of medical art was needed to improve upon natural processes. The essential question was when during the passage of the fetus through the birth canal was it necessary and safe to apply forceps.

The medical issue was a complex and serious one. Unlike the "low" forceps used today, so called because the fetus's head is low in the birth canal and already visible, many male attendants were using "high" or even "floating" forceps, which were applied before the fetal head was engaged in the mother's pelvis, or "mid" forceps, when the head was engaged in the curve of the birth canal, but not yet visible (see illustration below). These latter operations presented extreme danger to both mother and child, the possibilities of physical damage, infection in damaged tissue, hemorrhage, and a crushed fetal head.

Such medical questions, difficult in themselves, were to remain open to dispute for decades because the English had no means to

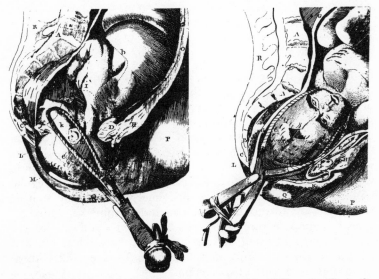

Mid-forceps (left) and high forceps (right) as used by William Smellie in the eighteenth century. Smellie's short-handled English forceps required strength to use because it lacked a pelvic curve so that the operator had to pull in a different direction from the curve of the birth canal.

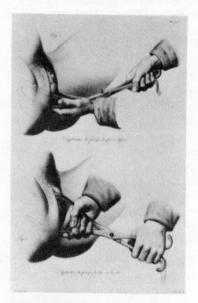

Long-handled French forceps in use. Note that these forceps are curved to fit the birth canal.

resolve them. In the first place, they did not have, as the French did, maternity hospitals in which to observe and evaluate the use of forceps. Deciding when forceps were necessary and safe to use remained a matter of impression rather than extensive clinical trial. Second, the English also had lacked a tradition of clinical training for birth attendants. Midwifery in England around 1750, whether male or female, was largely a self-proclaimed, individualistic, and competitive occupation, free of medical regulation. Just as traditional midwives had emerged randomly, so male midwives using forceps began with an undetermined and unregulated amount of learning about new birth science and with little or no experience in using the forceps. What they did in practice, whether right or wrong, useful or harmful, they did without supervision and without correction.

In addition to the fact that the theory and techniques of midwifery were not coherent in practice and that practicing midwifery was unregulated, the situation was further complicated be-

cause male midwives with forceps began to compete with midwives who were without forceps. It is a puzzle why the educated
midwives in the cities, and even traditional midwives, did not use
the forceps. Legal restrictions stemming from the power of surgeons' guilds may have prevented it, and the simple force of custom, which associated men with instrumental interference, may
have limited women's use of forceps. Men may also have refused
to sell forceps to women, or women may have found that using
early versions required a degree of physical strength they did not
have. At any rate, very few English midwives used forceps; most
never did.

It is also probable that many midwives associated the forceps
with the older, invariably destructive instruments used to perform
craniotomies. Elizabeth Nihell, a famous eighteenth-century
midwife who opposed both man-midwifery and forceps, wrote:

> A few, and very few indeed, of the midwives, dazzled with that
> vogue into which the instruments brought the men . . . attempted
> to employ them [but] soon discovered that they were at once
> insignificant and dangerous substitutes for their own hands, with
> which they were sure of conducting their operations both more
> safely, more effectually, and with less pain to the patient.[5]

There was apparently no legal prohibition at that time against
a midwife's use of forceps or other instruments, however, for
there were occasional reports of midwives' employment of them.
Sarah Stone, another famous midwife, reported using instruments (probably craniotomy instruments) in four out of three
hundred cases.[6] Margaret Stephens, a midwife who attended
George III's wife, Queen Charlotte, even advocated the use of
forceps. Stephens had her own school of midwifery in London in
the 1790s and demonstrated the forceps on a wooden manikin for
her women students.[7] She was distinctly in a minority, however,
for most English midwives rejected instruments entirely.

In America, where there were no surgeons' guilds and no legal
restrictions on the use of instruments, it was probably a combination of midwives' own noninstrumental tradition and the cost of
purchase that kept them from using forceps. Expense prevented
even some doctors from owning them.

The questions about forceps came to a boil after 1742, when
the unfortunately named William Smellie, a self-taught student of
the new midwifery, began to teach its theory and practice in a

short course in London. Smellie himself had a credible rationale
for using forceps, but at the outset of his teaching many of his
pupils and other male midwives were scandalizing both educated
doctors and some better-educated midwives with what appeared
to be the misuse of forceps and consequent abuse of mothers and
children. Several educated midwives—that is, women without a
formal medical education but who had attended doctors' lectures
or had aided doctors—published caustic attacks on male midwives' unnecessary use and misuse of forceps. Despite the midwives' obvious competitive self-interest, their public complaint
and ridicule, in an unregulated medical context, served to bring
the issue of forceps and the matter of adequate training to public
and medical attention.

Elizabeth Nihell described Smellie's pupils as:

... that multitude of disciples ... these self-constituted man-
midwives made out of broken barbers, tailors, or even pork
butchers, for I know one myself of this last trade, who having
passed half his life in stuffing sausage, is turned out intrepid
physician and man-midwife.[8]

Male midwives' intrepidity centered in their confidence that
the use of forceps was a talisman of ability and a panacea for every
difficulty in birth. They also regarded the forceps as a convenient
means to hasten along a labor that wasted their time. One physician noted that

... dispatch is the first object of consideration, and the maxims of
improved science as well as the dictates of humanity are disre-
garded from stronger views of interest. The moment a rider
comes for a man-midwife, he picks up his bag of tools, which may
be justly called the instruments of death; he mounts his horse,
and gallops away, resolved to hasten the process by all practicable
means, that he may sooner be ready to attend another call. At
whatever stage of labor he arrives, he spurs on nature with as
much eagerness as he had before spurred on his horse, though
the closely entwined lives of the mother and her offspring may
be endangered by his precipitancy. Yet such, perhaps, is the
impatience of the poor woman herself, and such very often the
ignorance of the bystanders, that the quicker he is in getting
through his work, if no *obvious* injury be done at the moment, the
greater reputation he undeservedly acquires, and the more he
enlarges the sphere of his murderous practice.[9]

This cartoon of a man-midwife may be a caricature of Smellie, who attended deliveries wearing a woman's nightcap and gown under which he concealed his instruments, so as not to frighten his patients.

Shortening the time of labor by the use of forceps thus gave the man-midwife a great competitive advantage over the midwife.

Smellie was a near genius in developing a rationale for using forceps and in teaching it during a short course, even if his pupils did not always learn and observe what he said. He could not always provide clinical experience of delivery for his pupils, how-

ever, although he tried to find poor expectant women whom he
might pay so that his pupils could observe his birth techniques.
More often he had to resort to a machine model of a woman in
order to demonstrate the theory and practice of birth. Part of his
genius was to represent the theory of birth in the form of a
"mock-woman" and child made of leather, beer, a doll, and a cork.
Here was the elegant French theory brought to the level of a trade
school. Mrs. Nihell described the "mock-woman" in a public exchange of insults with Smellie about which one of them did more
charity work. After claiming she had attended 900 women without charge, Mrs. Nihell said:

> I doubt much whether our critic can say as much, unless he
> reckons it for a charity when he exercises on his automaton or
> machine which served him for a model of instruction to his
> pupils. This was a wooden statue representing a woman with
> child whose belly was of leather, in which a bladder full, perhaps
> of small beer, represented the uterus. The bladder was stopped
> with a cork, to which was fastened a string of picket-thread to tap
> it, occasionally, and demonstrate in a palpable manner the flow-
> ing of the red-colored waters. In short, in the middle of the
> bladder was a wax doll to which were given various positions.
> Does it become a doctor to call us interested who himself for 3
> guineas in nine lessons makes you a man-midwife, or a female
> one, by means of this most curious machine, this mock-woman?[10]

The popularizing of the new midwifery in England after
1750 made it a contentious and incoherent medical and social
enterprise, operating in an open-market situation. Practitioners
did not disagree about the science of birth, largely French in
origin, although educated physicians honored it more than did
the man-midwives exposed to it in short courses such as Smellie's.
The beauty of the machine model was that nearly anyone, even a
sausage stuffer, could grasp the idea of birth. In regard to using
medical arts in birth, however, the lines were drawn. Educated
physicians, who had a long tradition of not using their hands, and
educated midwives, who did not use forceps, tended to argue that
nature was usually sufficient and should not be meddled with. But
new man-midwives, carrying on the rough-and-ready empirical
tradition of barber-surgery, found forceps useful to speed delivery, whether difficult or not, and to represent their triumph over
nature and over their own competitors. Smellie trained people in
the new midwifery, and they went out to practice as best they

A seventeenth-century drawing of a man-midwife delivering under a sheet to preserve his patient's modesty.

could without regulation or supervision. So the contention about technique continued, since entrance to midwifery practice was possible both from the short course and from medical education. After 1750 educated physicians also began to attend births, which they believed they now understood more fully than before—and which provided often handsome fees.

The inclusion of men in the new midwifery, the entrance of educated physicians into obstetrical practice, and the existence of an unregulated competitive situation not only made the question of using forceps unresolvable but also began to drive educated, middle-class midwives from practice. Only traditional midwives who attended the poor in the recesses of the cities and in outlying areas kept their clientele. Mary Wollstonecraft Godwin, author of the first feminist document, *Vindication of the Rights of Woman* (1792) and wife of the famous anarchist William Godwin, deplored the fact that women were losing their ancient occupation to men and insisted as a matter of principle upon having a woman attend her delivery in 1797. She gave birth to a healthy daughter, Mary (who married the poet Percy Bysshe Shelley and later wrote *Frankenstein*), but, when the placenta did not come, the Godwin family called a man-midwife, who inserted his hand to extract it, probably causing her to hemorrhage and eventually to die of puerperal fever.[11] Despite such consequences, male birth attendants were popularly perceived as more able than women, largely on the basis of custom, and gradually became the preferred attendants at middle- and upper-class births.

The Americans who were studying medicine in Great Britain at that time discovered that men could bring the benefits of the new midwifery to birth and thereby gain income and status. In regard to the unresolved question of what medical arts were appropriate, the Americans took the view of the English physicians, who instructed them that nature was usually adequate and intervention often dangerous. From that perspective they developed a model of the new midwifery suitable for the American situation.

From 1750 to approximately 1810 American doctors conceived of the new midwifery as an enterprise to be shared between themselves and trained midwives. Since doctors during most of that period were few in number, their plan was reasonable and humanitarian and also reflected their belief that, in most cases, natural processes were adequate and the need for skilled intervention limited, though important. Doctors therefore envisaged an arrangement whereby trained midwives would attend normal deliveries and doctors would be called to difficult ones. To implement this plan, Dr. Valentine Seaman established a short course for midwives in the New York (City) Almshouse in 1799, and Dr. William Shippen began a course on anatomy and midwifery, including clinical observation of birth, in Philadelphia. Few women came as students, however, but men did, so the doctors trained the men to be man-midwives, perhaps believing, as Smellie had contended, that the sex of the practitioner was less important than the command of new knowledge and skill.[12]

As late as 1817, Dr. Thomas Ewell of Washington, D.C., a regular physician, proposed to establish a school for midwives, connected with a hospital, similar to the schools that had existed for centuries in the great cities of Europe. Ewell sought federal funding for his enterprise, but it was not forthcoming, and the school was never founded. Herein lay a fundamental difference between European and American development of the midwife.

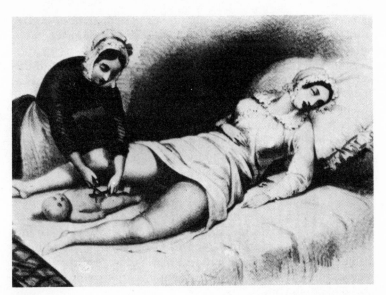

Midwife delivery in nineteenth-century America, from a text for Eclectic physicians. Eclectics, Thomsonians, and other "irregular" physicians advocated the use of midwives in normal cases.

European governments provided financial support for medical education, including the training of midwives. The U.S. government provided no support for medical education in the nineteenth century, and not enough of the women who might have aspired to become midwives could afford the fees to support a school. Those who founded schools turned instead to the potentially lucrative business of training the many men who sought to become doctors.[13]

Doctors also sought to increase the supply of doctors educated in America in the new midwifery and thus saw to it that from the outset of American medical schools midwifery became a specialty field, one all doctors could practice.

The plans of doctors for a shared enterprise with women never developed in America. Doctors were unable to attract women for training, perhaps because women were uninterested in studying what they thought they already knew and, moreover, studying it under the tutelage of men. The restraints of traditional modesty and the tradition of female sufficiency for the management of birth were apparently stronger than the appeal of a rationalized system for a more scientific and, presumably, safer midwifery system.

Not only could doctors not attract women for training in the new science and arts, but they could not even organize midwives already in practice. These women had never been organized among themselves. They thought of themselves as being loyal not primarily to an abstract medical science but to local groups of women and their needs. They reflected the tradition of local self-help empiricism that continued to be very strong in America. Americans had never had a medical profession or medical institutions, so they must have found it hard to understand why the European-trained doctors wished to organize a shared, though hierarchical, midwifery enterprise. How hard it was would be shown later, when doctors sought to organize themselves around the new science of midwifery, in which they had some institutional training. Their practice of midwifery would be governed less by science and professional behavior than by empirical practice and economic opportunity.

In the years after 1810, in fact, the practice of midwifery in American towns took on the same unregulated, open-market character it had in England. Both men and women of various degrees of experience and training competed to attend births. Some trained midwives from England immigrated to America, where they advertised their abilities in local newspapers.[14] But these women confronted doctors trained abroad or in the new American medical schools. They also confronted medical empirics who presented themselves as "intrepid" man-midwives after having imbibed the instrumental philosophy from Smellie's books. American women therefore confronted a wide array of talents and skills for aiding their deliveries.

Childbirth in America would not have any neat logic during the nineteenth century, but one feature that distinguished it from childbirth abroad was the gradual disappearance of women from the practice of midwifery. There were many reasons for that unusual development. Most obvious was the severe competition that the new educated doctors and empirics brought to the event of birth, an event that often served as entrance for the medical person to a sustained practice. In addition, doctors lost their allegiance to a conservative view of the science and arts of midwifery under the exigencies of practice; they came to adopt a view endorsing more extensive interventions in birth and less reliance upon the adequacy of nature. This view led to the conviction that a certain mastery was needed, which women were assumed to be unable to achieve.

Women ceased to be midwives also because of a change in the cultural attitudes about the proper place and activity for women in society. It came to be regarded as unthinkable to confront women with the facts of medicine or to mix men and women in training, even for such an event as birth. As a still largely unscientific enterprise, medicine took on the cultural attributes necessary for it to survive, and the Victorian culture found certain roles unsuitable for women. Midwives also disappeared because they had not been organized and had never developed any leadership. Medicine in America may have had minimal scientific authority, but it was beginning to develop social and professional organization and leadership; unorganized midwives were an easy competitive target for medicine. Finally, midwives lost out to doctors and empirics because of the changing tastes among middle- and upper-class women; for these women, the new midwifery came to have the promise of more safety and even more respectability.[15]

Midwives therefore largely ceased to attend the middle classes in America during the nineteenth century. Except among ethnic immigrants, among poor, isolated whites, and among blacks, there is little significant evidence of midwifery. This is not to say that there were no such women or that in instances on the frontier or even in cities when doctors were unavailable women did not undertake to attend other women. But educated doctors and empirics penetrated American settlements quickly and extensively, eager to gain patients and always ready to attend birth. The very dynamics of American mobility contributed to the break-up of those communities that had sustained the midwives' practices.

Because of continued ethnic immigration, however, by 1900 in many urban areas half of the women were still being delivered by immigrant midwives. The fact that ethnic groups existed largely outside the development of American medicine during the nineteenth century would pose a serious problem in the twentieth century.

Native-born educated women sought to become doctors, not midwives, during the nineteenth century. They did not want to play a role in birth that was regarded as inferior and largely nonmedical—the midwife's role—but wished to assume the same medical role allowed to men.

It is important to emphasize, however, that the disappearance of midwives at middle- and upper-class births was not the result of a conspiracy between male doctors and husbands. The choice of medical attendants was the responsibility of women, upon whom devolved the care of their families' health. Women were free to choose whom they wished. A few did seek out unorthodox practitioners, although most did not. But as the number of midwives diminished, women of course found fewer respectable, trained women of their own class whom they might choose to help in their deliveries.

In order to understand the new midwifery, it is necessary to consider who doctors were and how they entered the medical profession. The doctors who assumed control over middle-class births in America were very differently educated and organized from their counterparts in France or England. The fact that their profession remained loosely organized and ill-defined throughout most of the nineteenth century helps to explain their desire to exclude women from midwifery, for often women were the only category of people that they could effectively exclude. Doctors with some formal education had always faced competition from the medical empirics—men, women, and even freed slaves—who declared themselves able to treat all manner of illnesses and often publicly advertised their successes. These empirics, called quacks by the orthodox educated doctors, offered herbal remedies or psychological comfort to patients. Orthodox physicians objected that the empirics prescribed on an individual, trial-and-error basis without reference to any academic theories about the origins and treatment of disease. Usually the educated physician also treated his patients empirically, for medical theory had little to offer that was practically superior to empiricism until the development of bacteriology in the 1870s. Before then there was no convincing, authoritative, scientific nucleus for medicine, and doctors often had difficulty translating what knowledge they did have into practical treatment. The fundamental objection of regular doctors was to competition from uneducated practitioners. Most regular doctors also practiced largely ineffective therapies, but they were convinced that their therapies were better than those of the empirics because they were educated men. The uneducated empirics enjoyed considerable popular support during the first half of the nineteenth century because their therapies were as often successful as the therapies of the regulars, and sometimes less strenuous. Like the empirics, educated doctors treated patients rather than diseases and looked for different symptoms in different social classes. Because a doctor's reputation stemmed from the social standing of his patients, there was considerable competition for the patronage of the more respectable families.

The educated, or "regular," doctors around 1800 were of the upper and middle classes, as were the state legislators. The doctors convinced the legislators that medicine, like other gentlemen's professions, should be restricted to those who held diplomas or who had apprenticed with practitioners of the appropriate social class and training. State licensure laws were passed, in response to the Federalist belief that social deference was due to professional men. The early laws were ineffectual because they did not take into account the popular tradition of self-help. People continued to patronize empirics. During the Jacksonian Era even the nonenforced licensing laws were repealed by most states as elitist; popular belief held that the practice of medicine should be "democratic" and open to all, or at least to all men.[16]

In the absence of legal control, several varieties of "doctors" practiced in the nineteenth century. In addition to the empirics and the "regular" doctors there were the sectarians, who included the Thomsonian Botanists, the Homeopaths, the Eclectics, and a number of minor sects of which the most important for obstetrics were the Hydrotherapists.

The regular doctors can be roughly divided into two groups: the elite, who had attended the better medical schools and who wrote the textbooks urging "conservative" practice in midwifery; and the great number of poorly educated men who had spent a few months at a proprietary medical school from which they were graduated with no practical or clinical knowledge. (Proprietary medical schools were profit-making schools owned by several local doctors who also taught there. Usually such schools had no equipment or resources for teaching.) In the eighteenth century the elite had had to travel to London, or more often Edinburgh, for training. In 1765, however, the Medical College of Philadelphia was founded, followed by King's College (later Columbia) Medical School in 1767 and Harvard in 1782. Obstetrics, or "midwifery," as it was then called, was the first medical specialty in those schools, preceding even surgery, for it was assumed that midwifery was the keystone to medical practice, something that every student would do after graduation as part of his practice. Every medical school founded thereafter had a special "Professor of Midwifery." Among the first such professors wre Drs. William Shippen at Philadelphia, Samuel Bard at King's College, and Walter Channing at Harvard. In the better schools early medical courses lasted two years; in the latter half of the nineteenth century some schools began to increase this to three, but many two-year medical graduates were still practicing in 1900.

A prestigious medical education did not guarantee that a new graduate was prepared to deal with patients. Dr. James Marion Sims, a famous nineteenth-century surgeon, stated that his education at Philadelphia's Jefferson Medical College, considered one of the best in the country in 1835, left him fitted for nothing and without the slightest notion of how to treat his first cases.[17] In 1850 a graduate of the University of Buffalo described his total ignorance on approaching his first obstetrical case:

> I was left alone with a poor Irish woman and one crony, to deliver her child . . . and I thought it necessary to call before me every circumstance I had learned from books—I must examine, and I did—But whether it was head or breech, hand or foot, man or monkey, that was defended from my uninstructed finger by the distended membranes, I was as uncomfortably ignorant, with all my learning, as the foetus itself that was making all this fuss.[18]

Fortunately the baby arrived naturally, the doctor was given great praise for his part in the event, and he wrote that he was glad "to have escaped the commission of murder."

If graduates of the better medical schools made such complaints, those who attended the smaller schools could only have been more ignorant. In 1818 Dr. John Stearns, President of the New York Medical Society, complained, "With a few honorable exceptions in each city, the practitioners are ignorant, degraded, and contemptible."[19] The American Medical Association later estimated that between 1765 and 1905 more than eight hundred medical schools were founded, most of them proprietary, money-making schools, and many were short-lived. In 1905 some 160 were still in operation. Neither the profession nor the states effectively regulated those schools until the appearance of the Flexner Report, a professional self-study published in 1910. The report led to tougher state laws and the setting of standards for medical education. Throughout much of the nineteenth century a doctor could obtain a diploma and begin practice with as little as four months' attendance at a school that might have no laboratories, no dissections, and no clinical training. Not only was it easy to become a doctor, but the profession, with the exception of the elite who attended elite patients, had low standing in the eyes of most people.[20]

Many people registered their dissatisfaction with "regular" medicine by turning to the various "unorthodox" sects. One popular alternative was the Botanical Movement founded by Samuel Thomson, a poor farmer from rural New Hampshire who had learned his methods from a local "root and herb" doctoress. His *New Guide to Health* sold more than 100,000 copies between 1822 and 1839. Thomson rejected the two most commonly used treatments of regular medicine, calomel (a mercuric compound prescribed by regular doctors until the symptoms of mercury poisoning appeared) and bloodletting. He encouraged patients to think of themselves as equal to doctors in their medical knowledge and contended that regular medicine was not scientific but only pretended to be so.

Thomson's disenchantment with regular medicine had come about because of his wife's near-death from convulsions after childbirth. He called six doctors, all of whom prescribed different treatments. He told of this in his autobiography:

> I heard one of them say his experience in this case was worth fifty dollars. I found that they were trying their practice by experiments; and I was so dissatisfied with their conduct that at night I told them what I thought; and that I had heard them accusing each other of doing wrong; but I was convinced that all told the truth, for they had all done wrong.[21]

He dismissed the regular physicians, and his wife recovered under the care of two root-and-herb doctors. Thomson thereafter believed in self-help.

Because Thomson had learned his "system of botanic medicine" from an old-style empiric doctoress, he extolled "women's superior capacities for the science of medicine" and urged that women attend women.[22] He also opposed what he regarded as doctors' exploitation of midwifery for economic gain.

> Thirty years ago the practice of midwifery was principally in the hands of experienced women, who had no difficulty, but the

doctors have now got most of the practice into their own
hands.... These young, inexperienced doctors... have little
knowledge, except what they get from books, and their practice
is to try experiments.... The midwife's price was one dollar;
when the doctors began to practice midwifery in the country
rural areas, their price was three dollars, but they soon after
raised it to five; and now they charge twelve to twenty.[23]

If this trend continued, Thomson said, no one would be able to
pay the costs of birth.

Although Thomson urged his readers to "restore the business
into the hands of women, where it belongs," there is no evidence
that Thomsonianism prompted an upsurge of practice by midwives. The Botanic system was popular with women, however,
because it rejected bleeding and the practice of applying leeches
to the neck, where they left disfiguring marks.

Most of Thomson's many followers were loyal for reasons of
class; his rejection of banks and paper money along with "priest-
craft and doctor-craft" in the era of Jacksonian Democracy was
popular with the common people in the Midwest and the South.
The Thomsonians even founded their own medical schools in
those regions. An offshoot of Thomsonianism was Eclecticism,
which was founded by Wooster Beach in 1830 and prospered in
the Midwest from 1870 to 1890. Eclectics combined elements of
botanical and regular practice, founded their own medical
schools, and believed that women should be attended by midwives
or women doctors.

A very different sect, popular among the fashionable classes of
the Eastern cities, was Homeopathy, a therapeutic system based
on the theories of Samuel Hahnemann, a German physician.
Hahnemann prescribed extremely small dosages of drugs, down
to the ten-thousandth dilution, rather than the large doses given
by regular doctors. He believed that small dosages would stimu-
late the body to recover from disease. He also believed in fresh air,
bed rest, proper diet, washing, and public sanitation long before
they were popular among regular physicians. Homeopathy attracted the European nobility and was brought to America by
German immigrants in 1825. Because Homeopathy attracted
some of the upper classes, regular doctors accorded its practitioners more respect than they did the other sectarians.[24] Most
Homeopathic medical schools willingly admitted women, and
many of the women who obtained medical diplomas in the

A lecture room at the Medical College for Women in New York City, a Homeopathic school.

nineteenth century were actually homeopaths, or "irregular" physicians.

In addition to the three major sects, many smaller groups flourished. Phrenologists like O. S. Fowler not only presumed to diagnose moral and intellectual character by measuring people's skulls but also published popular manuals on maternity and preached self-help to women.[25] Hydrotherapy, or the "water-cure," consisted of a regimen of drinking mineral water and taking cold baths. The latter were believed to be particularly efficacious in preventing painful births. Under the motto "Wash and Be Healed," the *Water-Cure Journal* championed both women's rights and abolition, on the "medical" ground that all human beings were created equal. The water-cure spas had a predominantly female clientele and staff and were relatively sympathetic toward family limitation and abortion. Some women, like Catherine Beecher, a noted mid-century author on women's health and domestic matters, found the atmosphere of women's community so congenial that they continued to visit the spas long after they ceased to take the cure.[26]

Many of the sects were bolstered by a new interest expressed by laypeople in the workings of their own bodies and in developing healthy living habits, including moderate diet, exercise, non-constricting clothes, fresh air, and baths. Health was coming to be regarded as each person's individual responsibility. This "Popular Health Movement," as historians have labeled it, peaked in the 1830s and 1840s but remained influential throughout the century. Both women and men attended public lectures, held separately for each sex, on physiology, and many doctored themselves rather than turn to regular physicians. The various local "Ladies' Physiological Societies" were the backbone of the popular health movement. The lecturers were men and women doctors—regular, irregular, and empiric—and women and men with an interest in women's health, such as Mary Gove Nichols, a water-cure advocate, and Samuel Gregory, an opponent of man-midwifery. One of the most important influences of nineteenth-century feminism on birth was through the Popular Health Movement's admonition to women to know, and therefore implicitly to control, their own bodies. Such control eventually led to family limitation and to demands for less painful birth.

We have seen that nineteenth-century women could choose among a variety of therapies and practitioners. Their choice was usually dictated by social class. An upper-class woman in an Eastern city would see either an elite regular physician or a homeopath; if she were daring, she might visit a hydropathic establishment. A poor woman in the Midwest might turn to an empiric, a poorly-educated regular doctor, or a Thomsonian botanist. This variety of choice distressed regular doctors, who were fighting for professional and economic exclusivity. As long as doctors were organized only on a local basis, it was impossible to exclude irregulars from practice or even to set enforceable standards for regular practice. The American Medical Association was founded in 1848 for those purposes. Not until the end of the century, however, was organized medicine able to re-establish licensing laws. The effort succeeded only because the regulars finally accepted the homeopaths, who were of the same social class, in order to form a sufficient majority to convince state legislators that licensing was desirable.

Having finally won control of the market, doctors were able to turn to self-regulation, an ideal adopted by the American Medical Association in 1860 but not put into effective practice until after 1900. Although there had been progress in medical science and in the education of the elite and the specialists during the nineteenth century, the average doctor was still woefully undereducated. The Flexner Report in 1910 revealed that 90 percent of doctors were then without a college education and that most had attended substandard medical schools.[27] Only after its publication did the profession impose educational requirements on the bulk of medical practitioners and take steps to accredit medical schools and close down diploma mills. Until then the average doctor had little sense of what his limits were or to whom he was responsible, for there was often no defined community of professionals and usually no community of patients.

Because of the ill-defined nature of the medical profession in the nineteenth century and the poor quality of medical education, doctors' insistence on the exclusion of women as economically dangerous competitors is quite understandable. As a group, nineteenth-century doctors were not affluent, and even their staunchest critics admitted that they could have made more money in business. Midwifery itself paid less than other types of practice, for many doctors spent long hours in attending laboring women and later had trouble collecting their fees. Yet midwifery was a guaranteed income, even if small, and it opened the way to family practice and sometimes to consultations involving many doctors and shared fees. The family and female friends who had seen a doctor "perform" successfully were likely to call him again. Doctors worried that, if midwives were allowed to deliver the upper classes, women would turn to them for treatment of other illnesses and male doctors would lose half their clientele. As a prominent Boston doctor wrote in 1820, "If female midwifery is again introduced among the rich and influential, it will become fashionable and it will be considered indelicate to employ a physician."[28] Doctors had to eliminate midwives in order to protect the gateway to their whole practice.

They had to mount an attack on midwives, because midwives had their defenders, who argued that women were safer and more modest than the new man-midwives. For example, the *Virginia Gazette* in 1772 carried a "LETTER on the present State of MIDWIFERY," emphasizing the old idea that "Labour is Nature's Work" and needs no more art than women's experience teaches, and that it was safer when women alone attended births.

> It is a notorious fact that more Children have been lost since Women were so scandalously indecent as to employ Men than for Ages before that Practice became so general.... [Women mid-wives] never dream of having recourse to Force; the barbarous, bloody Crochet, never stained their Hands with Murder.... A long unimpassioned Practice, early commenced, and calmly pursued is absolutely requisite to give Men by Art, what Women attain by Nature.

The writer concluded with the statement that men-midwives also took liberties with pregnant and laboring women that were "sufficient to taint the Purity, and sully the Chastity, of any Woman breathing." The final flourish, "True Modesty is incompatible with the Idea of employing a MAN-MIDWIFE," would echo for decades, causing great distress for female patients with male attendants. Defenders of midwives made similar statements throughout the first half of the nineteenth century. Most were sectarian doctors or laymen with an interest in women's modesty.[29] No midwives came forward to defend themselves in print.

The doctors' answer to midwives' defenders was expressed not in terms of pecuniary motives but in terms of safety and the proper place of women. After 1800 doctors' writings implied that women who presumed to supervise births had overreached their proper position in life. One of the earliest American birth manuals, the *Married Lady's Companion and Poor Man's Friend* (1808), denounced the ignorance of midwives and urged them to "submit to their station."[30]

Two new convictions about women were at the heart of the doctors' opposition to midwives: that women were unsafe to attend deliveries and that no "true" woman would want to gain the knowledge and skills necessary to do so. An anonymous pamphlet, published in 1820 in Boston, set forth these convictions along with other reasons for excluding midwives from practice. The author, thought to have been either Dr. Walter Channing or Dr. Henry Ware, another leading obstetrician, granted that women had more "passive fortitude" than men in enduring and witnessing suffering but asserted that women lacked the power to act that was essential to being a birth attendant:

> They have not that power of action, or that active power of mind, which is essential to the practice of a surgeon. They have less power of restraining and governing the natural tendencies to sympathy and are more disposed to yield to the expressions of acute sensibility . . . where they become the principal agents, the feelings of sympathy are too powerful for the cool exercise of judgment.[31]

The author believed only men capable of the attitude of detached concern needed to concentrate on the techniques required in birth. It is not surprising to find the author stressing the importance of interventions, but his undervaluing of sympathy, which in most normal deliveries was the only symptomatic treatment necessary, is rather startling. Clearly, he hoped to exaggerate the need for coolness in order to discountenance the belief of many women and doctors that midwives could safely attend normal deliveries.

The author possibly had something more delicate in mind that he found hard to express. He perhaps meant to imply that women were unsuited because there were certain times when they were "disposed to yield to the expressions of acute sensibility." Doctors quite commonly believed that during menstruation women's limited bodily energy was diverted from the brain, rendering them, as doctors phrased it, idiotic. In later years another Boston doctor, Horatio Storer, explained why he thought women unfit to become surgeons. He granted that exceptional women had the necessary courage, tact, ability, money, education, and patience for the career but argued that, because the "periodical infirmity of their sex . . . in every case . . . unfits them for any responsible effort of mind," he had to oppose them. During their "condition," he said, "neither life nor limb submitted to them would be as safe as at other times," for the condition was a "temporary insanity," a time when women were "more prone than men to commit any unusual or outrageous act."[32]

The author of the anonymous pamphlet declared that a female would find herself at times (i.e., during menstruation) totally unable to manage birth emergencies, such as hemorrhages, convulsions, manual extraction of the placenta, or inversion of the womb, when the newly delivered organ externally turned itself inside out and extruded from the body, sometimes hanging to the knees. In fact, an English midwife, Sarah Stone, had described in 1737 how she personally had handled each of these emergencies successfully. But the author's readers did not know that, and the author himself could have dismissed Stone's skill as fortuituous, exercised in times of mental clarity.[33]

The anonymous author was also convinced that no woman could be trained in the knowledge and skill of midwifery without losing her standing as a lady. In the dissecting room and in the hospital a woman would forfeit her "delicate feelings" and "refined sensibility"; she would see things that would taint her moral character. Such a woman would "unsex" herself, by which the doctors meant not only that she would lose her standing as a "lady" but also, literally, that she would be subject to physical exertions and nervous excitements that would damage her female organs irreparably and prevent her from fulfilling her social role as wife and mother.[34]

Perhaps the epitome of this point of view about women was expressed by Dr. Charles Meigs of the Jefferson Medical College in Philadelphia in 1847 to his all-male gynecology class, in the form of a special introductory "Lecture on the Distinctive Characteristics of the Female." Meigs said, in part:

> The great administrative faculties are not hers. She plans no sublime campaign, leads no armies to battle, nor fleets to victory. The Forum is no threatre for her silver voice. . . . She discerns not the courses of the planets. . . . She composes no Iliad, no Aeneid. The strength of Milton's poetic vision was far beyond her fine and delicate perceptions. . . . Do you think that a Woman . . . could have developed, in the tender soil of her intellect, the strong idea of a Hamlet, or a Macbeth?
>
> Such is not woman's province, nature, power, or mission. She reigns in the heart; her seat and throne are by the hearthstone. The household altar is her place of worship and service. . . .
>
> She has a head almost too small for intellect and just big enough for love.[35]

In recent years some social historians have been examining the character of Victorian separate-sex culture, the reasons for it, its extent, and its consequences. That culture expected women to be primarily wives and mothers, homebound, pious, and dependent upon husbands and other males, and it seems that some women were content in this arrangement. Doctors as a group helped both to define and to enforce the boundary between what men and women were expected to do. Thus, arguing that women could not and should not be midwives or doctoresses, male doctors were expressing a cultural judgment as well as protecting their own professional and economic interests.[36] At the same time, they were also, of course, saying what men could and should sometimes do. Sex-linked attributes and prerogatives in birth became a central cultural event, a ritualistic definition of sexual place. In the most simple sense, it became unthinkable that a woman could both give birth and attend birth. Giving birth was the quintessential feminine act; attending birth was a fundamental expression of the controlling and performing actions suitable only for men.

Those women who sought to obtain medical training, despite the opposition of male doctors, were not merely attempting to serve the interests of female patients in modesty, morality, and more natural deliveries. They were also contesting the definition of social place determined by sex, as doctors and the dominant male culture defined and enforced it. When Harriot K. Hunt, a woman empiric who had been trained by apprenticeship to another woman, applied to Harvard Medical School in 1847, she was turned down. In 1850 she tried again and was admitted by the faculty, but the medical students' published objections forced her withdrawal. "We object," wrote the students, "to having the company of any female forced upon us, who is disposed to unsex herself and to sacrifice her modesty by appearing with men in the medical lecture room," where "no woman of any true delicacy" should be found.[37]

Elizabeth Blackwell had greater success; after applying to twenty-nine medical schools, she was finally accepted by Geneva (New York) Medical College, a "regular" school, in 1847. Her acceptance was not intended by the school. The faculty, hesitating to reject the request of the Philadelphia Quaker physician who sponsored her, had allowed the students to cast the decisive vote, feeling confident that they would reject her. Some of the class believed the application was a hoax, others thought that a woman's presence would enliven their education, and others argued that "one of the radical principles of a Republican Government is the universal education of both sexes," which statement appeared in the formal resolution adopted by the class after a unanimous vote to admit her. Blackwell attended three four-month terms, the usual length of a medical course in rural schools, and graduated at the top of her class. She had to go to Paris and London to obtain clinical experience, as no American hospital would allow her to practice. On her return she established, with Quaker backing, the New York Infirmary for Women and Children in 1856, not only to serve the poor but to give women doctors an opportunity for clinical experience. Dr. Marie Zackrzewska, who had been the head midwife at the Royal Maternity Hospital in Berlin, became one of the leading clinicians; she was later joined by Dr. Mary Putnam Jacobi, an ardent suffragist and notable researcher on menstruation. In 1864 Elizabeth Blackwell and her sister Emily opened a medical college for women in conjunction with the infirmary. Their college was notable for having the first professorship of "hygiene," or preventive medicine, in America, a chair first occupied by Elizabeth Blackwell.[38]

Blackwell was more interested in encouraging the entrance of women into the profession than in actually practicing medicine herself. She believed that her life work was "to open the profession to intelligent and cultivated women." The care of children, the sick, the wounded, and especially women in childbed, she argued, "has always been far more the special duty of women than of men," and "the medical practice of women is no new thing, but a necessity of society." She noted in 1855 that "the midwife has been entirely supplanted by the doctor," but she did not lament the passing of the "old midwife," who was "an imperfect institution" that "will disappear with the progress of society." "The midwife," she said, "must give place to the physician. Woman therefore must become physician." Women's practice of medicine would be a spiritual extension of maternity, which Blackwell considered women's "noblest thought," to all humanity, as the "great mothering spirit" was extended to patients.[39]

The difficulties of admission to regular medical schools spurred the establishment of special colleges for women. The first was New England Female Medical College, originally founded in 1848 as a school for midwives by Samuel Gregory. It quickly became a regular medical school but merged in 1874 with Boston University's Homeopathic medical school.[40] In Philadelphia, Quakers, who had always had an interest in the medical education of women, founded Woman's Medical College of Pennsylvania in 1850; it began as an Eclectic school, then became regular. Although no woman's name appeared on the opening announcement, the Quaker feminist Lucretia Mott was active in its establishment, and for many years Dr. Ann Preston, also a Quaker, was its moving spirit.[41]

Women also founded irregular schools. New York Medical College for Women, a Homeopathic school, was founded in 1863 with the help of the suffragist Elizabeth Cady Stanton. During the nineteenth century, at least seventeen women's medical schools were founded, some of them irregular, most of them below the standards of the elite schools. Only one, Woman's Medical College of Philadelphia, survived after the Flexner Report raised medical-educational standards.[42] Because the women's medical schools were mostly small, most women who sought medical degrees in the nineteenth century were forced to go to coeducational schools of irregular traditions such as Homeopathy, Botanism, Eclecticism, or Hydropathy, making their acceptance by the regular profession even more difficult. The first fully coeducational elite school was Johns Hopkins, opened in 1893, which had to accept women as a condition of its endowment by Mary Garrett.

Despite these problems, a number of women did acquire medical degrees of some sort during the nineteenth century. Blackwell estimated that there were two hundred women calling themselves doctors in 1855; by 1870 Federal Census records listed 527; by 1880, after some state university medical schools started admitting women, there were 2,432. In 1890 there were 4,557 and in 1900, 7,387. But these numbers seem less impressive when compared with the numbers of men in the profession. In 1905, for instance, out of 26,000 medical students, only about 1,000 were women.[43]

Women doctors faced obstacles at every turn. They were often refused membership in local medical societies, and even the men who supported or taught them were sometimes ostracized by the profession. Hospitals usually refused to give women clinical training. Therefore women had to found their own institutions, as had Blackwell. These included the New England Hospital for Women and Children in Boston, the Woman's Hospital in Philadelphia, and the Mary Thompson Hospital in Chicago, all founded in the 1860s as institutions where women could be "physicians unto their own sex." Women's practice was small, professionally segregated from men's, and often restricted to serving the poor because many notable women doctors regarded medicine as a public service rather than a scientific or a pecuniary endeavor.

Women never entered medicine in sufficient numbers to take over as physicians to their own sex, as Blackwell had hoped. One reason for this was that the development of nursing as a profession for upper-class educated women attracted many who might otherwise have gone to medical schools. Although the nurse appeared as a necessary figure in all the "matron's manuals of midwifery" published throughout the nineteenth century, she was portrayed as an uneducated practical helper, a servant hired by the family to clean up before and after the birth and to run errands for the doctor. Her virtue lay in her obedience to the doctor, according to the manuals. Possibly some women who might have become midwives in an earlier century became practical nurses in the nineteenth century, an occupation accorded little autonomy or esteem. Toward the end of the century, under the influence of Florence Nightingale, nursing schools were established for the educated upper- or middle-class woman who desired to work at service for others rather than stay at home. Blackwell and other pioneer women physicians applauded and encouraged the upgrading of nursing, but the new nursing schools siphoned off some women who might otherwise have tried to become physicians. Instead, they were trained to obey physicians.[44]

Women medical graduates specialized almost entirely in obstetrics and the diseases of women and children. They encountered difficulties in public acceptance, however, for they were sometimes confused with the "female physicians" who advertised in nineteenth-century newspapers and who were usually uneducated, illegal abortionists. Some male obstetricians lampooned women doctors as feminists, as unmarried, and, above all, as a threat to motherhood. The men implied that such women were promoting family limitation and abortion. In 1852 one doctor lecturing at King's College Medical School argued:

> We have lecturers and lecturesses, and female colleges, where the very large and highly intelligent classes are taught how to get children, and especially how not to get them. The Women's Rights Convention cannot see why women should bear children more than men, and while waiting some plan to equalize the matter, they refuse to bear them themselves.[45]

As a final irony, men doctors charged that women physicians were vulgar and coarse and used street language. Real ladies should prefer gentlemen doctors, who would be courteous and treat them with delicacy.

Many early women doctors were indeed feminists, and many hoped that obstetrics would become the province of women. It is questionable, however, whether feminism had any direct effect upon the therapies used by women physicians. The number of women who practiced was so small and so far outside the mainstream of research and teaching that women could have no effect on the course of obstetric medicine. It is possible that women may have intervened less frequently in birth than did men, but even if their practices differed, and it is uncertain whether they did, women did not establish and teach a distinctly "female" form of obstetrics. Their own training had been dominated by traditions established by men.

The exclusion of women from obstetrical cooperation with men had important effects upon the "new practice" that was to become the dominant tradition in American medical schools. American obstetric education differed significantly from training given in France, where the principal maternity hospitals trained doctors clinically alongside student midwives. Often the hospital's midwives, who supervised all normal births, trained the doctors in normal deliveries. French doctors never lost touch with the conservative tradition that said "Dame Nature is the best midwife." In America, where midwives were not trained at all and medical education was sexually segregated, medicine turned away from the conservative tradition and became more interventionist.

Around 1810 the new midwifery in America appears to have entered a new phase, one that shaped its character and problems throughout the century. Doctors continued to regard birth as a fundamentally natural process, usually sufficient by itself to effect delivery without artful assistance, and understandable mechanistically. But this view conflicted with the exigencies of their medical practice, which called upon them to demonstrate skills. Gradually, more births seemed to require aid.

Young doctors rarely had any clinical training in what the theory of birth meant in practice. Many arrived at a birth with only lectures and book learning to guide them. If they (and the laboring patient) were fortunate, they had an older, experienced doctor or attending woman to explain what was natural and what was not. Many young men were less lucky and were embarrassed, confused, and frightened by the appearances of labor and birth. Lacking clinical training, each had to develop his own sense of what each birth required, if anything, in the way of artful assistance; each had to learn the consequence of misdirected aids.[46]

If the doctor was in a hurry to reach another patient, he might be tempted to hasten the process along by using instruments or other expedients. If the laboring woman or her female attendants urged him to assist labor, he might feel compelled to use his tools and skills even though he knew that nature was adequate but slow. He had to use his arts because he was expected to "perform." Walter Channing, Professor of Midwifery at Harvard Medical School in the early nineteenth century, remarked about the doctor, in the context of discussing a case in which forceps were used unnecessarily, that he "must do something. He cannot remain a spectator merely, where there are too many witnesses and where interest in what is going on is too deep to allow of his inaction." Channing was saying that, even though well-educated physicians recognized that natural processes were sufficient and that instruments could be dangerous, in their practice they also had to appear to *do* something for their patient's symptoms, whether that entailed giving a drug to alleviate pain or shortening labor by using the forceps. The doctor could not appear to be indifferent or inattentive or useless. He had to establish his identity by doing something, preferably something to make the patient feel better. And if witnesses were present there was perhaps even more reason to "perform." Channing concluded: "Let him be collected and calm, and he will probably do little he will afterwards look upon and regret."[47]

If educated physicians found it difficult in practice to appeal before their patients to the reliability of nature and the dangers of instruments, one can imagine what less confident and less competent doctors did with instruments in order to appear useful. A number of horror stories from the early decades of the century have been retailed by men and women who believed that doctors used their instruments unfairly and incompetently to drive midwives from practice.[48] Whatever the truth may be about the harm done, it is easy to believe that instruments were used regularly by doctors to establish their superior status.

If doctors believed that they had to perform in order to appear useful and to win approval, it is very likely that women, on the other hand, began to expect that more might go wrong with birth processes than they had previously believed. In the context of social childbirth, which, we have noted, meant that women friends and kin were present at delivery, the appearance of forceps in one birth established the possibility of their being used in subsequent births. In short, women may have come to anticipate difficult births whether or not doctors urged that possibility as a means of selling themselves. Having seen the "best," perhaps each woman wanted the "best" for her delivery, whether she needed it or not.

Strange as it may sound, women may in fact have been choosing male attendants because they wanted a guaranteed performance, in the sense of both guaranteed safety and guaranteed fashionableness. Choosing the best medical care is itself a kind of fashion. But in addition women may have wanted a guaranteed audience, the male attendant, for quite specific purposes; namely, they may have wanted a representative male to see their pain and suffering in order that their femininity might be established and their pain verified before men. Women, then, could have had a range of important reasons for choosing male doctors to perform: for themselves, safety; for the company of women, fashion; for the world of men, femininity.

So a curious inconsistency arose between the principle of noninterference in nature and the exigencies of professional practice. Teachers of midwifery continued to stress the adequacy of nature and the danger of instruments. Samuel Bard, Dean of King's College Medical School, wrote a text on midwifery in 1807 in which he refused even to discuss forceps because he believed that interventions by unskilled men, usually inspired by Smellie's writings, were more dangerous than the most desperate case left to nature. Bard's successors made the same points in the 1830s and 1840s. Dr. Chandler Gilman, Professor of Obstetrics at the College of Physicians and Surgeons in New York from 1841 to 1865, taught his students that "Dame Nature is the best midwife in the world.... Meddlesome midwifery is fraught with evil.... The less done generally the better. Non-interference is the cornerstone of midwifery."[49] This instruction often went unheeded, however, because young doctors often resorted to instruments in haste or in confusion, or because they were poorly trained and unsupervised in practice, but also, as we have indicated, because physicians, whatever their state of knowledge, were expected to do something.

What they could do—the number of techniques to aid and control natural processes—gradually increased. In 1808, for example, Dr. John Stearns of upper New York State learned from an immigrant German midwife of a new means to effect the mechanics of birth. This was ergot, a powerful natural drug that

stimulates uterine muscles when given orally. Ergot is a fungus
that grows on rye and other stored grains. It causes powerful and
unremitting contractions. Stearns stressed its value in saving the
doctor's time and in relieving the distress and agony of long labor.
Ergot also quickens the expulsion of the placenta and stems
hemorrhage by compelling the uterus to contract. Stearns claimed
that ergot had no ill effects but warned that it should be given only
after the fetus was positioned for easy delivery, for it induced an
incessant action that left no time to turn a child in the birth canal
or uterus.

There was in fact no antidote to ergot's rapid and uncontrolla-
ble effects until anesthesia became available in later decades. So if
the fetus did not move as expected, the drug could cause the
uterus to mold itself around the child, rupturing the uterus and
killing the child. Ergot, like most new medical arts for birth, was a
mix of danger and benefit. Critics of meddlesome doctors said
that they often used it simply to save time. However true that was,
ergot certainly fitted the mechanistic view of birth, posed a di-
lemma to doctors about wise use, and enlarged the doctors' range
of arts for controlling birth. Doctors eventually determined that
using ergot to induce labor without an antidote was too dangerous
and limited its use to expelling the placenta or stopping hemorrhage.[50]

Despite the theory of the naturalness of birth and the danger
of intervention, the movement in midwifery was in the opposite
direction, to less reliance on nature and more reliance on artful
intervention. The shift appeared during the 1820s in discussions
as to what doctors should call themselves when they practiced the
new midwifery. "Male-midwife," "midman," "man-midwife,"
"physician man-midwife," and even "androboethogynist" were
terms too clumsy, too reminiscent of the female title, or too unre-
flective of the new science and skill. "Accoucheur" sounded better
but was French. The doctors of course ignored Elizabeth Nihell's
earlier, acid suggestion that they call themselves "pudendists"
after the area of the body that so interested them. Then an English doctor suggested in 1828 that "obstetrician" was as appropriate a term as any. Coming from the Latin meaning "to stand
before," it had the advantage of sounding like other honorable
professions, such as "electrician" or "geometrician," in which men
variously understood and dominated nature.[51]

The renaming of the practice of midwifery symbolized doctors' new sense of themselves as professional actors. In fact, the movement toward greater dominance over birth's natural processes cannot be understood unless midwifery is seen in the context of general medical practice. In that perspective, several relations between midwifery and general practice become clearly important. In the first place, midwifery continued during the first half of the nineteenth century to be one of the few areas of general practice where doctors had a scientific understanding and useful medical arts. That meant that practicing midwifery was central to doctors' attempts to build a practice, earn fees, and achieve some status, for birth was one physical condition they were confident they knew how to treat. And they were successful in the great majority of cases because birth itself was usually successful. Treating birth was without the risk of treating many other conditions, but doctors got the credit nonetheless.

In the second place, however, birth was simply one condition among many that doctors treated, and the therapeutic approach they took to other conditions tended to spill over into their treatment of birth. For most physical conditions of illness doctors did not know what processes of nature were at work. They tended therefore to treat the patient and the patient's symptoms rather than the processes of disease, which they did not see and were usually not looking for. By treating his or her symptoms the doctors did something for the patient and thereby gained approbation. The doctors' status came from pleasing the patients rather than from curing diseases. That was a risky endeavor, for sometimes patients judged the treatment offered to relieve symptoms to be worthless or even more disabling than the symptoms themselves. But patients expected doctors to do something for them, an expectation that carried into birth also. So neither doctors nor patients were inclined to allow the natural processes of birth to suffice.

There is no need to try to explain this contradiction by saying that doctors were ignorant, greedy, clumsy, hasty, or salacious in using medical arts unnecessarily (although some may have been), for the contradiction reflects primarily the kind of therapy that was dominant in prescientific medicine.

The relations between midwifery and general medical practice become clearer if one considers what doctors did when they confronted a birth that did not conform to their understanding of birth's natural processes. Their mechanistic view could not explain such symptoms as convulsions or high fevers, occasionally associated with birth. Yet doctors did not walk away from such conditions as being mysterious or untreatable, for they were committed to the mastery of birth. Rather, they treated the strange symptoms with general therapies just as they might treat regular symptoms of birth with medical arts such as forceps and ergot.

Bloodletting was a popular therapy for many symptoms, and doctors often applied it to births that seemed unusual to them. If a pregnant woman seemed to be florid or perspiring, the doctor might place her in a chair, open a vein in her arm, and allow her to bleed until she fainted. Some doctors bled women to unconsciousness to counter delivery pains. A doctor in 1851 opened the temporal arteries of a woman who was having convulsions during birth, "determined to bleed her until the convulsion ceased or as long as the blood would flow." He found it impossible to catch the blood thrown about during her convulsions, but the woman eventually completed her delivery successfully and survived. Bloodletting was also initiated when a woman developed high fever after delivery. Salmon P. Chase, Lincoln's Secretary of the Treasury and later Chief Justice, told in his diary how a group of doctors took 50 ounces of blood from his wife to relieve her fever. The doctors gave careful attention to the strength and frequency of her pulse, debating and deliberating upon the meaning of the symptom, until finally Mrs. Chase died.[52]

For localized pain, doctors applied leeches to draw out blood from the affected region. A distended abdomen after delivery might merit the application of twelve leeches; a headache, six on the temple; vaginal pain also merited several.[53]

Another popular therapy was calomel, a chloride of mercury that irritated the intestine and purged it. A woman suffering puerperal fever might be given extended doses to reduce swelling by purging her bodily contents. If the calomel acted too violently, the doctors could retard it by administering opium. Doctors often gave emetics to induce vomiting when expectant women had convulsions, for they speculated that emetics might be specifics for hysteria or other nervous diseases causing convulsions.

An expectant or laboring woman showing unusual symptoms might be subjected to a battery of such agents as doctors sought to restore her symptoms to a normal balance. In a famous case in Boston in 1833 a woman had convulsions a month before her expected delivery. The doctors bled her of 8 ounces and gave her a purgative. The next day she again had convulsions, and they took 22 ounces of blood. After 90 minutes she had a headache, and the doctors took 18 more ounces of blood, gave emetics to cause vomiting, and put ice on her head and mustard plasters on her feet. Nearly four hours later she had another convulsion, and they took 12 ounces, and soon after, 6 more. By then she had lapsed into a deep coma, so the doctors doused her with cold water but could not revive her. Soon her cervix began to dilate, so the doctors gave ergot to induce labor. Shortly before delivery she convulsed again, and they applied ice and mustard plasters again and also gave a vomiting agent and calomel to purge her bowels. In six hours she delivered a stillborn child. After two days she regained consciousness and recovered. The doctors considered this a conservative treatment, even though they had removed two-fifths of her blood in a two-day period, for they had not artificially dilated her womb or used instruments to expedite delivery.[54]

Symptomatic treatment was intended not simply to make the patient feel better—often the treatment was quite violent, or "heroic"—but to restore some balance of healthy appearances. Nor were the therapies given to ailing women more intrusive or different from therapies given to suffering men. The therapies were not, in most instances, forced upon the patients without their foreknowledge or consent. People were often eager to be made healthy and willing to endure strenuous therapies to this end. Doctors did believe, however, that some groups of people were more susceptible to illness than others and that different groups also required, or deserved, different treatments.

These views reflected in large part the doctors' awareness of cultural classifications of people; in other words, the culture's position on the relative social worth of different social classes influenced doctors' views about whose health was likely to be endangered, how their endangered health affected the whole society, and what treatments, if any, were suitable. For birth this meant, for example, that doctors believed it more important for them to attend the delivery of children by middle- and upper-class women than the delivery of children by the poor. It meant that doctors expected "fashionable" women to suffer more difficult deliveries because their tight clothing, rich diet and lack of exercise were unhealthy and because they were believed to be more susceptible to nervous strain. It also meant that doctors thought it fitting for unmarried and otherwise disreputable mothers not to receive charitable care along with other poor but respectable women.

There is abundant evidence that doctors came to believe in time that middle- and upper-class women typically had more difficult deliveries than, for example, farm women. One cannot find an objective measure of the accuracy of their perception, nor, unfortunately and more to the point, can one find whether their perception that some women were having more difficult deliveries led doctors consistently to use more intervention in attending them than in attending poorer women with normal deliveries. Doctors' perception of the relative difficulty of deliveries was part of their tendency to associate different kinds of sickness with different social classes. They expected to find the symptoms of certain illnesses in certain groups of people, and therefore looked for those particular symptoms or conditions. In the nineteenth century upper-class urban women were generally expected to be sensitive and delicate, while farm women were expected to be robust. Some doctors even believed that the evolutionary result of education was to produce smaller pelves in women and larger heads in babies, leading to more difficult births among civilized women. There is no evidence that these beliefs were medically accurate. Whether a doctor considered a patient "sick" or "healthy" depended in part upon class-related standards of health and illness rather than on objective scientific standards of sickness.

Treatment probably varied according to the doctor's perception of a woman's class and individual character. At some times and places the treatment given probably reflected the patient's class as much as her symptoms. Thus some doctors may have withheld the use of instruments from their upper-class patients in the belief that they were too fragile to undergo instrumental delivery. The same doctors may have used instruments needlessly on poor patients, who were considered healthy enough to stand anything, in order to save the doctor's time and permit him to rush off to the bedside of a wealthier patient. On the other hand, some doctors may have used instruments on the upper-class women in order to shorten labor, believing that they could not endure prolonged pain or were too weak to bring forth children unassisted, and also in order to justify higher fees. The same doctors may have withheld forceps from poor women whom they considered healthy enough to stand several days of labor. Unfortunately, there is no way of knowing exactly how treatments differed according to class, for very few doctors kept records of their private patients. The records now extant are for the small number of people, perhaps 5 percent of the population, who were treated in hospitals in the nineteenth century. Only poor women, most unmarried, delivered in hospitals, so the records do not cover a cross-section of classes. These hospital records do indicate a large number of instrumental deliveries and sometimes give the reasons as the patient's own "laziness" or "stupidity" in being unable to finish a birth. It is likely that doctors' expectations of lower-class performance are reflected here. Hospital records also reflect the use of poor patients for training or experimentation, another reason for a high incidence of instrumental deliveries.

The fact that doctors' tendency to classify patients according to susceptibility did not lead to consistent differences in treatment is an important indication that they were not merely slavish adherents to a mechanistic view of nature or to cultural and class interests. Doctors were still treating individual women, not machines and not social types. The possibility of stereotypical classification and treatment, however, remained a lively threat to more subtle discernments of individual symptoms and to truly artful applications of treatment in birth.

At the same time, it was possible that patients would find even unbiased treatments offensively painful, ineffective, and expensive, or would doubt that the doctor had a scientific reason for giving them. Such persons could seek other treatments, often administered by laypeople or by themselves. Yet those treatments, including treatments for birth, were also directed toward symptoms. At a time when diseases were unrecognized and their causes unknown, the test of therapy was the patient's whole response, not the curing of disease. So patients who resented treatments as painful, ineffective, or officious rejected the doctor and the treatments. A woman who gave birth in Ohio in 1846 recalled that the doctor bled her and then gave her ergot even though the birth was proceeding, in her view, quite normally. She thought he was simply drunk and in a hurry and angrily judged him a "bad man."[55]

The takeover of birth by male doctors in America was an unusual phenomenon in comparison to France and England, where traditional midwifery continued as a much more significant part of birth. Practice developed differently in America because the society itself expanded more rapidly and the medical profession grew more quickly to doctor in ever new communities. American mobility left fewer stable communities than in France or England, and thus networks of women to support midwives were more often broken. The standards of the American medical profession were not so high or so strictly enforced as standards in other countries, and thus there were both more "educated" doctors and more self-proclaimed doctors in America to compete with midwives. So American midwives disappeared from view because they had less support from stable communities of women and more competition from male doctors.

The exclusion of women from midwifery and obstetrics had profound effects upon practice. Most obviously, it gave obstetrics a sexist bias; maleness became a necessary attribute of safety, and femaleness became a condition in need of male medical control. Within this skewed view of ability and need, doctors found it nearly impossible to gain an objective view of what nature could do and what art should do, for one was identified with being a woman and the other with being a man.

The bias identified functions, attributes, and prerogatives, which unfortunately could become compulsions, so that doctors as men may have often felt that they had to impose their form upon the processes of nature in birth. Obstetrics acquired a basic distortion in its orientation toward nature, a confusion of the need to be masterful and even male with the need for intervention.

Samuel Bard, one of the few doctors to oppose the trend, remarked that the young doctor, too often lacking the ability to discriminate about natural processes, often became alarmed for his patient's safety and his own reputation, leading him to seek a speedy instrumental delivery for both. A tragedy could follow, compounded because the doctor might not even recognize that he had erred and might not, therefore, learn to correct his practice. But doctors may also have found the "indications" for intervention in their professional work—to hurry, to impress, to win approval, and to show why men rather than women should attend births.

The thrust for male control of birth probably expressed psychosexual needs of men, although there is no basis for discussing this historically. The doctor appears to history more as a ritualistic figure, a representative man, identifying and enforcing sexual roles in critical life experiences. He also provided, as a representative scientist, important rationalizations for these roles, particularly why women should be content to be wives and mothers, and, as a representative of dominant cultural morality, determined the classifications of women who deserved various kinds of treatment. Thus the doctor could bring to the event of birth many prerogatives that had little to do with aiding natural processes, but which he believed were essential to a healthy and safe birth.

Expectant and laboring women lost a great deal from the exclusion of educated female birth attendants, although, of course, they would not have chosen men if they had not believed men had more to offer, at least in the beginning decades of the century. Eventually there were only men to choose. Although no doubt doctors were often sympathetic, they could never have the same point of view as a woman who had herself borne a child and who might be more patient and discerning about birth processes. And female attendants would not, of course, have laid on the male prerogatives of physical and moral control of birth.

Instead, women gave birth before a male attendant in a culture that separated the sexes into widely divergent spheres of life. Birth thereby took on the additional problem of modesty; it became a social event that challenged codes of purity and privacy. Further, as an initiation rite for women, birth became a moral test and a physical trial in which the male doctor, not merely the company of women, judged a woman's passage into adult society.

Notes

1. Walter Radcliffe, *Milestones in Midwifery* (Bristol, England, 1967), pp. 19-63.
2. Lewis Mumford, *The Myth of the Machine.* Vol. 2:, *The Pentagon of Power* (New York: Harcourt Brace Jovanovich, 1970), pp. 51-76, discusses the importance of the machine metaphor.
3. Radcliffe, *Milestones in Midwifery,* pp. 30-33; K. Das, *Obstetric Forceps: Its History and Evolution* (St. Louis, 1929); Leonard Lause, *Obstetrical Forceps* (New York, 1968).
4. William Hunter, *The Anatomy of the Human Gravid Uterus* (London, 1774); George C. Peachey, "William Hunter's Obstetrical Career," *Annals of Medical History,* n.s., 2 (September, 1930):476-479.

5. Elizabeth Nihell, *A Treatise on the Art of Midwifery: Setting Forth Various Abuses Therein, Especially as to the Practice with Instruments* (London, 1760), p. 167n.
6. Sarah Stone, *A Complete Practice of Midwifery* (London, 1737).
7. J. H. Aveling, *English Midwives, Their History and Prospects* (London, 1872), p. 127.
8. Nihell, *Treatise on Art of Midwifery*, p. 71.
9. William Buchan, M.D., *Advice to Mothers* (Philadelphia, 1804), p. 68. First published in London, 1803.
10. Nihell, *Treatise on Art of Midwifery*, p. 50.
11. Eleanor Flexner, *Mary Wollstonecraft: A Biography* (New York: Coward, 1972), pp. 251–255.
12. Valentine Seaman, *The Midwives' Monitor and Mother's Mirror* (New York, 1800); Lewis Scheffey, "The Early History and the Transition Period of Obstetrics and Gynecology in Philadelphia," *Annals of Medical History*, Third Series, 2 (May, 1940), 215–224.
13. John B. Blake, "Women and Medicine in Ante-Bellum America," *Bulletin of the History of Medicine* 34, No. 2 (March–April 1965):108–109; see also Dr. Thomas Ewell, *Letters to Ladies* (Philadelphia, 1817), pp. 21–31.
14. Julia C. Spruill, *Women's Life and Work in the Southern Colonies* (New York: Norton, 1972), pp. 272–274; Jane Bauer Donegan, "Midwifery in America, 1760–1860: A Study in Medicine and Morality," unpublished Ph.D. dissertation, Syracuse University, 1972, pp. 50–52.
15. Alice Morse Earle (ed.), *Diary of Anna Green Winslow, a Boston Schoolgirl of 1771* (Detroit: Singing Tree Press, 1970), p. 12 and n. 24.
16. William G. Rothstein, *American Physicians in the Nineteenth Century: From Sects to Science* (Baltimore: Johns Hopkins Press, 1970), pp. 47–49.
17. J. Marion Sims, *The Story of My Life* (New York, 1888), pp. 138–146.
18. *Buffalo Medical Journal* 6 (September, 1850):250–251.
19. John Stearns, "Presidential Address," *Transactions of the New York State Medical Society* 1:139.
20. Sims, *Story of My Life*, pp. 115–116.
21. Samuel Thomson, *New Guide to Health* (Boston, 1832), pp. 130–131.
22. *Thomsonian Botanic Watchman* 1 (December 1, 1834):182.
23. Thomson, *New Guide to Health*, p. 130.
24. Martin Kaufman, *Homeopathy in America* (Baltimore: Johns Hopkins Press, 1971), pp. 4–11.
25. O. S. Fowler, *Maternity* (New York, 1868).
26. Kathryn Kish Sklar, *Catherine Beecher: A Study in American Domesticity* (New Haven: Yale University Press, 1973), pp. 206–207, 316–319.

27. Abraham Flexner, *Medical Education in the United States and Canada: A Report to the Carnegie Foundation for the Advancement of Teaching* (New York, 1910).

28. Anonymous, *Remarks on the Employment of Females as Practitioners in Midwifery* (Boston, 1820), pp. 4–6. See also Gregory, *Man-Midwifery Exposed*, pp. 13, 49; Donegan, "Midwifery in America," pp. 73–74, 240; Thomas Hersey, *The Midwife's Practical Directory; or, Woman's Confidential Friend* (Baltimore, 1836) p. 221; Charles Rosenberg, "The Practice of Medicine in New York a Century Ago," *Bulletin of the History of Medicine* 41 (1967):223–253.

29. Spruill, *Women's Life and Work*, p. 275; Samuel Gregory, *Man-Midwifery Exposed and Corrected* (Boston, 1848), pp. 13, 28, 36.

30. Samuel K. Jennings, *The Married Lady's Companion and Poor Man's Friend* (New York, 1808), p. 105.

31. Anonymous, *Remarks*, p. 12.

32. Horatio Storer, M.D., *Criminal Abortion* (Boston, 1868), pp. 100–101n.

33. Sarah Stone, *A Complete Practice of Midwifery* (London, 1737).

34. Anonymous, *Remarks*, p. 7.

35. Charles D. Meigs, *Females and Their Diseases: A Series of Letters to His Class* (Philadelphia, 1848), pp. 41–42, 46–47.

36. Barbara Welter, "The Cult of True Womanhood, 1820–1860," *American Quarterly* 18, No. 2 (1966):151–174; Carroll Smith-Rosenberg and Charles E. Rosenberg, "The Female Animal: Medical and Biological Views of Woman and Her Role in Nineteenth-Century America," *Journal of American History* 60 (1973):332–356; Donegan, "Midwifery in America," pp. 160–201.

37. Harriot Kezia Hunt, *Glances and Glimpses* (Boston, 1856), p. 270.

38. Esther Pohl Lovejoy, *Women Doctors of the World* (New York: Macmillan, 1957), pp. 41–76; Ishbel Ross, *Child of Destiny* (New York: Harper & Brothers, 1949); Peggy Chambers, *A Doctor Alone* (London: Bodley Head, 1956).

39. Elizabeth Blackwell, "Address on the Medical Education of Women," December 27, 1855 (New York, 1856), pp. 4–6.

40. Frederick C. Waite, *History of the New England Female Medical College* (Boston: Boston University School of Medicine, 1950).

41. Gulielma Fell Alsop, *History of the Woman's Medical College, Philadelphia, Pennsylvania, 1850–1950* (Philadelphia: J. B. Lippincott, 1950).

42. Lovejoy, *Women Doctors*, p. 120.

43. *Ibid.*, pp. 121–122.

44. Barbara Ehrenreich and Deirdre English, *Witches, Midwives, and Nurses: A History of Women Healers* (Oyster Bay, N.Y.: Feminist Press, 1973), pp. 32–36.

45. Augustus K. Gardiner, *A History of the Art of Midwifery* . . . (New York, 1852), p. 31.

46. Harold Speert, M.D., *The Sloane Hospital Chronicle* (Philadelphia: Davis, 1963), pp. 17–19; Donegan, "Midwifery in America," p. 218.

47. Walter Channing, M.D., *A Treatise on Etherization in Childbirth, Illustrated by 581 Cases* (Boston, 1848), p. 229.

48. Gregory, *Man-Midwifery Exposed*, pp. 13, 28, 36; Hersey, *Midwife's Practical Directory*, p. 220; Wooster Beach, *An Improved System of Midwifery Adapted to the Reformed Practice of Medicine* . . . (New York, 1851), p. 115.

49. Speert, *Sloane Hospital Chronicle*, pp. 31–33, 77–78.

50. Palmer Findlay, *Priests of Lucina: The Story of Obstetrics* (Boston, 1939), pp. 220–221.

51. Nihell, *Treatise on Art of Midwifery*, p. 325; Nicholson J. Eastman and Louis M. Hellman, *Williams Obstetrics*, 13th Ed. (New York: Appleton-Century-Crofts, 1966), p. 1.

52. Rothstein, *American Physicians*, pp. 47–49.

53. *Loc. cit.*

54. Frederick C. Irving, *Safe Deliverance* (Boston, 1942), pp. 221–225.

55. Harriet Connor Brown, *Grandmother Brown's Hundred Years, 1827–1927* (Boston, 1929), p. 93.

3

Modesty and Morality

Q. *What resource is there sufficient to enable the accoucheur always to diagnose*
pregnancy?
A. *Examination per vaginum.*
Q. *What is this process called in professional language?*
A. *The touch.*
Q. *What is the relative importance of this operation to the accoucheur in pregnancy*
and diseases of the uterus?
A. *By some high authority it is regarded as important to the accoucheur, as the lever*
to the mechanic, and the compass to the mariner.

Joseph Warrington, Obstetrical Catechism,
Philadelphia, *1842*

It is, perhaps, best upon the whole, that this great degree of modesty should exist even to
the extent of putting a bar to researches, without which no very clear and understand-
able notions can be obtained of the sexual disorders. I confess I am proud to say, that,
in this country generally, certainly in many parts of it, there are women who prefer to
suffer the extremity of danger and pain rather than waive those scruples of delicacy
which prevent their maladies from being fully exposed . . . but, nevertheless, it is true
that a greater candor on the part of the patient, and a more resolute and careful
inquiry on the part of the practitioner, would scarcely fail to bring to light, in their
early stages, the curable maladies, which, by faults on both sides, are now misun-
derstood, because concealed, and, consequently, mismanaged and incurable.

Charles D. Meigs, M.D., Females and Their
Diseases *(Philadelphia, 1848), p. 19*

ALL MEDICAL TREATMENT invades the patient's privacy. But the
entrance of male doctors into intimate medical relations with
female patients during the nineteenth century, when Victorian
sensibility emphasized purity and modesty, created stresses that
called for extreme delicacy and imaginative resolution. The physical examination during pregnancy, the manipulations in labor
and birth, and the presentations of other female complaints were
uneasy events, often causes for blushing shame and flustered apprehension in both patient and doctor. These intimate occasions

This famous illustration of "the touch" in a gynecological examination is from a nineteenth-century French text frequently used in America. Note the avoidance of eye contact between doctor and patient and the drapery shielding the woman's body from view.

also prompted public protests because of their unavoidable sexual implications, which many believed too often led to libertine fulfillment.

Taboos against revealing the body retarded clinical training in obstetrics until medicine learned to exchange with lower-class women the gift of treatment for the right to expose them to students. In time doctors devised rituals and a rationale for medical intimacy with more "refined" women, although some women were so acutely discomforted by male doctors that they chose continued illness over exposure or sought female attendants.

Yet the problem of modesty was fundamentally a matter of moral trust and moral control, for doctors called upon women to trust them completely, not only as heroes of self-restraint but as the ones who knew what was best for women.

During the 1820s, when man-midwives were beginning to attend more births, a wave of prudery engulfed American culture, so that sexual and physical matters elicited inhibition, embarrassment, and shame. Women were expected to embody innocence and piety, and many therefore felt it shamefully improper to expose any sexual or physical aspects of their nature. Such an emphasis cast pregnancy, for example, the all too obvious result of sexual intercourse, in an ambivalent light, for, although maternity was supposed to be woman's glory, pregnant women of the fashionable classes stayed indoors rather than show changes in their figures. They hesitated to tell even their husbands of their "condition" and worried so much about prenatal influence upon the child of things they had seen, done, read, or even thought about during pregnancy that they sometimes found it safest to do nothing at all.[1]

Susan B. Anthony's mother felt so much shame about her pregnancies that "before the birth of every child she was overwhelmed with embarrassment and humiliation, secluded herself from the outside world and would not speak of the expected little one."[2] Isabella Stewart Gardner and her Boston society friends of the 1860s "disappeared from the social scene" as soon as they suspected pregnancy, leaving their houses only when concealed within a carriage and under layers of shawls. Scarlett O'Hara, heroine of *Gone With the Wind,* lost her reputation in post-bellum Atlanta for "showing herself" while pregnant during an attempt to prevent her lumberyard from losing money throughout her socially enforced nine months' absence. The very term "pregnancy" was replaced in polite usage by such euphemisms as "in a family way," "expecting," or "in a delicate condition."

Agnes Smedley's autobiographical novel *Daughter of Earth* demonstrates that the shame associated with birth extended by the end of the century even to the rural poor; she told of the prudery she encountered in her childhood on a Missouri farm around 1900:

> A few days before a baby calf had been born and I had seen it. It was I who brought the news of the marvelous event; but then my father and mother forced me to keep out of sight of the field where the mother and calf were, and where I had been but a few moments before. The thing I had seen I dared not talk about or ask about without "deservin' to have my ears boxed."
>
> Even when my little brother was about to be born, we children were hurried off to another farmhouse, and secrecy and shame settled like a clammy rag over everything. At sunset, a woman, speaking with much forced joy and in a tone of mystery, asked us if we wanted a little brother. It seems a stork had brought him.[3]

The term "confinement," by which Victorians commonly described pregnancy and lying-in, expressed the shame and impropriety of exposure during pregnancy, for the expectant woman separated herself and kept to her home, indicating her need for rest and her unfitness for polite, mixed society. Colonial women, most of whom lived and worked on farms, could not remove themselves from view because their labor was essential to farm life, but leisured women of the nineteenth century embroidered the niceties of female conduct by withdrawing from social life. The word "confinement" pointed to the complex symbolism associated with their withdrawal, for the word also described the social separation of the dangerous criminal and the insane. "Confinement" never meant simply punishment or bland custody, however, even when applied to criminals or the insane; rather, it betokened society's hope to regenerate a self in institutions modeled upon the regularity, duty, and piety of the home. Thus confinement for childbirth was withdrawal to the supreme source of a woman's identity and purpose, the home. There, in her domain, a woman relearned who she was and, in maternity, performed her essential duty. Thereafter she might return, richly renewed, to society.

Women hid not only the physicalities of birth; they often feared as well to mention their physical distresses either to doctors or to one another. Almost unmentionable were such disorders as vaginal infections, prolapsed uteri, poorly healed perineal tears from past births, menstrual irregularities, and a host of "nervous" ailments that medicine then considered to be directly related to the generative organs but could do little to cure. Communicating about one's body and its ailments and being nude were unthinkable acts, because they revealed one's selfhood. Inhibition expressed not only protective innocence but guilty protection. A woman's body was a sacred vessel that she should navigate in all innocence; if that vessel wallowed and foundered it was certainly because she had lost her bearing. The exposed body revealed the course a woman had steered, perhaps errantly, for sickness was usually the sign of misbehavior and misguidance.

Prudery was not so complete, however, that women were not curious to learn about their sexuality and physiology; perhaps it even made them more so. Victorian ambivalence restricted public discussion and exposure but not necessarily private interest: Women seem to have read a host of books by both male and female authors that described human sexuality and offered a wide variety of counsel about ways to maintain health and to find personal, moral fulfillment.[4] Prudery therefore concealed a complex mix of public reticence and private concern, a hesitation about revealing one's self to social judgment, but also a desire for better knowledge and advice about a healthy and morally meaningful physicality. Who was able to offer such advice and what the proper advice was were matters that constituted a central cultural struggle between men and women during the nineteenth century. It was a struggle men generally won, and a principal means they employed was the leverage of advice about birth. But to attend to birth, men had to deal with modesty.

Intimate medical relations between male doctors and female patients required delicate maneuvering but were perhaps less cause for distress than is at first apparent. Man-midwifery by educated British and American physicians had been acceptable among upper- and middle-class women for a score of years before Victorian codes appeared. Although modesty had deterred easy male–female relations in the eighteenth century, attitudes toward the body had not been so cripplingly shameful that they prevented women from choosing male doctors to attend them. Women valued the doctors' reputed knowledge and skill more than their own modesty.

Moreover, in the centuries during which it was practiced, man-midwifery had devised methods by which to respect the modesty of female patients and male attendants during birth. In the sixteenth century a French doctor, Ambroise Paré, operated with the woman completely covered by linen cloths so that he could feel but not see what he was doing. Barber-surgeons in England probably practiced in a similar way. The Chamberlen family man-midwives kept their forceps a secret for three generations by covering themselves and the woman's body with a sheet and working in the dark. Smellie disguised himself as a woman, wearing a ruffled nightcap and gown, under which he concealed his instruments, so as not to alarm his patients with a man's presence. Some eighteenth-century doctors tied a cloth about their necks and draped it over their hands and lower bodies, thus separating themselves visually from their actions. Others preferred to have the woman lie on her side facing away from them so that they saw her only from behind. This position was comfortable for many women and preserved some degree of modesty, as there was no eye contact. Some American obstetrical textbooks advised the use of this "lateral," or "Sims," position as late as 1912, though by then most doctors preferred the "lithotomy" position, in which the woman lay on her back with legs apart.[5]

The touch, of course, had a medical rationale in measuring the size of the birth canal and in determining the dilatation of the cervix before birth, but whether women knew its purpose is uncertain. One medical writer indicated that the touch, far from being an affront, had such near-magical significance that it might be the occasion for a bit of flim-flam. He instructed doctors to act as if they caused all that happened in birth, even if they were not present:

> A patient, after the waters are discharged, requires a little management. It is not just to stay with her at the time; and yet it is necessary, if we leave her, to leave her in confidence. Therefore we may give her the idea of making provision for whatever may happen in our absence: we may pass our finger up the vagina or opening of the womb, and make a moderate degree of pressure, for a few seconds, or any part of it so that she may just feel it: after which we may say to her, "there ma'am, I have done something that will be of great use to your labor." This she trusts to: and if, when she sends for us, we get there in time, it is well: if later than we should be, we easily satisfy her. "Yes! You know I told you I did something which would be of great use to your labor!" If the placenta is not yet come away—"Oh, I am quite in time for the after-birth, and that, you know, is of the greatest consequence in labor!" And if the whole has come away—"We are glad that the after-birth·is all come away in consequence of what we did before we last left, and the labor terminated just as we intended it should."[6]

Here is an excellent example of symptomatic treatment that gave the doctor credit for birth's success, even though it was usually an inherently successful natural process.

Whatever immodesty medical gestures may have had was removed by claiming for them broader medical effects than they had, as doctors knew. But even immodest and often useless gestures symbolized the doctor's control of birth, as the *Obstetrical Catechism* indicated in calling the touch the doctor's "lever and compass." Students, however, had to learn to use the gestures delicately, as the following excerpt from the *Catechism* explains:

> Q. What conduct should the accoucheur observe when about to make this kind of examination?

A. That which has regard to the sense of delicacy, on the part of the female.

Q. To whom should he make the proposition for an examination?

A. To a third person, as a nurse, the husband, or some matronly female.

Q. How should he dispose of himself, while such a proposition is communicated to the patient?

A. He should retire into another room until the decision is made.

Q. What arrangements should be made in order to conduct the examination most satisfactorily?

A. The room should be darkened, and the patient lightly dressed, and placed in the suitable position.

Q. Should the physician insist upon having a third person present?

A. He should always do so if it be at all practicable.

Q. What is the rule for carrying the hand under the coverings?

A. The clothes should be properly raised at their lower edges, by the left hand, and then the right hand with the index finger lubricated, passed cautiously up under the clothes without uncovering the patient.

Q. To what portion of the genital fissure should the finger be carried?

A. Always to the posterior commissure, avoiding contact with the mons veneris if possible.[7]

By such procedures, doctors developed rituals to protect the patient's modesty and their own, for the doctor "should try to make a good impression in advance" and to

... carefully exhibit in his behavior the most refined delicacy, combining with a warm sympathy and kind consideration, thus soothing her scruples and enlisting her gratitude. He must also appear perfectly self-possessed under all circumstances, and then she will have full confidence in his skill and judgment.

The doctor should converse with the patient upon different subjects, such as the weather, and never upon the examination.

He should seat himself by the side of the bed, with his right hand next her, and his face opposite hers. Then passing his hand under the bedclothes, after having lubricated it with lard or oil, he can proceed with the examination as if it were a simple ordinary proceeding. By exhibiting no hurry, and appearing to think it nothing unusual or in any way strange, the female herself will cease to think it so and will not be flurried or shocked.[8]

The patient was of course fully clothed, and at no time did the doctor see her genitalia.

The medical profession claimed that a doctor who could not practice "by the sense of touch alone" was incompetent in midwifery, and American textbooks on midwifery, drawing from French originals, obligingly illustrated that point by showing drawings of the doctor on one knee before his standing patient, feeling under her long skirts, with his eyes averted and staring abstractly into the distance.[9]

The problem for modesty became not touch but sight, whether the male doctor could see the genitalia and whether the patient could see the doctor seeing her body. Exposure during physical examination and during delivery were the matters of most extreme delicacy in nineteenth-century America, for both doctors and patients. Exposure had been a problem in the previous century also, and British instructors in midwifery, such as Smellie, had to resort to using a "mock-woman" to demonstrate the processes of birth to most students, although occasionally

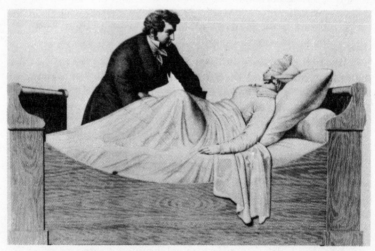

This nineteenth-century drawing illustrates another technique for preserving the patient's modesty: the doctor conducting a gynecological examination looks directly into the woman's eyes to assure her that her private parts are safe from his gaze.

Smellie, Shippen, and other instructors found poor women who were willing to allow male students to observe their deliveries. How much they actually saw is uncertain, but it is unlikely that the whole delivery occurred under cover. The reason such men found it hard to attract women students may have been that the women found the possibility of seeing birth in mixed company unthinkable.

The prohibition against exposure in nineteenth-century America was sufficiently strong to retard clinical training in midwifery, for until the middle of the century schools did not allow medical students to witness deliveries, and students had to learn how to deliver babies entirely from books. Professor Meigs of the Jefferson Medical School in Philadelphia wrote in 1848:

> I hope the day is far distant when the spectacle shall be seen in our hospitals, of troops of women, waiting in succession, for a public examination of their genitalia, in the presence of large classes of medical practitioners and students of medicine. I regard the public sentiment, as to the sanctity of female modesty and chastity, as one of the strongest safeguards of our public polity; . . . for woman, and man's respect for her, are truly at the basis, and are the very cornerstone of civilization and order. . . . He is but the pander of vice who parades his thousands of uterine cases before the public gaze; and is himself an unchaste man, who ruthlessly insists upon a vaginal taxis in all cases of women's diseases that, however remotely, may seem to have any, the least connection with the disorders of their reproductive tissues.[10]

Meigs was, of course, speaking of uterine examination as a part of treatment for sick women, but he expressed the dominant medical attitude about exposure, which in the natural event of childbirth was even less necessary.

Most doctors went forth to attend birth with no clinical experience; those from better medical schools associated with clinics or hospitals may have had experience of the touch alone. A desire to overcome the restriction on clinical training, which often created ignorance and mishap, prompted Dr. James White of Buffalo to demonstrate a delivery upon a living patient before a group of medical students in 1850. The woman was from the county poorhouse, was having her second illegitimate child, and was one of the recent Irish immigrants in Buffalo, a group of second-class citizens who had only shortly before won the right to enter the state legally. The presence of such a low-status female population may have been essential for clinical midwifery to proceed, for doctors could classify such women as not needing or deserving the same symptomatic treatment given to respectable women. It is curious that the protest that followed this event had little to say about the patient's feelings or the respect due to her but a great deal about the impropriety of the men's conduct and the effect their conduct would have upon the feelings of respectable women.

Twenty men observed for about five minues as Dr. White showed the correct technique while exposing only the birth canal to view. The students were grateful and proud that their school was the first to introduce clinical midwifery, but another Buffalo physician wrote newspaper articles charging that the students with their "salacious stares" had satisfied a "meretricious curiosity." Delicacy forbade him to say what the students had done, yet he implied that they had become sexually aroused and jocular and that the tedium of what he called long hours of exposure "was relieved by such methods as a congregation of boys would know how to employ."[11]

In order to protect his reputation from that kind of innuendo, White initiated a libel suit, which he lost on technical grounds. During the trial many local doctors indicated their opposition to White's clinical teaching; one testified that all the "essentials of instruction could be learned by watching the deliveries of cows and sheep in a barnyard." Seventeen doctors signed a letter to the local medical journal expressing their belief that clinical instruction was unnecessary, unprofessional and "grossly offensive alike to morality and common decency."[12]

A committee of the American Medical Association deprecated the exposure of a patient during delivery as unnecessary since a physician had to learn to conduct labor by touch alone or he was unfit to practice. Other national responses were more varied, some pointing out that clinical training in obstetrics had long been common in foreign countries and had contributed to new knowledge and better skills for complications of birth and other female conditions. Other doctors feared, however, that, if men could not perform obstetrical operations (including catheterization, forceps, and even embryotomy) "as well without the eye as with it," obstetrical practice would so offend women that they would choose female attendants and thus ruin many male doctors' practice.[13]

The fit doctor was to be essentially a blind man. Clinical demonstration threatened the medical image of physicians as moral men, and the misbehavior of one doctor could contaminate the entire profession in the eyes of women, who might come to fear that a doctor would expose them to view at any moment. The need to keep women's trust conflicted with the need for better training and research; doctors' authority rested fundamentally upon the approbation of patients and not yet upon science.

At mid-century modesty and fear of patients' disapproval blocked clinical training in midwifery even in hospitals. In Boston in 1845 Doctors John C. Warren and Jacob Bigelow of the Massachusetts General Hospital requested a committee to consider adding a maternity ward to the hospital so that medical students might no longer be deprived of clinical training and thus "be called to their first case without ever having seen a delivery or possessing more knowledge of the science than can be gathered from books." The committee agreed to the wisdom of the proposal but rejected it. Although a few women had delivered in the hospital, they were not objects for teaching and were attended as if they were in their own homes. The committee explained why clinical training was impossible and in doing so revealed a clear sense that the hospital could not change the society's classificatory scheme for women since its status came from patronage by the respectable.

"Respectable married women," the committee said, could not be expected to deliver where they would be subject to exposure and publicity. Their own self-respect, "regard for their families and friends and other strong feelings and prejudices" would keep them away. Even poorer women would prefer to be at home. If only unmarried mothers were taken, then no respectable woman would ever attend the hospital to deliver. And even unmarried women would not want publicity, for most came from respectable families, and though "they have lost their claim to virtue, they still retain its image in their hearts." That would leave for patients only "fallen" women, those who have "become fixed in a vicious course of life," "kept mistresses, women of notoriously loose habits and girls of the town, so called." In this group also were women reared without any moral or religious instruction, those in whom "every bad passion and feeling has been fostered and indulged." But most of those would still retain enough scruples to prevent them from allowing exposure. Those who had no such

In this French nineteenth-century drawing, the woman lies in expulsive agony while the doctor reaches in to guide the baby's head. Many French clinicians, unlike their American counterparts, believed that exposure of the patient was necessary for the training of students, but the patients so exposed were rarely of the higher classes.

scruples—are they yet "deserving of sympathy and protection" by a charitable institution? Perhaps yes, the committee said, for they need "moral as well as medical treatment." But the effect of admitting such maternity patients of "bad reputation" would be to empty the hospital of all reputable patients, to lose the good will of philanthropic donors, and to increase greatly the hospital expenses.[14] At that time hospitals, like doctors, had to exemplify moral rectitude to gain and retain status.

In the early decades of the nineteenth century in many cities doctors and philanthropic patrons did establish separate maternity hospitals as charitable asylums for poor or unmarried women who the doctors and patrons believed deserved a clean, comfortable, and moral environment in which to deliver and to rehabilitate themselves. Many of those expectant women were servants of wealthy families, just as general hospital patients were often servants or employees of wealthy patrons, for it was inconvenient for domestic servants to deliver or be sick in their masters' homes. Patrons and doctors were also willing to admit unmarried mothers, as victims of ignorance and urban living, for first deliveries, but they did not welcome repeaters, whom they regarded as morally degraded and culpable. Women usually stayed in such hospitals as long as two months (one month before and one after delivery). In offering a simulated home delivery, the hospital provided not only for their health but for their moral rehabilitation. Expectant and newly delivered women were often asked to work to keep the hospital clean, for example, thus learning the housewife's chores while also supporting the institution. The hospital attempted to treat the whole woman: body, behavior, and belief.[15]

After the Civil War doctors realized that maternity hospitals provided occasions for clinical obstetrics; students might learn and professors teach and research. Doctors therefore struck a bargain with the charity patients in such hospitals; in exchange for medical treatment, the women would allow themselves to be exposed to the eye of medicine. Doctors could do this because respectable women patrons supported such institutions for the deserving poor, who were valuable to the patrons as object lessons about the redeemability of the poor and the value of charity.

The maternity hospital was an interesting example of the exchange of benefits between social classes, for what the doctors learned in treating the poor they could use in treating respectable women in their homes. A number of obstetrical and gynecological procedures were perfected, occasionally taught to students, and made available to other women. Doctors could study birth more intently in the light of growing scientific knowledge than was possible in home deliveries, for they could disregard the scruples and feelings of poor charity patients more readily than those of respectable women. Since doctors acquired little status from treating the poor, the maternity hospital allowed obstetrics to transcend the barrier of modesty and to begin to transform itself into a science that looked primarily at the physical processes of birth rather than at patients. Of course the transformation was incomplete in the second half of the nineteenth century, and even scientifically inclined hospital doctors continued to explain difficulties in birth by referring to differences in patients' moral character and social behavior. In fact, the doctors and patrons could not have institutionalized the disregard for modesty in poor women if they had not assumed that modesty was somehow a less real or valuable attribute among the poor.

The number of American doctors interested in advancing the science of obstetrics and gynecology was small, however, just as the number of women they treated in hospitals was small throughout the century. The vast majority of doctors were engaged in private practice, which meant treating women in their homes, and most of these doctors reacted against medical advances whose use in treating respectable women might disturb the moral ethos of the medical relationship. For example, the vaginal speculum, an ancient instrument which was further developed in France in 1801, permitted full visual inspection of the vagina and cervix and made possible the earlier discovery of abnormalities, such as tumors, not disclosed by the touch. But doctors themselves, as the quote from Dr. Meigs at the outset of this chapter indicates, felt deeply ambivalent about using a potentially beneficial technique that required exposure. The American Medical Association in 1851 recommended against use of the speculum as too embarassing to women and hazardous for the doctors' reputation and status.[16] Doctors did not routinely use such visual techniques in private practice; the women who benefited from them were those who sought out scientifically inclined physicians to treat some aggravated gynecological condition.

While scientific insights about birth increased and while more doctors used technical aids to assist birth, most doctors did not regard birth scientifically but in a fundamentally different way; that is, they sought to understand why some women had difficult births or organic troubles by examining and speculating about

The vaginal speculum (left) which permitted full visual examination of the cervix, was considered an affront to modesty during much of the nineteenth century.   Speculum developed by J. Marion Sims for use in operations to repair vesico-vaginal fistulas, tears between vagina and bladder resulting from difficult births.

those women's entire life situation, which the doctors suspected to be deviant in such a way as to cause their troubles. In practicing what remained essentially prescientific medicine, most doctors assumed that female troubles came from defects in the woman's behavior, environment, and moral disposition—in the broadest sense, from her "personal being." Exactly which social, cultural, religious, moral, and physical laws the woman had supposedly disobeyed to cause her particular trouble was a highly intuitive perception that varied from one doctor to another. But each saw the fault primarily in the woman's person although it was expressed in her body. The doctor's task was always twofold: to treat the trouble once it had appeared, and to attempt to prevent trouble by advising women so they might not become errant, inadequate, and ultimately physically defective persons.[17]

Doctors did not invent this moralistic perspective about sickness and health, for it was a general cultural perception, but they gave it content that had profound effects upon women. Most people explained sickness, except for a few recognizably contagious diseases, according to this moralistic perspective. The female authors of books about female physiology shared this view, for example, though their advice to women about prevention and treatment often differed from men's advice. Irregular doctors of various persuasions, both male and female, shared the moral view. In fact, modesty itself expressed more than a simple reluctance to expose the genitalia; it showed how widespread and real was the cultural belief that revealing the bodily condition would reveal as well the state of the person indissolubly linked with it.[18]

The whole culture was oriented toward counsels of perfection that would prevent trouble; doctors' advice to women about how to avoid difficult births and other female problems amplified this view. People expected medical practitioners to define the types of behavior that produced good or bad health in women and also to treat women's troubles, once they appeared, not only with physical therapies to alleviate symptoms but also with moral regimens to rehabilitate the person. Male doctors therefore had abundant opportunities to become counselors and "friends" to women, guides to "correct" behavior, who helped women find personal fulfillment. Nonetheless, the doctors' opportunities were not without difficulty, for they had to contend with women's modesty, with the many other advisers and counselors to women, and with women who doubted the doctors' wisdom or authority itself.

Nineteenth-century male doctors handled the problem of modesty by the rituals against exposure already mentioned and by cloaking themselves in cultural roles promising that doctors were not only blind but asexual as well. Dr. Meigs lectured his class in obstetrics on the importance of being Christian gentlemen in their practice: "With woman as his companion, he acts not only that he may live, but that he may live like a Christian and like a Gentleman."[19] The historian Charles Rosenberg has suggested that the nineteenth-century gentleman

> ... was an athlete of continence, not coitus, continuously testing his manliness in the fire of self-denial. This paradigmatic figure eschewed excess in all things, and, most important, allowed his wife to dictate the nature of their sexual interaction.[20]

This idea may well have fortified doctors to touch lady patients without becoming aroused and, at the same time, may have encouraged patients and their husbands to trust Christian gentlemen-doctors to be self-restrained if not sexually benign. Doctors also thought of themselves as "angels of mercy, and priestly confidants," thus bringing to the relation with women the promise of the secrecy and confidentiality of the confessional.[21]

Not until many years later would doctors and patients come to think that the doctor was looking at the woman with the impartial gaze of science. In that interim, both had to conceive of the relation in terms of trustworthy roles the culture provided, such as: guardian with ward, father with daughter, priest and confessee, counselor and counselee, teacher and pupil. These roles emphasized paternalism and its opposite, childish innocence and dependency.

The role-playing that was essential for the relation to begin soon pervaded it entirely, strengthening the doctor's authority and the woman's dependency. Doctors stressed that women's innocent trust was a helpful therapy in itself, an indispensable step to the recovery of health. They were saying that if a woman trusted them to be blind, asexual, and confidential, then the doctors would be able to bring their intellect, their capable and decisive medical techniques, their firm and reliable moral advice to control the woman for her own good. The woman should therefore submit, reveal, rest, and recover—entrusting herself entirely to the purposeful control of the fatherly doctor. S. Weir Mitchell,

a prominent nineteenth-century physician to women, described
the ideal patient thus:

> Wise women choose their doctors and trust them. The wisest ask
> the fewest questions. The terrible patients are nervous women
> with long memories, who question much where answers are dif-
> ficult. The nervous woman should be made to comprehend at
> the outset that the physician means to have his way unhampered
> by the subtle distinctions with which bedridden women are apt to
> trouble those who most desire to help them.[22]

Modesty was like a psychological hurdle for women, but once
over it women found themselves in the arms of men who said,
"Now that we know you, we will be able to do what is best for you."
The doctors' claim that they knew best, that trust in them was
worthwhile, was not new, of course; it had been fundamental to
their opposition to midwives early in the century and had prompted
many upper-class women to choose the doctors. What the doctors
did was expand the claim that they knew better about birth
mechanics than midwives, and thus could give women safer and
speedier deliveries, to include the claim that they knew better than
others how to prevent trouble and how to remedy it. The doctors
were claiming that their moral therapy—a vast amount of culturally
influenced, scientifically unsubstantiated, and essentially speculative knowledge—would ensure a woman's having healthy reproductive organs, less painful and unsafe births, and a generally happier,
more fulfilling life. Thus doctors encouraged women to make the
leap of faith, for they had everything to gain from doctors' care.

The doctors' strategy, therefore, was to tell women that safe
delivery was such a deeply imperiled event that they needed doctors' constant advice in order to make it a planned and conscious
success. At the same time, the doctors endlessly reiterated that
each woman's individual and social fulfillment turned basically
upon becoming a mother. By calling women to a necessary but
threatened destiny, which doctors were best able to aid, doctors
made themselves indispensable comforters of women.

Doctors did not invent the nineteenth-century cultural views
about women's proper place and behavior, what historians have
termed "the cult of the 'true' woman," but these views focused the
doctors' concern and mandated their intrusion into the lives of
women. The "true" woman was meant to be pious and pure, a

domestic creature who would submit herself to her husband; most important, she was meant to be a mother. Motherhood was her special glory and purpose, her deepest reward and justification, and also her means to power. If the crux of women's place and behavior was maternity, then both doctors and women shared a common goal: to bring women to this fulfillment.[23]

Many women and their doctors believed that fulfillment was imperiled, however, by a deteriorating condition in women's health. By the middle of the nineteenth century women seemed to be in greater pain, to be more nervous, to be simply limper and weaker than women had been before. In 1855, for example, Catherine Beecher, as a self-styled hygienist for women, was convinced "that there was a terrible decay of female health all over the land." She conducted, therefore, an amateur survey of women's health by inquiring of her friends in various cities about their friends' health. What she learned confirmed her perception that remarkably few women felt in even fair health; most complained of fatigue, backache, headache, excruciating pains in various parts of the body, coughs, chills, or nervousness. Some were completely invalided. Beecher concluded that good health was so rare that most women did not even know what it was like.[24] While doctors might have dismissed Beecher's evidence as being only a summary of upper-class women's affectations, doctors were well aware that American women of all classes were more susceptible than men to such illnesses as consumption. So both women and doctors came to think mid-century women less healthy than their mothers and grandmothers had been. Women were suffering a plague of unhealthy conditions, which not only threatened their maternal purpose but often appeared to originate in women's reproductive organs themselves. This perception caused doctors to speculate increasingly about the behavioral, environmental, and biological causes that distinguished women from men and endangered women's destiny.

Doctors devised a vast litany of specific dangers to women's health, which was centered of course in their sexual organs. The effect of their increasingly urgent and widespread advice was to teach women that their biology was not only different from men's but also so sensitive that they must live a cautious life shaped by the demands of their inward parts, which were the keys to their own physical and social fulfillment. Women were warned that since they were the creature and the prisoner of their female organs they must keep to the social roles of wife and mother for which their biology was fitted and in which they were safe. To venture beyond the domain of the home was to risk danger, for they were not equipped for the wider world's strenuous demands and would irreparably "unsex" themselves by incautious behavior. The world of intellect and business was too full of nervous shocks for women to enter it without endangering their physical being and personal character; nervous shocks directly transmitted themselves to the reproductive organs, harmed them, and thus distorted the emotions and moral perceptions. Damaged organs meant that a woman could not love and feel as a woman should and, worst of all, could not bear healthy children.

Doctors rang many changes on the alarm system of female biology, for the boundary between safe and dangerous behavior was subtle even if a woman did not stray far from the safety of home. Late parties, romantic novels, card playing, money worries, auto-eroticism, marriage too early or too late, too much intercourse in marriage or too little—these were some of the diverse and confusing dangers to fulfillment. Throughout most of the century doctors did not (and could not) distinguish precisely among the causes of illness but assumed that health and ill health resulted from patterns of moral choice. They held women responsible for generating many of their illnesses by having behaved so as to harm their physiological systems. At the same time, doctors held women to be simply more susceptible than men to disease. Either way, doctors made women deeply fearful and eager for aid.

Although doctors blended physical and moral treatment for male patients also, they did not usually assume that the sexual organs in men were so central to their being or so susceptible to ailment as those in women, and doctors also did not have the same opportunities to impose their advice upon men as upon women. It is not unlikely, in fact, that the many natural occasions doctors had to treat women—in puberty, menstruation, pregnancy, birth, and menopause—gave rise to their beliefs about the centrality of the female organs to women's health and personal fulfillment. At any rate, these occasions gave the doctors periodic medical rituals in which to impose their treatment, judgment, and advice.[25]

Doctors pictured women as the bearers of a physiological system that was like a complex but sensitive machine, one that had a will of its own—as shown by menstruation—but needed guidance as well. The woman was to oversee herself, and her failures were her own, but because her physiology affected her ability to control herself, she ultimately had to rely upon the guidance of her doctor. Doctors therefore claimed the widest therapeutic modality: the unique ability to steer women day by day to physical and social fulfillment. Fearing mistakes of choice or behavior, fearing failure in childbirth or in other womanly roles, women increasingly turned to male doctors as "counselors" and "friends."[26]

For many people, however, these rituals and roles, promises and practices, did not ring true, and they objected vigorously to male doctors' invasion of the privacy of female patients. Objections came from varied sources: women who considered themselves hygiene experts, such as Catherine Beecher and Thomsonian doctors; angry husbands; self-styled lecturers on what was good for women, like Samuel Gregory of Boston; and even some regular physicians. According to Beecher, examination and treatment happened "with bolted doors and curtained windows, and with no one present but patient and operator." She claimed that all too often the doctors believed in free love, were not Bible-reading Christians, and exercised undue power over the morals of all-too-submissive patients who looked to them for wisdom and guidance. "How can a woman *ever know* to whom she can safely entrust herself in such painful and peculiar circumstances?" Beecher perceived doctors' actions as typifying aggressive male superiority that took advantage of women's dependent position in the culture, rather than treatments based upon medical necessity.[27]

Beecher's objections may appear simply paranoid, yet it is possible to see her protests as reasonable in view of current conventions about medical practice. If doctors disobeyed the ritual of having a third person present, if they did not evidence Christian character and morality that would restrain their behavior, if they appeared to be medically unreliable, or if their moral advice was distastefully infantilizing, then doctors were out of line and dangerous to women. Beecher's protest indicates what were issues for many justifiably apprehensive women confronted by a new experience.

Sectarian doctors opposed male midwifery on grounds of modesty also, regarding the presence of men in the labor and delivery rooms as an affront not only to women but to the whole order of nature. They protested fundamentally because they did not credit the medical value of man-midwifery, believing that midwives had innate skills for attending birth, and because they resented and questioned the medical authority regular doctors had. Since doctors, in their view, had no practical value or authority deserving of respect, their presence was an affront not only to modesty but to common sense and the pocketbook.[28]

The most common protest about immodesty was based on the belief that male doctors could not and did not restrain themselves as gentlemen should but too often allowed medical license to become sexual exploitation. Dr. Thomas Ewell of Virginia, a regular doctor himself, charged that the practice of calling men to examine women was an "imposition on the credulity of women" and an attack against chastity. In his view, the thought was the same as the deed: "Every situation which causes an internal blush is a real prostitution." He went on to tell of instances of scandal:

> Many of those modest looking doctors, inflamed with the thoughts of well-shaped bodies of the women they have delivered, handled, hung over for hours, secretly glorying in the privilege, have to their patients, as priests to penitents, pressed for accommodation, and driven to adultery and madness where they were thought most innocently occupied. In one case, I was well assured that a physician in Charleston, infuriated with the sight of the woman he had just delivered, leaped into her bed before she was restored to a state of nature.

In another "well-known case," the wife of a Congressman from South Carolina was followed everywhere by her doctor, who finally "attained his game," only to be killed by the woman. Ewell knew of a husband so jealous as to warn the doctor that if he touched his wife or so much as looked at her "he would demolish him."[29] Samuel Gregory recited instances where New England doctors had made indecent approaches or where women became passionately attached to the men who had delivered them.[30]

Charges about illicit acts and emotions were probably not entirely imaginary, but, even if none was true, they indicated the stress the medical situation placed upon both doctors and patients unless clear rules and roles for behavior were articulated and observed. Interestingly, husbands also found it difficult to believe that a doctor's attentions were entirely professional and not also salaciously motivated. A nineteenth-century broadside entitled "LET EVERY MAN HAVE HIS OWN WIFE, AND EVERY WOMAN HER OWN HUSBAND" pointed out that midwives had attended women for five thousand years "in a safe, modest and well-disposed manner," until Satan "vomitted up a set of reptiles," calling themselves midwife-doctors, who set out to tempt women once again by deceiving and flattering them. It continued:

> My blood boils in my veins, when I behold the time has come that our loving companions who are bone of our bone and flesh of our flesh, our dearest treasures on earth, nearest to our hearts, must be torn from our bosoms and be delivered into the paws of these hell-deserving monsters to be handled to gratify their abominable and wanton desires, and then take from us our hard earnings as a recompense for their behaviour. Will not Sodom rise in judgment against this generation, if we sit down quietly and let these abominations reign among us?

The broadside concluded with an appeal to midwives to awake and to take up again their God-given assignment, so that "modesty may be again heard in our land."[31]

In its echoes of the sectarian doctors' doubts about the validity of the "vile presumptuous crew" and its echoes of the charges of sexual wantonness, this religious damnation of doctors and plea to midwives probably expressed the bewilderment many people in rural America felt when they first encountered man-midwifery. These people might not have understood the medical rationales for examination, the rituals of behavior devised to protect modesty, or the restraints doctors imposed upon themselves. Of course, some new, half-educated man-midwives may not have known or observed the rules of behavior and may have given genuine offense. Perhaps in many instances doctors who were strangers to their patients had to reassure them by teaching them why and how doctors were medically and morally reliable; yet it was always possible that the reasons, the rituals, and the roles that made man-midwifery possible for some women were not sufficient to make it possible for others. The "startle effect"—in the first examination and delivery by a man—must have been considerable no matter how elaborately the doctor or another woman justified it. Critics of man-midwifery contended that some women were so upset that their labor stopped as long as the man was present. That may have been true. Man-midwifery was undoubtedly disconcerting or uncomfortable, even when it was a finely tuned ritual.[32]

Although today the medical rationale for the prenatal examination is well established, it still requires structure and ritual to control its sexual implications. When man-midwifery was newer, less understood by women, and lacking in full scientific authority, the examination needed the broadest justification, and that was moral advice and counsel. But the advice, which many women and doctors felt to be entirely appropriate and necessary, was an even greater threat to some women than exposure or sexual assault, for it diminished their autonomy, rendered them childlike, and reinforced cultural stereotypes about proper behavior that limited their freedom.

Seeking medical care from male doctors became itself the principal moral choice confronting women, as doctors intended it to be. There is little doubt that doctors won the struggle—with its cultural, economic and professional dimensions—to define and control female sexuality. Doctors were in a position to publicize their view of women, to limit rigidly medical practice by women, and to keep to themselves whatever new benefits for parturient women medical science developed. Yet it would be naive to assume that women therefore were invariably made dependent or childlike by the medical relation. In the first place, nineteenth-century women had a much wider variety of practitioners and therapies from which to choose than do women today, and many women unquestionably picked and chose until they found welcome comfort and care. Also, although regular physicians shared the view that moral rehabilitation was a part of treatment, they did not all necessarily have the same rigid view of what moral behavior was correct and therapeutic. Women could shop even among the regulars for the most suitable style—what else, after all, was the "bedside manner?" And some women turned to female physicians, although regular male doctors said female doctors could not bring sufficient moral authority to female patients to elicit rehabilitation. Some doctors disagreed and willingly trained women to be doctors.[33] And some women continued, no doubt, to seek out largely untrained female practitioners, even though regular male doctors made the worst charges of all against them, claiming they were likely to be immoral, dirty, and unreliable.

It is unfortunate that so little information remains about what occurred in the female patient–male doctor encounters. Yet even on a speculative basis it is possible to imagine many reasons why, even if most women trusted their male doctors, the doctors did not therefore dominate them.[34] Medicine proceeded speculatively rather than scientifically, that is, it assumed there were certain links between behaviors and conditions, but medicine had few independent physiological proofs for such linkages. Therefore, a doctor knew only as much about his patient's condition as she chose to reveal by behavior. Modesty often prevented the doctor from examining her, which would seldom have revealed any independently meaningful physiological information anyway. Doctors were in the position of estimating patients' conditions by their outward manner—as in phrenology—or by their social class. This is what "treating the patient" rather than "treating the disease" meant in prescientific medicine. The doctor's moral advice tended therefore to be general and often medically irrelevant. If a woman of the middle- or upper-class seemed "fit"—in tune with whatever the doctor thought proper for her class, age, and family situation—he had little more to offer, except a ritual blessing.

The female patient had many kinds of leverage in that encounter, for the doctor could not do anything to threaten the "fitness" she already had. That was why modesty was such a problem, and why "the bedside manner" was more important than physiological examination. The woman could ask, for example, for means to keep her health, which could mean, in the broadest sense, means to restrict fertility and hence to stay in the social class already attained. It is hard to understand the persistent drop in fertility unless some doctors assisted in birth control. But the strongest weapon woman carried was the right to judge the doctor himself "unfit" to attend her, "improper" in his own moral condition and sensitivity. Moral therapy worked both ways, for prescientific medicine often involved the encounter of class equals. Only when such medicine was as ignorant of its effects as were its patients, such as in the spread of puerperal fever, was it truly tragic.

More important to the limitation of the authority of medicine's moral therapy than women's leverage in it was the achievement of effective relief and cure for some of the unpleasant, disabling, or socially stigmatized physical conditions by new gynecological practices developed before the Civil War. Once doctors could relieve such conditions in women their authority rested on new and unquestionably acclaimed grounds. The most notable example of such success and authority was Dr. J. Marion Sims, a once bumptious country practitioner in the South who, through persistence and skill, found a surgical procedure to heal tears (fistulas) between the bagina and bladder and vagina and anus, which often

resulted from operative delivery and rendered a woman so uncomfortable and odorous she was isolated thereafter from friends
and family. Sims had experimented repeatedly on a number of
black slave women, who had such fistulas, and who agreed to
allow him to try to heal them even though the pain of repeated
suturing without anesthesia—not available to Sims—was unspeak-
able. Sims for his part bought the women from their owners and
fed and housed them for a number of years while continuing to
operate experimentally. When he finally succeeded, his discovery
and skill brought him world-wide fame, including the establishment of the first women's hospital in New York City, where his
practical aid to women of such condition was made available to all
classes. Sims toured the world performing this operation on
wealthy and deserving women. The gratitude of women everywhere was symbolized by the action of New York matrons in erect-
ing a statue to Sims in Central Park.[35]

Such concrete practical benefit put the authority of medicine
on an entirely different footing, and, not surprisingly, the uterus
became the object of increased attention. Doctors were eager to
experiment with it and women to forego modesty in order to
improve unpleasant conditions related to it. In 1867 Dr. W. H.
Buck, President of the New Hampshire Medical Society, called it
"outrageous" that some physicians had made the vagina a
"Chinese toy-shop" filled with mechanisms. He pointed to the
"burning and cauterizing, cutting and slashing, and gouging, and
spitting and skewering, and pessarying" that were likely to make
the "old-fashioned womb... cease to exist, except in history."
Buck compared the excesses of the uterine specialists to the practices of an earlier set of specialists who returned from training in
Paris thinking that the anal sphincters of most New York young
men were too large and needed puckering up by surgical stitching. A similarly ill-informed and unnecessary raid was now being
made upon the uterus. Whereas "our grandmothers" never knew
they had a uterus until it became filled with a healthy fetus, even
young women today had to have their "wombs shored up with a
pessary." There were now, he said, 123 kinds of such mechanisms,
"from a simple plug to a patent threshing machine, which can
only be worn with the largest hoops. They look like the drawings
of turbine water-wheels, or a leaf from a work on entomology."[36]

Whereas Charles Meigs had worried about unnecessary physical examinations as affronts to modesty. Buck was concerned

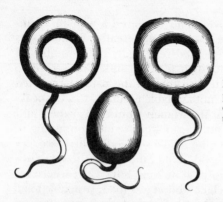

Pessaries were used to support prolapsed uteri, not as birth-control devices. The tails were attached to the wearer's belt.

about unnecessary mechanics as affronts to common sense and serious medical achievement. Yet the promise of medical relief has always had its excesses and its quackeries. What is important to note is that after mid-century more and more women found the ability of medicine—or at least the expectation of it—more important than its potential threat to modesty or to ideology about female sufficiency. The somewhat random advances of gynecological surgery brought compelling power to medicine yet, interestingly, doctors still could not always explain why conditions arose even if they could correct them, and thus the opening for moral advice remained as wide as before. Even in the era before the emergence of scientific medicine, therefore, Victorian women were confronted with additional evidence to validate cultural assumptions about male prerogatives and abilities and with significant reasons for "trusting the doctor." If women shrank from male doctors it was not because of their supposed inability but because of lack of sympathy for women. Female doctors made this supposed lack their own *raison d'etre*. Yet this was essentially a backward-looking rationale, for the moral authority of medicine would soon rest on scientific ability and practical benefit.

In addition to the fact that women may have been less powerless in the medical relation than rhetoric suggests, and in addition to its promise of relief, women sought out what was essentially a male service because they could depend less after mid-century upon supporting networks of female friends and relatives. Families were more scattered and urban life was often inimical to the agrarian traditions of social childbirth. More isolated from other women, the expectant woman turned to her doctor for the array of help the supportive female networks had offered. Now the doctor became the woman's "friend," giving the comfort and guidance, the reassurance and strength, that women had once offered to one another. Toward the end of the century accounts of childbirth depicted it as a family event attended only by the doctor (and nurse, sometimes) while the husband stood nearby.

When the novelist Frances Parkinson Keyes delivered her first child at her home in Haverhill, Massachusetts, the doctor came from Boston by train. By the time he arrived, she had been in labor for 18 hours but was still walking about the house. As the

EVERY PHYSICIAN IS AWARE

of the trouble to himself and the discomfort to his patient in the treatment of uterine displacements by the old appliances, such as rings; pessaries, etc. Cases treated with pessaries and rings held in position by pressure against the vaginal walls receive no permanent relief from their use. The womb is held in place so long as the pessary or ring is in use, but on removal the case is worse than before, the walls of the vagina are dilated and weakened, the womb has lost its natural support from this course and falls lower in the pelvic cavity, and the only relief by the old method is to use a larger ring or pessary. By the new method, the McIntosh Supporter will raise the womb to its proper position in the pelvic cavity, allow the vagina and ligaments of support to contract and gain their normal tone, and although the instrument has been worn but a short time the uterus will keep its normal position if it be removed, though to insure a permanent result the supporter should be worn longer.

No instrument has ever been placed before the medical profession which has given such universal satisfaction as

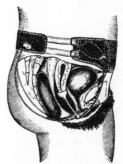

THE NATURAL UTERINE SUPPORTER   THE NATURAL UTERINE SUPPORTER APPLIED.

DR. McINTOSH'S Natural Uterine Supporter.

Over 200 devices for the treatment of uterine displacement were marketed in nineteenth-century America. Some were so elaborate that they were derisively called "threshing machines" and were designed to be worn only under hoop skirts.

labor continued, the doctor and Mrs. Keyes's husband sat in the den with her, timing the pains. When the birth began, the doctor offered forceps and ether to reduce pain; she accepted ether as the head was born. Despite her protracted labor, she felt she gave birth at the "most ideal time in history . . . after anesthetics had come into general use but before mothers were wrested from their homes and hurried off to hospitals."[37] Behind her delivery was her unspoken confidence in her doctor.

It is probable that the embarrassment of the relationship often gave way to collaboration, so that the male doctor as a "friend" helped the woman to effect changes that both thought desirable. It is likely, we have said, that such quiet collaboration reduced fertility. There is no doubt at all that doctors appeared medically and morally satisfying because they gave women narcotics to ease "female" pains and discomforts. Modesty and moral therapy presented no obstacles if the doctor's advice and therapy suited the woman's own purposes.

If the male doctor–female patient relation did not always lead to dominance, it did further the process whereby the female body became an object to medicine and to women themselves. That process began when early birth science spoke of the reproductive

This illustration, purportedly showing "the position of the child at nine months," is from a Victorian birth-control manual, one of the first of its kind. Some middle-class nineteenth-century women had an avid interest in learning about their own physiology, although many were quite willing to leave such matters to their doctors.

organs as a mechanical pump. Nineteenth-century medicine added a moral dimension, holding that the healthy functioning of a woman's organs was a measure of her personal and social worth. Each new gynecological or obstetrical advance treated the body as an object to be manipulated according to the wishes of the patient and the doctor. Modesty was an issue, because women could not easily adapt to regarding themselves as *having* a body rather than *being* a body, yet as women did adopt this view of themselves they were able to imagine themselves to be, along with their physicians, in control of the functioning of their female potentiality. The timing and the number of conceptions, for example, could be regarded no longer as inevitable but henceforth as managed choices.

As the nineteenth century came to a close, the question women confronted was not whether they would choose a male doctor but for what purpose they would choose him. The question was not particularly whether he was blind, asexual, and confidential but what changes or choices did he offer to women in dealing with their female potentiality. For, while modesty before men and moral advice from men had once constituted serious problems for women, they had learned from the difficult relation to regard themselves as carrying a reproductive function for which they were also responsible and over which they themselves should exercise control.

The conceit of many male doctors early in the century had been that they alone should have the leverage to direct and advise women, but the effect of their exclusivism in treating women was to generate in women a psychological distance from their own bodies and a habit of choosing what their bodies should be and do.

A woman writing to *Good Housekeeping* magazine in 1915 expressed this attitude very succinctly in regard to why women should have painless births:

> In those ages when women felt the religious significance of giving birth—just as men felt the religious significance of going into battle—they so frequently regarded the act as a great, mystical freeing of the life from the womb—not merely a birth but a resurrection—that they completely lost consciousness of pain, just as men were sometimes unconscious of their wounds in the exhilaration of battle. Today, on the other hand, and particularly in this country, we are all, men and women alike, inclined to think of our bodies, not as instruments of cosmic forces, but as

personal possessions of ourselves, tools of our own desires—very exalted desires in many cases, but still merely personal. We take care of our bodies, study them, worry about them, treat them, in short, much as one does a favorite horse, and then demand that they serve us absolutely... to inflict upon the modern woman many burdens and sufferings which a cruder type of woman took as a matter of course is unnatural.[38]

Notes

1. George Napheys, *The Physical Life of Woman* (Philadelphia, 1880), pp. 183-184; O. S. Fowler, *Maternity* (New York, 1868), p. 183.

2. Ida Husted Hrper, *The Life and Work of Susan B. Anthony* (Indianapolis, 1899), pp. 12-13.

3. Agnes Smedley, *Daughter of Earth* (Old Westbury, N.Y.: Feminist Press, 1973), p. 201.

4. Charles E. Rosenberg, "Sexuality, Class and Role in Nineteenth-Century America," *American Quarterly* 25, No. 2 (May, 1973):133.

5. Walter Radcliffe, *Milestones in Midwifery* (Bristol, England, 1967), pp. 32-33; Julius Jarcho, *Postures and Practices* (New York, 1934).

6. Wooster Beach, *An Improved System of Midwifery*... (New York, 1851), p. 19.

7. Joseph Warrington, *Obstetrical Catechism* (Philadelphia, 1854), pp. 113-114.

8. Frederick Hollick, *Matron's Manual of Midwifery* (Boston, 1848), pp. 222, 224.

9. Editorial, "Demonstrative Midwifery," *New York Medical Gazette* 1, No. 1 (July 6, 1850):5; Jacques Pierre Maygrier, *Midwifery Illustrated*, trans. with notes by A. Sidney Doane (New York, 1833), Plates 29, 30, 31, 33.

10. Harold Speert, *The Sloane Hospital Chronicle* (Philadelphia, 1963), p. 79; Charles D. Meigs, *Introductory Lecture... November 4, 1841* (Philadelphia, 1841), p. 8.

11. Jane Bauer Donegan, "Midwifery in America, 1760–1860: A Study in Medicine and Morality," unpublished Ph.D. dissertation, Syracuse University, 1972, pp. 206–209; Herbert Thoms, *Chapters in American Obstetrics* (Springfield, Ill., 1961), p. 103.

12. Speert, *Sloane Hospital Chronicle*, p. 79.

13. Donegan, *Midwifery in America*, pp. 210-222.

14. Frederic A. Washburn, *The Massachusetts General Hospital: Its Development, 1800–1935* (Boston, 1939), pp. 357-364.

15. Frederick Irving, *Safe Deliverance* (Boston, 1942); Frederick P. Henry, ed., *Founders' Week Memorial Volume* (Philadelphia, 1909).

16. Donegan, "Midwifery in America," p. 226.

17. Carroll Smith-Rosenberg and Charles E. Rosenberg, "The Female Animal: Medical and Biological Views of Woman and Her Role in Nineteenth-Century America," *Journal of American History* 60 (1973):332–356.

18. Among the many manuals of advice, the following were some of the most influential. Alice B. Stockham, M.D., *Tokology: A Book for Every Woman* (Chicago, 1885); Mrs. P. B. Saur, M.D., *Maternity: A Book for Every Wife and Mother* (1891); Elisabeth Robinson Scovil, *Preparation for Motherhood* (Philadelphia, 1896); Mrs. Emma F. Angell Drake, M.D., *What a Young Wife Ought to Know* (Philadelphia, 1901); Fowler, *Maternity;* Napheys, *Physical Life of Woman.*

19. Charles Meigs, *Females and Their Diseases* (Philadelphia, 1848), p. 39.

20. Rosenberg, "Sexuality, Class, and Role," p. 139.

21. Daniel S. Smith, "Family Limitation, Sexual Control, and Domestic Feminism in Victorian America," M. S. Hartman and L. Banner, eds., *Clio's Consciousness Raised: New Perspectives on the History of Women* (New York: Harper & Row, 1974), pp. 119–136; Hugh L. Hodge, *On the Non-Contagious Character of Puerperal Fever* (Philadelphia, 1852), pp. 10–13.

22. S. Weir Mitchell, *Doctor and Patient* (Philadelphia, 1888), pp. 84–85; Regina Morantz, "The Lady and Her Physician," in Hartman and Banner, *Clio's Consciousness Raised,* pp. 38–53.

23. Barbara Welter, "The Cult of True Womanhood, 1820–1860," *American Quarterly* 18, No. 2 (1966):151–174.

24. Catherine Beecher, *Letters to the People on Health and Happiness* (New York, 1855), pp. 121–133.

25. Smith-Rosenberg and Rosenberg, "Female Animal," pp. 332–356.

26. Vern Bullough and Martha Voght, "Women, Menstruation, and Nineteenth-Century Medicine," *Bulletin of the History of Medicine* 47, No. 1 (January–February, 1973):37.

27. Samuel Gregory, *Man-Midwifery Exposed . . .* (Boston, 1848), pp. 43–44; Beecher, *Letters to the People,* pp. 136–138.

28. Samuel Thomson, *New Guide to Health* (Boston, 1832), pp. 131–134.

29. Thomas Ewell, *Letters to Ladies* (Philadelphia, 1817), p. 194.

30. Gregory, *Man-Midwifery Exposed,* pp. 13, 19.

31. Broadside, no date, place or author, probably 1800–1850, Yale Medical School Library.

32. Fowler, *Maternity,* p. 183; Gregory, *Man-Midwifery Exposed,* p. 20.

33. Hollick, *Matron's Manual,* p. vi; S. Weir Mitchell, *Fat and Blood* (Philadelphia, 1877), p. 39.

34. Donegan, "Midwifery in America," pp. 236–240, 244; Morantz, "Lady and Her Physician," pp. 48–51.

35. J. Marion Sims, *The Story of My Life* (New York, 1888); Seale Harris, *Woman's Surgeon* (New York, 1950), pp. 177–185, 243–249.

36. W.D. Buck, M.D., "Extract from the address of the President of the New Hampshire Medical Society for 1866," *New York Medical Journal* 5 (August, 1867):464–465.

37. Frances Parkinson Keyes, *All Flags Flying* (New York, 1972), pp. 27–30, 33. See also Paul Blanshard, *Personal and Controversial* (Boston: Beacon Press, 1973), pp. 1–2.

38. Charlotte Tell, "The Neglected Psychology of Twilight Sleep," *Good Housekeeping* 41 (July, 1915):17–24.

4

The Wounds of Birth:
Birthpain and Puerperal Fever

There are doubters in the profession, of the propriety or expediency of etherization; and there are clergymen who say it is a violation of "the curse of God"—if such language be not blasphemy—to mitigate or remove human suffering. From my heart do I wish that such had been in that poor woman's only room, and witnessed what occurred in it,—its perfect peace and pleasure, where before was agony; and the joy which so largely and richly replaced that former wretchedness and fear!

Dr. Walter Channing, *1848*

Whatever indulgence may be granted to those who have heretofore been the ignorant causes of so much misery, the time has come when the existence of a private pestilence in the sphere of a single physician should be looked upon, not as a misfortune, but a crime.

Dr. Oliver Wendell Holmes, *1855*

CHILDBIRTH in nineteenth-century America was strongly marked by concern for pain in delivery and by bewilderment about puerperal fever, which appeared mysteriously after some deliveries and often led to a quick death. While birthpain and childbed fever were old and well-known conditions, in Victorian America they seemed more prevalent than before: More women were suffering more pain or were dying after delivery. Although doctors had the means to relieve pain after the 1840s, they did so selectively; by the end of the century women became insistent that doctors eliminate pain as a symptom of birth. Puerperal fever confounded doctors for decades, but by the 1880s they were finally able to combat it with success. The struggles to rid birth of these conditions entailed a fundamental transformation.

For the Victorian woman, pain in parturition was likely to be more than "simple" physical suffering: She might have had untreatable physical ills that augmented pain; she might have felt victimized by a conception and birth she had not wanted; she might have chosen to suffer in order to mark herself as a lady or to limit future conceptions. Birthpain thus had many sources and was a complex of physical, psychological, and social conditions. The culture expected women to suffer, and suffer they did, but the reasons were not simple.

Some women had indisputable physical causes of birthpain. Types of fashionable behavior, such as wearing corsets, for example, made birth difficult; yet, because the constricted waist marked one's middle-class status and one's liberation from the working class, women sought to achieve the ideal waist of 15 to 18 inches even though they might faint from the effort of walking in devices intended to minimize nature's bounty. The practice of binding the waists of pre-adolescent girls resulted in compressed and permanently deformed lower ribcages. Women wore corsets during pregnancy to support the child and after delivery to regain the figure. The corset aptly symbolized the confined, economically unproductive middle-class woman. Lack of exercise and improper diet among such women and their life in stuffy rooms also contributed to physiological ill health.[1]

Female organs could be a source of pain for which medicine had little beneficial treatment. Low-grade vaginal infections, which burned, itched, or caused frequent urination, not only were embarrassing, uncomfortable, or debilitating but often persisted until organic damage occurred. Venereal disease found its way into many households, even the most respectable, usually because husbands had consorted with prostitutes. Frequent births and the demands of child care exhausted many women who had no servants. Some women suffered from prolapse of the uterus, a condition that caused constant discomfort if the uterus had dropped down upon the bladder. This may have been the unnamed complaint that permanently removed so vigorous a warrior as Angelina Grimké from the antislavery campaign after the birth of her first child. The precise reason for the condition remains unknown, though operative interventions in childbirth were probable causes.[2] Still worse was the vesicovaginal fistula, a tear in the wall between vagina and bladder caused by protracted labor or by the clumsy use of instruments. Continuous seepage of urine brought agonizing discomfort, intolerable odors, and consequent social isolation. Vague Victorian references to a woman's being "invalided" actually could mean that she suffered any one of these painful physical disabilities.[3]

Nineteenth-century physicians conducted a campaign against the wearing of corsets as detrimental to child-bearing. Women of the upper classes, however, preferred the fashionable wasp waist to the healthier, but considerably larger, natural silhouette.

On the other hand, women of the upper classes found certain ailments to be fashionable. Being weak, invalided, nervous, or subject to fainting spells marked one as being above the common clay, which was thought, without much justice, to be vulgarly robust. Women were expected to be weaker than men, and upper-class women often prolonged or exaggerated their debility as a mark of distinction. One doctor caustically commented:

> Unfortunately, custom and false notions have given this melancholy state the stamp of propriety, and thrown around it the charm of fashion. The suffering invalid is called *interesting*, and the pale-faced, debilitated creature, scarcely able to crawl about, is styled, *genteel*, while robust health and physical capability is termed *coarseness* and *vulgarity*.[4]

Many doctors of course believed that women's illnesses were signs of moral failure, a kind of malingering that kept them from their domestic duties.

Weakness, pain, and suffering were more than a culturally approved way of achieving status. Many women were caught up in cultural expectations about female behavior that were contradictory or demeaning, and a breakdown in their health could resolve a role that had become too complex, demanding, and even, occasionally, disgusting. Women were trapped, for example, between the need to be pure and the need to submit to their husbands, between the belief that sexual desire was limited to males and the belief that women should somehow train men to control those desires. Contradictory expectations could generate anxiety and distress and cause illness; on the other hand, illness might be a conscious way of dealing with, and limiting, male sexuality.[5]

Some women did not find maternity to be the fulfillment the culture had promised; they did not receive the honor or acquire the power that motherhood was supposed to confer. They felt deprived and regarded the prospect of further conceptions and births as troublesome, unwanted duties; if their husbands insisted upon their bearing more children, such women became anxious and even angry, a situation that contributed to pain.

Birthpain was not only an indication of women's fated physical, psychological, and social condition, however, for women could employ pain as a means to achieve their own wishes, particularly the limitation of conceptions and births. The marked decline in fertility throughout the whole society during the nineteenth century indicated that husbands and wives were increasingly reluctant to have large families. Economic aspirations were unquestionably part of the reason, but husbands also cooperated in limiting conceptions because they thought more births, and more child care, would be detrimental to their wives' health. Women used their supposed weakness as an excuse for continence; their fear of painful birth was cause for both contraception and abortion. Some doctors became alarmed about the frequency of abortion and railed against it, claiming it was a crime brought about by women's too great love for "fashion" and for "society." Other "trifling reasons" were "the dread of suffering, fears respecting their own health and strength, the trouble and expense of larger families and professedly, also, the responsibility incurred in the education of children."[6]

Historians have no way of knowing how much of the emphasis on pain pointed to real, imagined, or simulated experience. Victorian culture encouraged women to be more sensitive to pain than men and to express openly their aches and illnesses. Thus many women suffered exquisitely as ladies should. Doing so often served practical purposes as well as needs for status. Moral and medical expectations about women, however, gave women many reasons to be anxious and fearful about birth, conditions that induce pain. Many doctors described birthpain as one of the worst agonies known to them, greater than the terrible agonies of soldiers in the Civil War. Medicine would find means to palliate the agony of birth, but the matter of pain continued to be discussed. What did it mean that women seemed to suffer more than before?

The physiology manuals and women's handbooks carried on a cultural discussion about the meaning of pain and showed the same ambivalence about it as about women's sexuality. On the one hand, to suffer pain was to be feminine, for weakness and sickness were built into the female animal; on the other, pain in childbirth was somehow unnatural, for not all women suffered. The women who gave birth in their sleep and first awakened when the baby cried appeared frequently as an illustration that childbirth *could* be painless. Some books made this archetypical woman an English noblewoman, to show that good breeding need not require pain. Another common illustration of painless birth was the proverbial Indian squaw, the unspoiled child of nature, whose pregnancy occasioned no special attention or worry and who performed her usual drudging chores up to the very hour of labor:

> When she realizes that the hour of delivery is at hand, she enters her cabin or betakes herself to some stream or spring, gives birth, washes the young "injun" in the cold water, straps it on her back, and before she has been scarcely missed, has returned a full-fledged mother, and resumes her labors.[7]

The Indian woman, however, was a double-edged symbol. All the manuals pointed to her as exemplifying childbirth in the primitive state of nature, before "civilization" caused women to feel the dreadful pains of birth. Yet the woman who did not feel pain was open to the accusation of being less civilized than her neighbors who did, for pain was not only the price but also, unfortunately, the mark of progress, of escape from the drudgery of nonindustrialized society. The experts did not consider a return to primitive society either possible or desirable, nonetheless. Why, then, make so much of the Indian woman?[8]

Both male and female writers agreed that civilization had harmed women's health in several respects that were essentially unnecessary even in an industrialized society. Tight corsets, lack of exercise, airless rooms, late hours, and sexual overindulgence— many of the fashionable "vices" —were offenses against health that led to painful births. Male and female writers used the Indian woman and other symbols of painless birth to encourage women to behave differently, preferably like their female ancestors who were close to nature in their lives, but male and female authors did not really agree about what that desirable life was.[9]

Male authors used the symbols of painless birth to imply that women had pain because they were not truly feminine, because civilization had rendered them too "sexually aggressive, intellectually ambitious, and defective in proper womanly submission and selflessness." Pain in childbirth followed the woman's desertion of True Womanhood, her failure to remain in her rightful place in the home and her choice of the fashionable and flirtatious social life. Unfeminine women did not rest during their menses, as Indian women supposedly did, and thus suffered organic damage that caused painful deliveries. The English noblewoman was the creature of leisured refinement; she did not exhibit the unfeminine eagerness, the nervous bustle, of American women. Men's palliative for birthpain was the return of women to their properly subordinate, nonaggressive household role. The Indian woman and the English noblewoman represented women in the "natural"—that is, rightful—cultural roles.[10]

To female authors, the Indian woman symbolized the autonomous sufficiency of women to care for themselves outside of and despite the social roles culture laid on them. The Indian woman not only did not need male attention in giving birth, but she was like men in being strong and self-determined. While male authors urged women to give up bad health habits in order to become properly submissive, female authors urged women to live healthier lives so that they would be stronger and more independent than before. A lecture by Elizabeth Cady Stanton, a feminist and the mother of seven, became the favorite text for female writers:

> If you suffer, it is not because you are cursed of God, but because you violate his laws. What an incubus it would take from woman could she be educated to know that the pains of maternity are no curse upon her kind. We know that among Indians the squaws do not suffer in childbirth. They will step aside from the ranks, even on the march, and return in a short time bearing with them the new-born child. What an absurdity, then, to suppose that only enlightened Christian women are cursed.
>
> But one word of fact is worth a volume of philosophy; let me give you some of my own experience. I am the mother of seven children. My girlhood was spent mostly in the open air. I early imbibed the idea that *a girl is just as good as a boy,* and I carried it out. I would walk five miles before breakfast, or ride ten on horseback.... I wore my clothing sensibly.... I never compressed my body.... When my first four children were born, I suffered very little. I then made up my mind that it was totally unnecessary for me to suffer at all; so I dressed lightly, walked every day ... and took proper care of myself. The night before the birth ... I walked three miles. The child was born *without a particle of pain.* I bathed it and dressed it myself.

In other words, if a woman regarded herself as the equal of a man and lived sensibly, she should not have pain. Embedded in this point of view was a vivid recollection of the earlier sufficiency of colonial women's simple but vigorous life. Many women sought a painless birth as a sign of their own release from feminine roles that made them weak and dependent.[11]

Dr. William P. Dewees, a famous obstetrician of the 1830s, said that pain in childbirth was a morbid symptom, and that, if women would not pervert their "systems," a healthy regimen might be counted on with certainty to do away with pain. This statement was quoted repeatedly; as a generalization it covered the specific suggestions of everyone. Birth could be painless if women would only do what they should. The trouble with this attitude was that it was too romantic about the plasticity of nature and encouraged people to regard painless birth as a sign of femininity, however defined. When women continued to suffer pain they felt like failures, if they had tried to be independent, and men took comfort that independent women were bringing pain upon themselves. Birthpain did not vanish according to the various prescriptions of cultural politics; it remained a complex and enduring physical fact.[12]

Pain was actually more difficult to overcome than shame, for although exposure was never exactly pleasant, pain was incorrigibly resistant to ritual and suggestion. However doctors and female authors lectured women on healthy attitudes and behavior, pain usually persisted.

The relief of female suffering was a prominent feature of nineteenth-century medicine, and this humanitarian concern encouraged doctors to apply the new anesthesias—chloroform and ether—to the relief of birthpain in the 1840s. The techniques

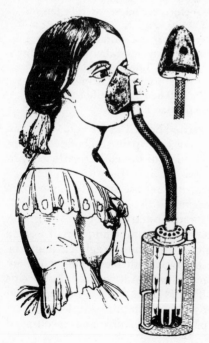

The chloroform mask was introduced in the mid-nineteenth century to alleviate the pains of labor.

disturbed many people who thought of birthpain as a religious curse upon women or, at least, as salutary suffering that induced motherlove. After Dr. James Simpson of Edinburgh used chloroform in childbirth in 1847, he had to reply to the objections of religious spokesmen for having removed Eve's curse. He employed some skillful Biblical exegesis to justify the dulling of pain as a religious act—God meant men to use natural means to benefit humankind—but he did not really silence his opposition until 1853, when Queen Victoria elected chloroform for her delivery. In 1848 Dr. Walter Channing of Boston first used ether for childbirth and encouraged other physicians to try it. His motives were clearly humanitarian, and he challenged doubters in the medical and clerical professions to witness the serenity, pleasure, and joy that ether produced where before there was only agony, wretchedness, and fear.[13]

Although some physicians were enthusiastic about the use of anesthesia for every birth and even regarded it as a panacea for such conditions as puerperal fever, hemorrhage, and weak contractions, most American doctors used anesthesia infrequently in the second half of the century. Doctors had both moral and medical qualms about drugs. Some feared the drugs would excite the laboring woman to voluble and unguarded actions that might be mistaken as eroticism, so that the woman would fear the doctor's control over her behavior. (The doctor had to protect the patient as well as himself from impropriety.) Others probably agreed with Dr. Charles Meigs, who thought birthpain was a desirable evidence of the life force that ensures a mother's love for her offspring, a kind of psychological imprinting. A modern-sounding objection was to the obliteration of the consciousness of birth itself:

> The female, at the most interesting period of her life, the time of labor, should, all other things being equal, have her mind unclouded, her intellect undisturbed, her judgment fully adequate to realize and appreciate the advent of a new and important era in her existence—the birth of her child.[14]

Many educated physicians were uncertain about the necessity and the safety of anesthesia in most births. Having observed the increased number of deaths during surgery under anesthesia, even though they resulted more from experimental procedures than from the drug, was a cautionary experience. Moreover, the

medical claims about how and when to use anesthesia were contradictory. Most doctors who used it at all therefore limited it to
first deliveries, and then only to create an analgesic effect, a dulling of pain without full unconsciousness before the birth of the
child's head. Doctors thought this was the most painful moment in
birth, although the greatest pain actually occurs earlier as the
cervix expands. Occasionally they used drugs to obliterate the
extraordinary pain involved in inserting a hand to turn the fetus
in the womb or in using instruments, whereas other doctors believed the woman had to be conscious at those moments in order
to warn the doctor against damaging her tissues by being able to
express untoward pain. Most doctors found the advice about the
proper use of anesthesia so confusing that they never sought to
use it in most births or, if they used it, did so not to induce
unconsciousness but only to dull pain.[15]

It is probably fortunate that anesthesia was not excessively
used, for the health and life of many babies would have been
endangered. But the restricted use meant that the great majority
of women in the nineteenth century endured pain as the inevitable and elemental climax to pregnancy. One woman, signing
herself "the wife of a Christian physician," wrote to the prestigious
Boston Medical and Surgical Journal in 1866 that doctors who complained about the increased frequency of abortion might consider
the more generous use of anesthesia:

> One great reason for the aversion to child-bearing is the
> thousand disagreeable and painful experiences which attend the
> long months of patient waiting, and the certain agony at the
> end—agony which is akin to nothing else on earth—agony which
> the tenderest susceptibilities and sympathies of the noblest physi-
> cian can but faintly imagine—agony which, in not one case in a
> hundred, is mitigated by anesthesia. If the blessed, benevolent
> suggestion of the use of chloroform could be adopted, the world
> would hear less of abortions.[16]

In 1879 the President of the newly formed American
Gynecological Society suggested that doctors consider using the
forceps to expedite delivery, rather than standing by the an-
guished, laboring woman and crooning to themselves that meddlesome midwifery was bad. In the closing decades of the century
some educated doctors offered women the option of forceps and
anesthesia as their labor neared conclusion; they also generously
supplied them with morphine for the afterpains and complaints

of births. Yet few doctors sought to relieve pain throughout labor, and women were often ready to try any new method that promised less painful delivery.[17]

The fruit diet and the water cure were methods frequently described in popular literature. The fruit diet attempted to produce a fetus with small and flexible bones by removing from the mother's diet all substances thought to form bone, particularly wheat. Ideally, the woman was to subsist on apples, oranges, lemons, potatoes, and rice. In the oft-quoted example of success, the labor was easy and "the child—a boy—was finely proportioned and exceedingly soft, *his bones being all in gristle.*" Some doctors cautioned that the diet was harmful to the health of both mother and child.

The water cure had many adherents and advocates; it was a welcome release from traditional confinement, for it prescribed fresh air, long walks, and the plentiful use of cold water for drinking and bathing. The regime seemed new and radical in 1850, when most people wondered whether a weekly bath might damage their health. The water cure also had its celebrated successes in easing birthpain. Harriet Robinson, a former mill girl who had become a feminist, reported in her diary in 1854 that she had had a pregnancy free from sickness and a swift recovery from using cold water. Later in the century women would advocate hot water, in the form of sitz baths. Such methods were attempts not only to diminish birthpain but also to free women from dependent contact with doctors, who often emphasized how painful birth was but did little to ease it. By the end of the century many women were looking for methods that would remove pain entirely.[18]

Most women experienced birthpain, but fortunately not all had to endure puerperal fever, which was the great tragedy for maternity during the nineteenth century. Medicine was slow to understand and to avert this condition, actually a wound infection in the birth passages, although its symptoms had been known for centuries and in some years during the seventeenth and eighteenth centuries had achieved epidemic prevalence in foreign hospitals. American women, who delivered almost always at home, were spared these infectious epidemics, but after 1840 the fever began to appear even in some home deliveries, and for the next fifty years it perplexed and agitated physicians.

In retrospect, the causes for the fever are readily apparent. Pasteur was the first to point out that parturients are "wounded women," for during labor the cervix, vagina, and perineum may be lacerated and torn while the inner surface of the uterus is always an open wound caused by the cleavages of birth and offers many excellent breeding grounds for bacteria. Any pathogenic bacteria that enter the birth passages have favorable conditions to enter the bloodstream and cause deadly infection. In a few instances the genitalia's own bacteria may be harmful, but most infectious bacteria enter from the outside, via the doctor's hand or instruments. In the absence of sterile procedures, a doctor or nurse could bring staphylococcus aureus from another patient's wound or abscess or carry, from autopsy matter, the most deadly bacterium, beta hemolytic streptococcus, group A. This bacterium is so virulent that medical personnel could transmit it on clothes, or instruments and even from nasal passages. In a hospital it was easily carried from one infected woman to others and could be transmitted by a doctor or nurse from one home to another. Only the most rigorously sterile procedures prevent its appearance and spread. In the "wounds of birth" it causes widespread inflammation of the abdominal cavity, blood poisoning, and death within a few days.

Foreign doctors were deeply concerned by the "childbed fever" that occasionally left hospitals with many sick and dead maternity patients. Some doctors began, after 1770, to initiate prophylactic regimens to combat the epidemics of fever. Dr. Charles White of Manchester, England, argued in 1773 that the fever stemmed from self-poisoning by vaginal fluids that were not allowed to drain. He urged that women not be confined to beds without clean linens in stuffy, unclean wards. Under his regime the number of fever deaths dropped dramatically in the Manchester hospital. Alexander Gordon of Aberdeen, Scotland, practiced during the epidemic of 1790–1793, after which he wrote the first epidemiological study of the fever, arguing that the disease was a contagion spread by medical people rather than, as some thought, a result of some noxious element in the air. He claimed to be able to trace the spread of fever from patient to patient as doctors and nurses visited them and urged medical personnel to wash themselves and their clothes and to provide clean linens for sickbeds.[19]

Dr. Oliver Wendell Holmes was the first American physician to call puerperal fever a contagion spread by doctors in private practice. When his colleagues in the Boston Society for Medical Improvement recounted occasions of women's deaths in home deliveries and the deaths of doctors after having performed autopsies, Holmes concluded that certain doctors were carrying a contagious presence from home to home, perhaps from autopsy material. He published his empirical conclusions in 1843, advising doctors to cease practice when they or their patients became ill with the fever.[20]

A Hungarian doctor, Ignaz Philipp Semmelweis, was the first to demonstrate the contagiousness of the fever statistically and to prove certain antiseptic means effective in preventing it. He worked in Vienna's large maternity hospital, where medical students attended births in one ward and midwives in another, and he observed that mortality in the students' ward exceeded mortality in the other by 437 percent in 1846 (459 deaths versus 105)—and that women who delivered on the hospital steps or in corridors before they could reach the wards never contracted the fever. He concluded that those women did not die because they were not touched. When a colleague died with the symptoms of puerperal fever after performing an autopsy, Semmelweis decided that decomposed matter caused the disease, and thereafter he required all birth attendants to wash their hands in a chloride of lime solution before attending women. The result was that in 1848 only 45 women out of 3,556 died in the medical students' ward and 43 out of a similar number in the midwives' ward. This rate of infection was as high as it was because Semmelweis did not realize that it was necessary for each new bed patient to have clean sheets.[21]

After Semmelweis published his systematic examination, Holmes issued a monograph, *Puerperal Fever as a Private Pestilence,* in 1855, reprinting his earlier piece and responding to American critics who disbelieved the contagiousness of puerperal fever and who had ridiculed the young Boston doctor for his outrageous suggestion that doctors were instruments of death. Holmes's monograph is one of the most important documents in American medicine, clear, logical, and forceful.

Two well-known Philadelphia physicians, Dr. Hugh L. Hodge and Dr. Charles Meigs, had rejected the idea that the fever was contagious. Dr. Hodge found the idea incompatible with his image of the doctor as comforter and "minister of mercy" to women, and he urged his students to avoid any fear that they could convey to women so horrible a thing as the fever. The stress of birth itself was enough to upset women without their having to bear the "cruel, very cruel" suggestion that their trusted doctor might bring deadly contagion; "it is far more humane ... to keep her happy in ignorance of danger." Hodge believed that Holmes's hypothesis lacked proof and was simply a reprehensible supposition that threatened the comfort and happiness of families.[22]

Dr. Meigs was more direct and more abusive of Holmes, attacking him as sophomoric and judging his idea of the contagiousness of the fever

> ... as one injurious to the profession of medicine, pernicious to the people, by filling the minds of interested parties with alarm, and as propagating, from age to age, a vile, demoralizing superstition as to the nature and causes of many diseases. . . . I prefer to attribute them to accident or Providence of which I can form a conception rather than to a contagion of which I cannot form any clear idea. . . .
>
> I have practiced midwifery for many long years. I have attended thousands of women and passed through epidemics of childbed fever, both in town and hospital; I have made many researches of childbed fever. . . . Still, I certainly never was the medium of its transmission.

Meigs particularly resented Holmes's suggestion that doctors' hands were not clean, by which Holmes seemed to imply that they were both dirty and culpable. Meigs retorted that doctors were gentlemen and that gentlemen's hands were clean![23]

Holmes responded in 1855 with caustic reserve, saying there could no longer be a question in the unprejudiced mind about how the fever was spread, the empirical evidence being conclusive. Adherents of science could not neglect his evidence if the science of medicine was not to be a sham. Those who spoke of being ministers of mercy to "their" families had to face the "question whether or not the 'black death' of childbed is to be scattered broadcast by the agency of the mother's friend and adviser."

Holmes was less gentle with Meigs not only because Meigs had been more abusive but because Meigs had emphasized his own attempts to treat puerperal fever, which he believed to be a self-generating disease. To this approach Holmes replied that, "for my own part, I had rather rescue one mother from being poisoned by her attendant, than claim to have saved forty out of fifty patients, to whom I had carried the disease." Meigs had remarked that the eminent Dr. James Y. Simpson of Edinburgh had

had cases of the fever in his practice, implying that a gentleman could not have spread the fever. Holmes simply said:

> Dr. Simpson attended the dissection of two . . . cases and freely handled the dissected parts. His next four childbed patients were affected with fever and it was the first time he had seen it in his practice. As Dr. Simpson is a *gentleman* (Dr. Meigs as above), and as a gentleman's hands are clean (Dr. Meigs as above), it follows that a gentleman with clean hands can carry the disease.

Holmes concluded that there were certain rules of practice that would decrease the instances of fever. He urged doctors attending women not to take an active part in post-mortem examinations of puerperal fever; if a doctor could not avoid doing so, he should thoroughly wash himself, change his clothes, and wait a day before attending a woman. Similar precautions were necessary after attending other autopsies or treating certain surgical cases. If a doctor had one case of fever in his practice, he should consider the possibility that he would infect the next; if he had two instances, he should stop practice for a month; three cases were *prima facie* evidence that he was a vehicle of contagion. Finally, Holmes said that doctors could no longer be excused for ignorantly causing puerperal fever; henceforth, "the existence of a private pestilence in the sphere of a single physician should be looked upon, not as a misfortune, but a crime."[24]

Learning to deal with puerperal fever was to be even more difficult than Holmes suggested. In the first place, most American doctors were not looking for disease but for symptoms that they might treat. Holmes was an exceptionally well-educated doctor who had studied abroad, where he learned to observe and catalog specific diseases; many American doctors might not even recognize puerperal fever. In the second place, if recognized at all, the fever was extraordinarily persistent even when doctors took measures to prevent its spread. A colleague of Dr. Meigs, a Dr. Rutter of Philadelphia, after having forty-five cases in his private practice during a year, left the city for ten days, burned his clothes, shaved his head, beard, and mustache, pared his nails, and scrubbed himself thoroughly. Nevertheless, his next patient died of the fever. Altogether, he had ninety-five cases in four years, of whom eighteen died. Often, of course, the infection only made women very sick. Meigs said he had no other explanation for Rutter's misfortune except "God's Providence," adding that Rutter must somehow have carried "the essence of disease." So mysterious was the spread of the fever, in spite of sanitary precautions in private and hospital practice, that a few early believers in contagion saw it as a malignant halo or aura surrounding an unlucky doctor. Later writers attributed Rutter's cases to a chronic nasal infection he had that made him "unclean" despite continual washing. This was only one of many ways in which a conscientious and "gentlemanly" doctor could unknowingly cause fever.[25]

In the third place, doctors were consequently unable to prevent or control the fever because they did not yet know its exact cause and did not have a specific to cure it. They were left with prevention alone, but prevention was never completely effective while the cause was uncertain. Doctors speculated endlessly about what generated puerperal fever, and many resisted the notion that they were agents in spreading contagion.

The elaboration of theories was rich and illustrated how environmental models of disease were overcoming older behavioral explanations even before bacteriological theory. Some doctors—Holmes, for example—thought puerperal fever was like erysipelas, an infectious skin disease. Others suggested that it was a specific disease that struck only lying-in women and resulted from some morbidity in their condition, such as putrefaction of portions of placenta retained in the womb. Others believed that it was really several different diseases, distinguishable by varying symptoms. Some thus thought it to be "autogenic," proceeding from causes within the woman; others thought it "heterogenic," originating from causes outside, such as the decomposed animal matter Semmelweis had blamed. European doctors sometimes favored the "miasma" theory, according to which bad air—perhaps sewer gas from improperly installed plumbing—or some other environmental influence carried the disease to some but not other women. English and Scottish physicians favored "contagion," the transmission from person to person, although this left open the question of what was transmitted. Some doctors in America, having observed changes in blood chemistry in pregnant women, argued for a "crasis" theory, a spontaneous origin of fever in the blood; but why some women's changes produced fever and others did not was uncertain. As late as 1875 one American, Dr. Fordyce Barker, wrote a book supporting "crasis" as an alternative to microbial theory.[26] Many doctors suggested that some common disease touched the pregnant and parturient woman and transformed itself because of birth conditions into the deadly fever.

The most colorful theory reverted to explaining the disease on the basis of the woman's moral and mental conditions. In 1877 the president of the American Gynecological Society said:

> The mortality in lying-in hospitals must always be larger than in the city, outside their walls. . . . The majority of patients who seek the lying-in asylums are unmarried . . . this circumstance has a bad effect on their recovery . . . a poor girl who is ashamed of her condition, who is anxious as to what will become of herself and her offspring, who has been driven away from her place when her state could not be longer concealed, and who has suffered from cold and hunger, is more apt to become infected with puerperal fever, and certainly more apt to succumb to its attack on her feeble and worn-out body.[27]

There was a measure of truth in this also.

Until approximately 1880 it was uncertain what caused the fever. Then Louis Pasteur demonstrated that the microbial chains he had first discovered in 1860 and called streptococci were its major cause, and he showed that parturient women, having wounded genitalia, were particularly susceptible to the virulent bacterial infection.

Physicians' reluctance to think themselves agents for transmitting "a private pestilence" is understandable, not only because many were untrained to observe disease, but also because, as Hodge remarked, contagion threatened their self-understanding as professionals bent upon helping women. And so long as the exact cause of the fever was unknown, its baffling character perplexed even those doctors who were interested in scientific medicine. Nonetheless, most doctors, even if they were not believers in contagion, tried to prevent puerperal fever in both private and hospital practice by following the advice of White, Gordon, and Holmes.

Exact statistics for morbidity and mortality from puerperal fever before 1885, when antisepsis began to be used in hospitals, are not available, because causes of death were not accurately recorded. A Philadelphia doctor said in 1873 that doctors naturally shrank from reporting their fatal midwifery cases as such and resorted to calling death from puerperal fever by many other, obscuring names.[28] Yet, even without exact statistics, it is clear that puerperal fever was continually present during that period and often reached epidemic proportions.

Holmes mentioned several doctors who had lost four to six patients in a short time. Meigs admitted to seeing many cases. Channing estimated that thirty-six women had died in Boston of the fever in 1847 and twenty-two more by June of the next year. Dr. Fordyce Barker of New York said that the fever had reached epidemic scale in 1873, being twenty times as great as in the previous twenty years. Moreover, it was striking the wealthy twice as often as the poor and killing four times more women in home deliveries than in hospitals. He also said that the fever was present in Cincinnati, where it took 130 lives, whereas in previous years it had never taken more than twenty. Another doctor in New York estimated in 1885 that 75 percent of deaths in childbed resulted from puerperal fever; he guessed the mortality from the fever might be as high as 40 per 1,000 in private practice, given the doctors' unwillingness to acknowledge its presence.[29]

The records of fatalities in lying-in hospitals are not entirely reliable, but they do indicate that the fever caused much sickness and death during sporadic outbreaks. The State Emigrants' Hospital on Ward's Island in New York admitted 574 women during 1852, of whom 124 contracted the fever and 68 died of it. In 1883 in Boston's Lying-In Hospital 75 percent of the patients had the fever and 20 percent died of it.[30]

Even though many doctors did not fully agree with the microbial explanation, they were prepared to draw upon Joseph Lister's successful use of antiseptics during surgery in order to prevent infection during childbirth, particularly in hospital deliveries. Preventive antisepsis as well as regimens of prophylaxis became the object of continuous experiment in some hospitals. One New York hospital treated the woman's vulva after birth as though it were a wound caused by a "capital operation" and four times a day put on a new dressing after injecting the genitalia with carbolic acid.[31]

In 1883 Boston's Lying-In Hospital had been following White's prophylactic regimen and using injections of carbolic acid. Yet the syringe used for douching patients was not itself disinfected, just as the hands of examining students and doctors were not. The means of transmission were still open, and thus the hospital had another epidemic.[32]

A recent study comparing the practice of male and female doctors in Boston hospitals suggests that women doctors lost fewer patients to puerperal fever than men did because the women doctors exercised more professional discipline, more regularly scrubbing themselves, and because the women used instruments to hasten deliveries less frequently than did male doctors, who often adjudged patients uncooperative or lazy.[33]

Carelessness in antiseptic routine made puerperal fever a continuing problem for both hospital and home deliveries until the 1930s and 1940s, when sulfa and penicillin became available to cure infection. Many general practitioners simply gave little credence to the virulence of bacteria and contented themselves, for example, with sterilizing a needle or probe by running it through a bar of soap and with cleaning their hands by wiping them on a towel. Self-studies by the profession in the 1930s pointed out that uneducated immigrant midwives of New York had septicemia rates no worse than those of doctors in home and hospital deliveries.[34]

Although carelessness contributed to the continuance of the fever into the twentieth century, the increase in traumatic interventions was equally important. Pasteur had shown that the presence of bacteria alone was not enough to cause infection; a wound had to be present to allow bacteria to enter the bloodstream. Although all puerperal women were "wounded women," those who had additional trauma from operative interventions were even more susceptible to infection. This was forgotten by many hospitals, which hoped to prevent infection by asepsis alone. There were types of bacteria already present in the genitalia that could become virulent when operative interventions created the right tissue medium for their growth. The increased number of high- and mid-forceps operations, induced labors, versions, and Caesarean sections created the "traumatized, devitalized tissues" that allowed the anaerobic streptococci already present to develop into infections, despite the creation of a sterile operating environment. It is quite possible that the fact that hospitals had infection rates as high as 11 percent in 1934 was the result not of carelessness about asepsis but of needless operations. Some physicians believe that the reduction in such operative interventions was as important as the new antimicrobial drugs in reducing the incidence of infection after the mid-1930s. Other facts were blood transfusions, which kept up a woman's strength and rendered her less susceptible; a shortening of excessively long labors that exhausted a woman and gave bacteria easier access after the breaking of the amniotic sac; better aseptic technique; and a general improvement in women's health. The "magic bullets" of sulfa and penicillin, though very useful, were not entirely responsible for the drastic reduction of infection after 1935.[35]

Puerperal fever is probably the classic example of iatrogenic disease—that is, disease caused by medical treatment itself. It is useless to speculate about whether fewer women would have sickened and died if midwives, who were less likely to carry bacteria and to intervene operatively, rather than doctors had continued to attend births, for the basis of comparison is missing. But it is clear that doctors' need to prevent puerperal fever contributed to the dehumanization of birth. Doctors not only had to control more carefully the processes and contexts of birthcare, they also had to bring preventive treatment to each pregnant and parturient woman, however healthy, because each woman was susceptible to infection from the doctor and the medical environment. Doctors had to regard each woman as diseased, because birth provided the occasion and medicine the cause for infection. Excessive interventions only increased the chances for sickness and infection. Until specific cures for puerperal fever were available in the late 1930s, each woman had to be judged a potential victim needing preventive, and dehumanizing, treatment.

More women were attracted to hospitals, however, because after 1900 hospitals offered painless birth not readily available in home deliveries. Women gained release from birthpain, at the expense of being processed as possibly diseased objects. Thus began the major transformations in birth: from home to hospital, from suffering to painlessness, from patient care to disease care.

Notes

1. Andrew Sinclair, *The Emancipation of the American Woman* (New York: Harper & Row, 1965), p. 137; Elizabeth R. Scovil, *Preparation for Motherhood* (Philadelphia, 1896), p. 137; Celia D. Mosher, *Woman's Physical Freedom* (New York, 1923), pp. 1, 29; Page Smith, *Daughters of the Promised Land* (Boston: Little, Brown, 1970), pp. 131–139.
2. Gerda Lerner, *The Grimké Sisters from South Carolina* (Boston: Houghton-Mifflin, 1967), p. 290.

3. Harold Speert, *Obstetric and Gynecologic Milestones* (New York: Macmillan, 1958), pp. 442–443.
4. Frederick Hollick, *The Matron's Manual of Midwifery* (Boston, 1848), pp. v–vi.
5. *Ibid., p.* 16; Charles E. Rosenberg, "Sexuality, Class and Role in Nineteenth-Century America," *American Quarterly* 25, No. 2 (May, 1973):138–139; Alice Stockham, *Karezza: The Ethics of Marriage* (Chicago, 1896), p. 77; Carroll Smith-Rosenberg. "The Hysterical Woman: Sex Roles and Role Conflict in Nineteenth-Century America," *Social Research* 39 (1972):656.
6. Hugh L. Hodge, *Foeticide* (Philadelphia, 1872), p. 32; Linda Gordon, "Voluntary Motherhood," in M. S. Hartman and L. Banner, *Clio's Consciousness Raised* (New York: Harper & Row, 1974), pp. 54–71.
7. John H. Dye, *Painless Childbirth* (Buffalo, 1884), pp. 53–54.
8. Hollick, *Matron's Manual*, pp. v–vi.
9. Dye, *Painless Childbirth, pp.* 79–80; Mary S. Nichols, *Experience in Water-Cure* (New York, 1850), p. 74.
10. Ann Douglas Wood, "The Fashionable Diseases," *Journal of Interdisciplinary History* 4 (1973):36; George H. Napheys, *The Physical Life of Woman* (Philadelphia, 1880), p. 169.
11. Quoted in Mrs. P. B. Saur, *Maternity* (Philadelphia, 1891), pp. 199–200, and in Alice B. Stockham, *Tokology* (Chicago, 1889), pp. 96–97.
12. Dye, *Painless Childbirth*, p. 52; Stockham, *Tokology*, p. 20.
13. Palmer Findlay, *Priests of Lucina* (Boston, 1939), pp. 234–248; Harvey Graham, *Eternal Eve* (New York: Doubleday, 1951), p. 476; Walter Channing, *A Treatise on Etherization in Childbirth* (Boston, 1848).
14. Quoted without attribution by Fordyce Barker, *On the Use of Anesthetics in Midwifery* (New York, 1861), p. 253; Graham, *Eternal Eve*, p. 476.
15. Henry Miller, "Report ... on Anaesthesia in Midwifery," *Transactions of the Kentucky State Medical Society* (Louisville, 1853), pp. 14–15; Dye, *Painless Childbirth*, p. 151; Horatio Storer, *Eutokia* (Boston, 1863); Benjamin E. Cotting, "Anaesthetics in Midwifery," *Boston Medical and Surgical Journal* 59, No. 19 (December 9, 1858):372; Barker, *On Use of Anaesthetics*, pp. 255–268; H. Culbertson, *Prize Essay on Use of Anaesthetics in Obstetrics* (Cincinnati, 1862); "Report of the Committee on Obstetrics," *Transactions of the AMA* (Philadelphia, 1848), pp. 228–231.
16. "Why Not? A Book for Every Woman: A Woman's View," *Boston Medical and Surgical Journal* 75, No. 14 (November 1, 1866):273–276.
17. Harold Speert, *The Sloane Hospital Chronicle* (Philadelphia, 1963), p.

83; William G. Rothstein, *American Physicians in the Nineteenth Century* (Baltimore: Johns Hopkins Press, 1970), pp. 188–194; Frances Parkinson Keyes, *All Flags Flying* (New York, 1972), p. 27.

18. Dye, *Painless Childbirth*, p. 85; Hollick, *Matron's Manual*, p. 445; M. L. Holbrook, *Parturition Without Pain* (New York, 1891); Sinclair, *Emancipation of American Woman*, pp. 128–129; Stockham, *Karezza*, p. 189.

19. Charles White, *A Treatise on the Management of Pregnant and Lying-in Women* ... (London, 1773); Alexander Gordon, *Treatise on the Epidemic Puerperal Fever of Aberdeen* (London, 1795).

20. Irving S. Cutter and Henry R. Viets, *A Short History of Midwifery* (Philadelphia: Saunders, 1964), pp. 130–133; Oliver Wendell Holmes, "The Contagiousness of Puerperal Fever," *New England Quarterly Journal of Medicine and Surgery* 1 (April, 1843):503–530.

21. Graham, *Eternal Eve*, pp. 403–408; Cutter and Viets, *Short History of Midwifery*, pp. 136–143.

22. Hugh L. Hodge, *On the Non-contagious Character of Puerperal Fever* (Philadelphia, 1852), pp. 10–13, 26–27.

23. Charles Meigs, *Obstetrics* (Philadelphia, 1852) p. 631; idem, *On the Nature, Signs and Treatment of Childbed Fever* ... (Philadelphia, 1854), pp. 102, 104.

24. Oliver Wendell Holmes, *Puerperal Fever as a Private Pestilence* (Boston, 1855), pp. 6, 12, 24, 56–57, 60.

25. *Playfair's Midwifery* (Philadelphia, 1898), p. 619; also 1885 edition, p. 605; Theodore Cianfrani, *A Short History of Obstetrics and Gynecology* (Springfield, Ill.: Charles C. Thomas, 1960), pp. 306–316.

26. Fordyce Barker, *The Relation of Puerperal Fever to Infective Diseases and Pyaemia* (Louisville, 1875); idem, *The Puerperal Diseases* (New York: D. Appleton, 1884), p. 399. Barker believed that bacteria were "a product of changes effected in the blood," ... "rather than a cause of the morbid phenomena which appear in septicaemia."

27. Address by Henry J. Garrigues, quoted by Speert, *Sloane Hospital Chronicle*, p. 81.

28. William Goodell, *On the Means Employed at the Preston Retreat* ... (Philadelphia, 1874), p. 14.

29. Channing, *Treatise on Etherization*, pp. 375–380; Fordyce Barker, *The Relation of Puerperal Fever to the Infective Diseases* ... (Lousville, 1874), p. 11; Joseph Kucher, *Puerperal Convalescense and the Diseases of the Puerperal Period* (New York, 1886), pp. 224–227.

30. Frederick Irving, *Safe Deliverance* (Boston, 1942), pp. 143, 161, 167.

31. Henry J. Garrigues, *Prevention of Puerperal Infection* (New York, 1884), pp. 10–11.

32. Irving, *Safe Deliverance*, pp. 140–184.

33. Alice B. Crosby, *The Story of the New England Hospital, 1862–1937*

(Boston, 1937); Laurie Crumpacker, "Female Patients in Four Boston Hospitals: Sex, Class and Science in Late Nineteenth-Century Medicine," unpublished paper in Schlesinger Library, Radcliffe College.

34. D. W. Cattell and W. T. Cattell, *Book on the Physician Himself* (Philadelphia, 1902), p. 27: New York Academy of Medicine, *Maternal Mortality in New York City: A Study of Puerperal Deaths, 1930– 1932* (New York, 1933), pp. 191, 211.

35. Nicholson J. Eastman and Louis M. Hellman, *Williams Obstetrics,* 13th ed. (New York: Appleton-Century-Crofts, 1966), p. 957.

5

Birth in the Hospital

Everything, of course, depends on what we define as normal.
                                        Dr. Joseph B. DeLee, 1920

> *"But is the hospital necessary at all?" demanded a young woman of her obstetrician friend. "Why not bring the baby at home?"*
> *"What would you do if your automobile broke down on a country road?" the doctor countered with another question.*
> *"Try and fix it," said the modern chauffeuse.*
> *"And if you couldn't?"*
> *"Have it hauled to the nearest garage."*
> *"Exactly. Where the trained mechanics and their necessary tools are," agreed the doctor. "It's the same with the hospital. I can do my best work—and the best we must have in medicine all the time—not in some cramped little apartment or private home, but where I have the proper facilities and trained helpers. If anything goes wrong, I have all known aids to meet your emergency."*
>
> The Century Illustrated Magazine, *February,*
> *1926*

NINETEENTH-CENTURY maternity hospitals were urban asylums for poor, homeless, or working-class married women who could not deliver at home but who doctors and philanthropists believed deserved medical treatment and the chance to recuperate in an atmosphere of moral uplift—what lying-in at home was thought to provide for more fortunate women. After the Civil War, such institutions could no longer overlook the large numbers of *un*-married expectant women, often young girls, who were "neither vicious nor depraved" but often victims of rapacious city life, and whom doctors and patrons wished to save from "degenerating into depravity." The fascination with rehabilitating social degradation expressed an optimism that the disorders of industrial society might be healed.[1]

Those hospitals were never large and attracted only a small percentage of pregnant women, for most poor and genteel women delivered in their homes. Maternity hospitals had obvious liabilities: the danger of puerperal fever and the stigma of being an unconfined, homeless woman, if not worse. But once the specter of the fever was generally banished in the 1880s and hospital-based obstetricians developed new medical skills, the hospital's image improved. Women of all classes selected it for difficult births and gradually came to consider it a safer, more comfortable, and cleaner place than their homes for all deliveries. The hospital specialists of course preferred it; later, general practitioners sent their patients to hospitals.

While less than 5 percent of women had delivered in hospitals in 1900, the numbers increased and became a flood in the 1920s. As Rose Kennedy remarked, the "fashion changed." Urban life made the hospital the necessary resort of many poor women, but middle- and upper-class women also chose hospitals. By 1921 more than half the births in Minneapolis–St. Paul, Spokane, San Francisco, Hartford, the District of Columbia, and Springfield, Massachusetts, took place in hospitals, as did between 30 and 50 percent of the births in a dozen other cities, including Philadelphia, Newark, and Cincinnati. Urban areas with a smaller percentage of hospital births had larger immigrant populations, which preferred midwives, but, as midwives ceased to practice, hospital births increased. In Cleveland hospital deliveries jumped from 22 percent in 1920 to 55 percent in 1930 and 76 percent in 1937. By 1939 half of all women and 75 percent of all urban women were delivering in hospitals. In rural areas where midwives and general practitioners had long attended home births, the automobile's increasing availability enabled women to travel considerable distances to hospitals even after labor began.[2]

The marked transformation in birth practice occurred because both women and doctors found hospital birth more efficient than home birth for accomplishing what they wanted. Although women and doctors had somewhat different social and cultural expectations about hospital birth, both agreed that it was safer than home birth. Moreover, it appeared to offer the best of the old and the new rituals without loss to either. The hospital was a hotel that provided the practical services associated with social childbirth and the chance for recuperation; it was a place where the doctor could personally relate to his patient, provide the old moral care, and yet use new skills to make birth safer and more comfortable, to cure disease if necessary. From 1900 into the

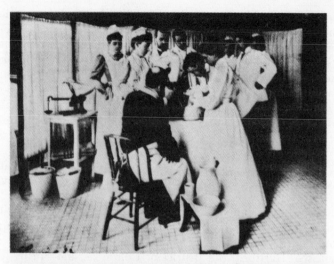

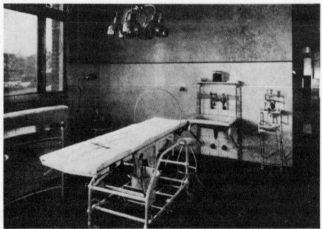

Top: A forceps delivery in 1892 by Dr. James W. McLane, first Director of New York City's Sloane Maternity Hospital. The resident listens to the fetal heart. Note that no gloves or masks are used and that Dr. McLane is seated. *Bottom:* Maternity operating room, Bridgeport (Conn.) Hospital, *circa* 1918.

1930s women and doctors shared the view that birth was best and safest if women entrusted themselves to specialists' care in hospitals. Only gradually after 1930 did people realize that centralizing birth had altered it fundamentally and brought new problems. Doctors began to worry because hospital birth had not produced notably better results; women began to feel that the medical treatment and institutional care had alienated them from important birth experiences.

In this chapter we shall try to explore why women and doctors sought hospital delivery and examine the nature of the "new" medical and institutional birth.

In the decades after the Civil War, maternity hospitals achieved no outstanding success in overcoming social degradation, but they did begin to benefit doctors and patrons in other ways. By their association with a few of the better medical schools, maternity hospitals became clinical laboratories and schools, places for testing new knowledge and skills, for training students and trying new operations. Perhaps because charity patients and

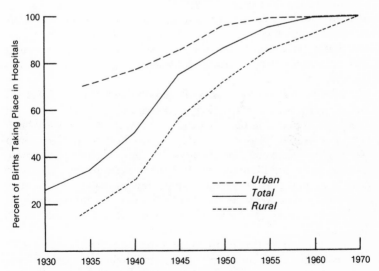

Estimated Percentages of Births Taking Place in Hospitals, 1930-1970

Sources: Donnell M. Pappenfort, *Journey to Labor,* Chicago, 1964, Table 15, p. 49; AMA Council on Medical Education and Hospitals, *Hospital Service in the U.S., IX-XV* (Chicago: 1936).

unmarried women had less social claim on doctors than middle- and upper-class genteel women had, doctors looked more readily at them as "cases," instances of difficult or diseased birth, and less as persons. But it was also simply the nature of scientific medicine to focus its attention more narrowly upon the natural process, healthy or diseased, rather than upon the whole person. It was the process that interested the doctor; it was curing the "diseased" process or aiding the "difficult" process that gave him satisfaction and status. The line of development for the scientific doctor was more exact attention to and more precise control over a selected natural process *within* the patient. As he was able to control that process more skillfully for the patient's benefit, he tended to become less interested in the rest of the patient's life. The zeal for moral therapy waned. Doctors were pleased, therefore, to have charity patients whose reproductive processes they might observe with a steady, clinical eye. Doing so with genteel women would have been difficult, if not impossible, not only for reasons of modesty but because such women would have expected more generally supportive care. But what doctors learned from practicing with charity patients they might apply to other women when emergency needs arose.

The corollary to the narrowing of doctors' interest was their need to control the patient more completely in order to give treatment. Treatment itself became a series of more precise and effective manipulations and interventions, both to prevent and to cure disease.

Doctors were on the lookout for trouble in birth. That seemed to them to be their primary purpose. They found a lot of trouble—so much, in fact, that they came to think that every birth was a potential disaster and that it was best to prepare each woman for the worst eventualities. In line with that perception, doctors increased their control over the patients during labor and delivery, rendering them more powerless to experience or participate in birth. Women acceded to the doctors' increasing control because they also believed that their methods would make birth safer.

The realization that many of the dangers in birth originated in the environment of the hospital or in the medical treatment itself was very slow in coming. A good example was the standardization of birth rituals in order to combat puerperal fever in maternity hospitals.

Standard procedures arose before the exact sources of the

death-dealing germs were known. Drawing on the advice of Gordon of Manchester and from practices in military hospitals during the Civil War, maternity hospitals established routine methods to prevent the disease. The medical posture became one of manipulation, intervention, and active combat. Doctors assumed that the disease might originate in the hospital environment, so they had wards aired and washed with carbolic acid at regular intervals and required nurses to bathe and change their uniforms on schedule. They also assumed that the patient herself might be carrying the germs that could kill her, so, despite her individuality, each woman had to be treated as if she harbored them. Patients from the slums might carry filth on their clothing or lice in their hair; there was good reason for removing their personal belongings and cleaning or shaving their hair. The enema was an ancient practice, but it became routine because doctors thought accidental bowel movement might be the contaminating cause of the fever. Cleaning, shaving, and purging the patient were not merely training in cleanliness; they constituted preventive treatment, a broad prophylactic program to eliminate disease.

William Goodell, physician in charge of the Preston Retreat in Philadelphia and professor of the diseases of women at the University of Pennsylvania, explained in 1874 his system for cleaning out the fever. What is striking about the system is that it treated each woman *as if* she was diseased. When the patient came to the hospital, some days or weeks before delivery, she was put on a regular dosage of quinine, then a kind of all-purpose preventative. Each woman received drugs for constipation, headaches, and sleeplessness. When labor began, each received a cathartic and a bath. The staff then ruptured the amniotic sac, used forceps to expedite delivery, gave ergot when the head appeared, and hurried the expulsion of the placenta by pressing on the stomach. After cutting the cord and bathing the woman again, they gave her morphine each hour until she felt no more afterpains and gave her quinine "until the ears rang." Anesthesia was not used.

In Goodell's view, these routines for cleansing and for manipulating birth made hospital delivery safer and more comfortable than home delivery. He was convinced that he had had greater success in eliminating the fever than most physicians had in their private practices in homes, for they concealed its evidences. The comfort of his system derived from the drug regimes that eased pain after birth.[3]

Another example of the fight against sepsis, after its causes were known, is found in the routine at Sloane Maternity Hospital in New York. Preventive measures were still needed, of course, since the germs were virulent and no real cure was available until the 1940s. In 1900 each patient at Sloane received an enema immediately upon admission and then a vaginal douche with bichloride of mercury, the favored antiseptic. Nurses then washed the woman's head with kerosene, ether, and ammonia, her nipples and umbilicus with ether; they shaved the pubic hair of charity patients, assuming that poor people harbored more germs, and clipped it for private patients. They gave women in labor an enema every twelve hours and continued to douche the vagina during and after labor with saline solutions to which whisky or bichloride of mercury was added. The zeal against infection led to more douching than was really necessary or safe, for the solutions were ineffective against the germs and served to spread any infection that was already present. But the broad-gauged prophylaxis resulted in increased manipulations of the patient.[4]

Sloane had an epidemic in 1927 that killed 15 percent of its patients. The irony that hospitals had to undertake more antiseptic and aseptic routines because they were bacterially "dirtier" and more likely to be a reservoir for hardy strains of resistant bacteria than a home only gradually became apparent to doctors. The "safe" hospital was the product of extremely vigilant and ritualized manipulations and interventions. The hospital environment itself had contributed materially to defining birth as a dangerous event and to the treatment of each pregnant woman as if she might die.

Another reason for the development of a readiness to intervene in birth was the nature of the patients in maternity hospitals in the closing decades of the nineteenth century. Doctors saw these women—the charity patients and the unwed mothers who sometimes paid for part of their care—as defective both in health and in moral ability, and thus as in greater need of assistance from medical arts than were healthy and respectable women. A doctor trained in Vienna reported in 1886 that he needed to use forceps in only 5 percent of his cases in Vienna, but in New York he found it necessary to use them in 40 percent of his cases, partly because his colleagues advised him to do so, and partly because he believed that his patients were less healthy.[5] A recent study of case reports in a Boston maternity hospital in the 1890s found that instrumental interventions were often justified with moral judgments about

the patients as too lazy or too stupid to deliver by themselves.[6]
How often interventions were expressions of impatience, of
therapy for weak women, or even of punitive treatment for having "fallen" cannot be known, but doctors seem to have felt
licensed to do what was best for the women who were not in a
social position to complain.

Many interventions were of course humanitarian attempts to
apply the best treatment. One class of interventions involved
using new procedures for very difficult deliveries. There was an
inevitable element of experimentation in this, for doctors had to
test the appropriateness of the procedure for the condition and
also learn how to do it properly. The Caesarean section was an
example. An old operation, nearly always fatal, it was revived in
1882 by a German named Max Sänger and developed into a
largely successful method to deliver women with deformed
pelves. Sänger had found that by using aseptic methods and
suturing the uterine wall with silk thread as well as the abdominal
wall he had success in 80 percent of the operations. American
doctors then had to learn when and how to do the operations. The
first Caesarean section in Boston occurred in 1894 upon a small
woman with a tiny pelvis who had previously lost two babies. A
witness described the successful operation:

> Haven made an incision in the abdominal wall about a foot long
> and lifted the uterus through it, so that it rested upon the skin
> and the towels that were placed about it. This enormous organ,
> the color of a ripe plum, was a sight that filled the eyes of the
> beholders with wonder and respect. A quick slash through its
> wall brought a gush of liquid and blood which shot halfway
> across the room. The baby and the afterbirth were rapidly ex-
> tracted, the uterus contracted well at once, and there was no
> further hemorrhage. Haven sutured the uterus in the approved
> Sänger manner, using silk ... and closed the abdomen in the
> same way.[7]

The director of the Sloane Hospital left word that he was to
be called whenever a patient appeared with symptoms indicating
the need for a section. By 1913 he had performed the operation
112 times and had accumulated enough experience to know when
and how to perform it. He offered a few dicta, one of which,
"Once a Caesarean always a Caesarean," has been well heeded
ever since. Such operations were often dangerous; they remained
experimental until doctors developed a consensus about when it

was necessary to operate and when it was not, when was the correct time in labor to begin, and how to cut. Sections were often done too late, after the woman was dehydrated, starved, exhausted, or even infected by repeated examinations. The great value for specialists in having a continuous supply of clinic patients lay in the opportunities they provided for acquiring case experience. Sometimes specialists decided that a procedure was useless because the results were poor. Thus, Boston doctors concluded that induced labor and the use of forceps were not suitable for treating eclampsia, which caused puerperal convulsions, after six of ten patients died from the treatment. Rather, they determined that rest and sedation were better.[8]

By 1910 prenatal care had become more meaningful than ever before, for not only had doctors found that a woman showing the danger signals of eclampsia could be treated to prevent its development by a combination of rest, diet, and drugs; they also could take her blood pressure and examine the urine for albumin, which served as positive diagnoses for the beginning of eclampsia. Furthermore, with the Wassermann test, doctors could diagnose maternal syphilis, and prompt treatment with the new arsenical "Salvarsan" might prevent congenital syphilis in the fetus. The importance of the prenatal Wasserman test was underscored by studies in St. Louis and New York indicating that 10 percent of pregnant married women were actively syphilitic and that 5 to 6 percent of infants among the poor were congenitally syphilitic. The Children's Bureau estimated that there was a total of 73,000 infant deaths (including 41,700 stillbirths) in the year 1916 due to syphilis alone. Gonorrhea, though rarely a killer, could cause blindness if the gonococcus came into contact with the baby's eyes as it passed through the birth canal. Pediatricians estimated that 25 to 30 percent of adult blindness was due to gonococcal infection at birth, and some estimates ranged as high as 50 percent. Although it was not possible to diagnose the presence of gonorrhea in the mother with any accuracy, by the early 1900s gonococcal blindness had become entirely preventable by dropping a 1-percent silver nitrate solution in each eye immediately after birth. Doctors realized that such preventive treatment had to be given to every baby, since gonorrhea frequently presented no symptoms in women. These preventive measures, both prenatal and postnatal, convinced doctors further that routine medical intervention was necessary to prevent diseases associated with birth.[9]

By 1920 doctors believed that "normal" deliveries, those without convulsions, deformed pelves, protracted and difficult labor, the threat of sepsis or of tears in the woman's perineum, were so rare as to be virtually nonexistent. The doctors saw every birth as varying from the normal, and thus as potentially pathogenic, or disease-causing. They concluded, therefore, that routine interventions should be made during every labor and delivery in order to prevent trouble. One finds many statements such as the following in medical journals:

> It is a common experience among obstetrical practitioners that there is an increasing gestational pathology and a more frequent call for art, in supplementing inefficient forces of nature in her efforts to accomplish normal delivery.[10]

A Boston obstetrician, addressing a large women's group in 1923,

> ... re-defined birth, not as "something natural and normal, and not worth the time of obstetricians and specialists' charges," but as "a complicated and delicately adjusted process, subject to variations from the normal which may be disastrous to the mother or baby, or both."[11]

Doctors had known for many decades that labor and delivery could result in serious gynecological conditions, which then required surgical repair. Preventing such conditions seemed a necessary and humane objective. American obstetrical textbooks at the turn of the century had begun to recommend that the "second stage of labor," when the fetus passes through the birth canal, be allowed to last no longer than two hours. Probably the most influential exponent of routine interventions in normal birth was Dr. Joseph DeLee of Chicago, whose 1920 article entitled "The Prophylactic Forceps Operation" became a benchmark for obstetrical practice. DeLee urged that two interventions, outlet forceps and episiotomy, be made routine in normal delivery. The procedure he commended involved sedating the woman and allowing her cervix to dilate, giving ether when the fetus entered the birth canal, making a cut of several inches through the skin and muscles of the perineum, the area between vagina and anus, applying forceps to lift the fetus's head over the perineum while monitoring the fetal heart via stethoscope, using ergot or one of its derivatives to contract the uterus, and then extracting the expelled placenta with a "shoehorn maneuver." Finally, the doctor should stitch up the perineal cut.[12]

DeLee's rationale for this procedure was that episiotomy, the perineal cut, prevented the tearing of the perineum as the baby's head stretched it, an event that could cause "permanent invalidism," such as prolapsed uteri, vesico-vaginal fistulas (tears in the vaginal wall), and sagging perineums. His operation, DeLee said, restored "virginal conditions." Likewise, the brief and timely application of forceps prevented potential damage to the baby's brain caused by the contractions pushing the head against the perineum. He presented a lengthy list of possible injuries caused by "natural, spontaneous labor" and claimed that 4 or 5 percent of babies died from such damage. Long, hard labors were often responsible, he said, for epilepsy, idiocy, imbecility, and cerebral palsy, conditions that Americans had begun to fear very greatly during the previous decades, partly because the conditions had been associated with criminal behavior.[13] DeLee argued that his prophylactic operation prevented gynecological trouble for the mother, even restored her to "better than new," and saved the child from brain damage and a life of crime.

DeLee employed several vivid similes to express the dangers of unaided birth. He compared it to the mother's falling on a pitchfork and to the baby's head being caught in a door jamb:

> It always strikes physicians as well as laymen as bizarre, to call labor an abnormal function, a disease, and yet it is a decidedly pathologic process. Everything, of course, depends on what we define as normal. If a woman falls on a pitchfork, and drives the handle through her perineum, we call that pathologic—abnormal, but if a large baby is driven through the pelvic floor, we say that it is natural, and therefore normal. If a baby were to have its head caught in a door very lightly, but enough to cause cerebral hemorrhage, we would say that it is decidedly pathologic, but when a baby's head is crushed against a tight pelvic floor, and a hemorrhage in the brain kills it, we call this normal, at least we say that the function is natural, not pathogenic.
>
> In both cases, the cause of the damage, the fall on the pitchfork, and the crushing of the door, is pathogenic, that is disease-producing, and in the same sense labor is pathogenic,

disease-producing, and anything pathogenic is pathologic or abnormal.

DeLee said that "only a small minority of women" escaped damage and many babies were killed or damaged "by the direct action of the natural process itself":

> So frequent are these bad effects, that I have often wondered whether Nature did not deliberately intend women to be used up in the process of reproduction, in a manner analogous to that of the salmon, which dies after spawning.[14]

DeLee's procedure represented the preventive disposition and best intentions of obstetrics, and it came to have a great influence upon hospital delivery. By the 1930s his routine was normative in many hospitals, for his rationale to prevent tears seemed reasonable: Many women delivering in hospitals *were* experiencing tears. But obstetricians did not ask whether tears resulted from the failings of nature or from hospital practices, which often immobilized a woman on her back with legs raised in stirrups. DeLee's procedures did not become routine in foreign countries that had a higher proportion of home deliveries and fewer perineal tears. As late as 1973 doctors were looking for scientific proof of the validity of DeLee's hypothesis that episiotomy and outlet forceps protected the baby's head also.[15]

It is impossible to know whether births around 1920 were really more pathological or whether doctors saw more pathology in birth because they were looking for it and had more means to prevent and cure it. Doctors believed, however, that women should deliver in hospitals in order to receive the preventive treatments that seemed to protect birth from itself. Interventions grew steadily in number after 1900. In one Boston maternity hospital, for example, procedures such as forceps, versions, Caesarean sections, and mechanical induction increased between 1910 and 1921 from 29 percent to 45 percent of all deliveries, largely because of greater use of forceps and sections. Birth was more malleable, more a product of medical skill and technique.[16]

Doctors had social and cultural reasons for promoting hospital delivery as well as medical ones. Some commentators have suggested that doctors sought to centralize all medical care in hospitals because of the model of industry, which had taught them that control of a work space would make them a new elite,

like the "captains of industry." Perhaps doctors were aware that
institutionalizing medicine would bring them power and prestige,
but in the decades after 1900 they had more immediately practical
reasons for centralizing care.[17]

One was convenience. Obstetrical specialists, who had developed their skills in hospitals, wished no part in the cottage
industry of home delivery. Traveling to women's homes, remaining during the period of labor, and becoming involved in family
life were time-consuming and a compromise of medical authority.
The doctor had to defer to family wishes about intervention and,
inevitably, could not have with him the tools with which to demonstrate his skills. Carrying forceps, scissors, and lancet was one
thing; going with X-ray equipment, transfusion equipment, anesthesia, drugs, sterilizing equipment, and the like was impossible.
The doctor's skill nested within the hospital. Women had to come
to the specialists' work place, the hospital.

Home delivery had also been associated with the generalized
moral therapy that sought to prevent troubles in birth by advising
women about correct behavior. As doctors learned more about
the scientific causes of disease and acquired more technical means
to prevent or cure it, they lost interest in behavioral and environmental causes of illness and difficulty in birth. They were convinced that the disease was in the patient's natural processes;
moreover, doctors believed that they could do little effectively to
prevent the social and environmental causes of disease and more
to cure it once evident. Hospital rather than home delivery was a
more efficient use of medicine's ability, which had been shown to
be more effective in treating disease than in advising people.

This shift of preventive efforts from moral advice to medical
treatment never implied to doctors a requirement that they cease
offering "care," that is, the administration of comfort, support,
and sympathy that constituted the old bedside manner. Doctors
believed that they could continue to offer such care in the hospital
as well as they had in the home. In fact, however, they found it
difficult to do so, not only because their own status was no longer
derived primarily from giving care and advice but from providing
skilled cure, but also because the hospital staff inevitably took over
some of those functions in the doctor's absence. Doctors were
often not aware of it, but they preferred hospital delivery because
the hospital was a center not only of skill but of social care, which
relieved the doctors of the need to provide it and allowed them to

use their skill more efficiently. Nurses, social workers, chaplains, and cleaning women could provide sympathy and the comforts of social childbirth.

Another reason specialists were eager to have women deliver in hospitals was that doctors needed a regular supply of patients in order to train students more efficiently in the science of obstetrics. The hospital was to become a laboratory and school around which the profession of obstetrics might be upgraded and organized.

Scientific medicine made rapid strides in the years around the turn of the century, and the medical profession faced the problem of bringing education and practice into line with advances in knowledge and technique. Obstetrics had been an informal specialization for a few doctors for several decades and a part of medical education and practice for most doctors for a century, but both education and practice soon fell far behind the standards of new knowledge and technique after 1900. Obstetrics had a low reputation as a field of practice, even among medical students. Sinclair Lewis captured its low status in *Arrowsmith* by having the dunce of the medical class, Fatty Pfaff, choose obstetrics as his specialty: "He was magnificently imbecile; he knew nothing; he could memorize nothing."[18] J. Whitridge Williams, Professor of Obstetrics at Johns Hopkins, the best medical school of the time, said in 1911: "The student . . . cannot be blamed for believing that obstetrics is a pursuit unworthy of broadly educated men, but is suitable only for midwives or physicians of mediocre intelligence." And he said of his own students: "I would unhesitatingly state that they are unfit on graduation to practice obstetrics in its broad sense, and are scarcely prepared to handle normal cases,"[19] by which he meant the students had not been required to acquire sufficient clinical experience to be competent in the latest procedures.

The belief of well-educated specialists, such as Williams, that obstetrics required much more than patient waiting while women delivered, that it required, in fact, a scientific medical education and extensive clinical experience, led them to survey the state of training and practice. Williams examined the teaching of obstetrics in medical schools in 1911 and found it deplorably inadequate. Most professors were poorly prepared to teach, were incompetent to handle abnormal births, lacked adequate facilities for clinical training, and confessed that their students were no better than untrained midwives. At that time there were 120 medical schools giving a full four-year course, but only half of them were accredited by the American Medical Association. Ninety percent of American doctors in 1900 had only a high school education before entering medical school; in 1911 most medical schools still required only a high school degree. Most were also proprietary schools—that is, doctors owned them and taught in them to make a profit. Most of the instructors had the slimmest competence, taught out of books, and offered no clinical experience at all, except perhaps in anatomy.

Williams showed that even the best medical schools, which required a college degree for admission and had respected faculty, still offered insufficient clinical experience in obstetrics. In the best situations a graduate might have attended thirty births. In most, he had attended none or one. Williams believed that no graduates could handle difficult labors, even if they could recognize them; they had no training that related obstetrics to gynecology or surgery; they attended home deliveries without supervision. He reported that professors of obstetrics thought general practitioners lost as many women to infection as did midwives and also thought ill-judged and improperly performed operations by general practitioners killed as many women as died from infection. These beliefs constituted "a railing indictment of the average practitioner and of our methods of instruction."[20]

Williams argued that there should be fewer medical schools and that those schools should have better equipment, higher standards of admission, and qualified instructors; he said that obstetrics should be recognized and taught as a fundamental part of scientific medicine, that the general practitioner should be trained only to attend normal births and to leave all others to obstetrical specialists "in control of abundant hospital facilities"; he pleaded that general practitioners be licensed as having seen at least ten women delivered in a clinic, that medicine should educate the laity that most doctors were dangerous in birth and that most of the ills of women resulted from poor obstetrics; he urged doctors to tell women that they were likely to receive better care in maternity hospitals than at home; he suggested that more hospitals be built for both charity and private patients; finally, he urged that midwives, who attended immigrant women, be abolished. Williams's program paralleled the famous Flexner Report of the same time, undertaken to bootstrap American medicine into conformity with new developments in medical science.[21]

The centerpiece of Williams's proposed reforms was the maternity hospital itself. It, rather than the medical school or private practice, held the promise of improved treatment for women and advanced training for doctors. For a superior obstetrics to emerge, Williams said, expectant mothers should go to hospitals, where they would receive better care, so that medical students might learn the science and the skills to be better general practitioners and specialists. Medical schools should give up the "extern" programs in which unsupervised students delivered the poor in their homes; rather, poor women should deliver in hospitals so that students might attend them while learning new skills.

The desire to upgrade obstetrical education by having a flow of patients as "teaching material" did not produce exactly the results Williams wished. The upgrading took several decades, because of the egalitarian nature of the profession, but the flow of patients began. Williams's message that hospital delivery was safer was heard not only by the poor but by middle- and upper-class women as well; it was broadcast by women's magazines, by women's groups, and by advocates of women's health. The advent of scientific medicine induced an outpouring of philanthropy for building new hospitals, which now included maternity wards as a matter of course. Women of all social classes wanted hospital delivery, and doctors encouraged it. Hospital delivery became the standard of practice.

Williams's proposals gradually improved obstetrical training for new students but did nothing to prevent poorly trained practitioners from sending their patients to hospitals and attempting new procedures that they were unqualified to perform. Williams had hoped that general practitioners would relearn basic obstetrics and attend normal births in home deliveries, leaving difficult births to specialists in hospitals, but neither he nor the profession could enforce this wise division of labor according to skills. For many decades the egalitarian ethos of the profession kept the medical elite from establishing or enforcing credentials for hospital practice or for attempts to do specialist's tasks without training in specialist's skills. Delivering babies had been the prerogative of the generalists for more than a century, and many such doctors, suspicious or resentful of specialists' claims, sought to do what specialists did. Thus, women were attracted to hospitals by the "promise" of better care, which, unfortunately, they often did not receive.[22]

In the years before 1920 specialists and general practitioners had formulated many reasons why hospital delivery was desirable. The primary reason was of course safety, but implicit in that were many other nonmedical aspirations, such as convenience, upgrading of the profession, and the excitement of scientific advance and perfecting of skills. Hospital delivery became normative, however, because women also had aspirations, including safety, which the hospital seemed able to fulfill.

Around 1900 women adopted new attitudes toward bearing and rearing children, which for more than a century had been their primary social responsibility. Contraception had proved to many that it was possible to have fewer children and to engage in other social activities. The home no longer needed to be a shrine to continuous maternity. Many women rejected the rituals of confinement along with the exclusive definition of their lives by maternity. Their interests shifted to encompass events and duties outside the home—in the work place, for example, and in the new, buoyant society of abundance: automobiles, movies, dancing, shopping.[23]

An interesting example of the emergence of pregnancy from confinement was the appearance in 1904 of the first maternity clothes. A young immigrant dressmaker named Lena Bryant designed a "tea gown" for at-home entertaining, featuring accordion pleats from bust to ankle that allowed for expansion. The dress became so popular that it established the fashion house of Lane Bryant. By 1910 the firm offered maternity clothes for street wear, advertising them as healthful because they enabled women to "live normally" and to "go about among other people." The firm urged pregnant women to continue their social activities, to "go out into the health-giving air and sunshine right up to the day of confinement," and to do so "for your baby's sake."[24]

Bottle-feeding also answered women's desire for freedom, for breast-feeding simply extended the period of confinement, rendering women socially and physically immobile, as even the most discreet nursing in public was unthinkable. Besides, breast-feeding was impracticable for working mothers. In order to go about or to go to work, women hired wet-nurses, purchased human milk, or experimented with commercial milk formulas.

Sunshine or Shadow?
Which Do You Choose?

Here are two pictures. They are as nearly opposite as two pictures could possibly be.

One of them shows your life the next few months as it may be. The other as it ought to be. Which, dear mother, will you choose?

Will you be the "shut-in" mother? Hiding in darkness and gloom? Thinking only of things that depress?

Or will you be the carefree one? Out in the brightness and sunshine? Out where gloomy thoughts are banished? Out where friends and happiness make every day a day of joy?

You can put yourself in whichever picture you choose. And Oh, how much the choosing means to you! To choose right means a lifetime of health and happiness. To choose wrong may mean a lifetime of regret.

So choose, dear mother, with care. Choose sunshine, not shadow. Choose happiness, not gloom. Choose health, not misery.

Lane Bryant Will Help You

The choice is not easy, we know. Embarrassment tempts you to seek the shadows. False modesty urges you to hide. Pride forces you to unhealthful dress.

But pay no attention to these tempters. Cling to the other, the better way. Do as your doctor will tell you. Continue every normal activity. Lane Bryant has made it easy for you to do so.

We picture in this book a complete line of Lane Bryant Maternity garments. In these you can face the world without embarrassment. You can continue your social activities. You can go out into the health-giving air and sunshine right up to the day of confinement. You can be as proud of your appearance as you ever were in your life.

So study these garments, today. Study their beauty, their style, their marvelous figure-concealing lines, their health-promoting construction.

And then, for your own sake—for your baby's sake—take the first step on the road to health and happiness. Order now, TO-DAY, the garments that you need to drive the shadows from your life and to bring the sunshine in.

The introduction of maternity clothes made it possible for expectant mothers to lead normal lives and did much to dispel Victorian notions of proper behavior during the gestation period.

Many bottle-fed infants died from "summer complaint," or diarrhea (thus explaining doctors' and hospitals' emphasis upon breast-feeding during the 1920s and 1930s), before women learned to sterilize the bottles. Educated women were especially eager for bottle- rather than breast-feeding, which was not only confining but symbolic of low social status. Mrs. Hartshorn in Mary

McCarthy's novel *The Group* contemptuously rejected nursing as "Lower East Side." She told her daughter, Priss, who was anxiously, unfashionably, and unsuccessfully trying to breast-feed in 1936, "The bottle was the war cry of my generation. We swore by the bottle."[25]

Women's central complaint about birth, however, had less to do with its confinement than with its pain and suffering. Women would gladly have given up home delivery, which they valued less anyway, for hospital delivery if it meant the relief of birthpain. In fact, women themselves campaigned for the acceptance in America of a hospital-based technique for painless birth, developed in Germany and called "Twilight Sleep."

This technique involved injecting the woman with morphine at the beginning of labor and then giving her a dose of an amnesiac drug, called scopolamine, which caused her to forget what was happening; once the fetus entered the birth canal, the doctor gave ether or chloroform to relieve the pain caused by the birth of the head. Altogether, the procedure dulled awareness of pain and, perhaps more important, removed the memory of it. A few American doctors had tried the technique around 1900 and rejected it as unreliable and unsafe, but several American women were so excited by the prospect of a completely painless delivery that they went to Freiburg, Germany, during the opening months of the Great War to have such a delivery. They returned to initiate a newspaper and magazine campaign for American women's liberation from suffering.[26]

Women with feminist and suffragist sympathies spearheaded this drive. One such person was Dr. Eliza Taylor Ransom, a homeopathic doctor in Boston. She herself had "gone through hell" twice in giving birth and had become disgusted with what she considered the medical profession's indifference to women's pain and aversion to anything new. In 1914 Ransom founded her own maternity hospital in Boston's Back Bay in order to provide the painless method for women; she eventually attended 3,000 women there. She insisted that women would not get relief unless they demanded it, and she began the New England Twilight Sleep Association in order to force hospitals to offer the procedure. In 1915 she arranged to show healthy babies born under this method to a large group of "stylish" women in a Boston theater; later the association produced films showing the method and featuring the healthy babies. The films were circulated to women's groups throughout the nation.

"Twilight Sleep" and anesthetics were eagerly adopted by fashionable women who sought painfree deliveries.

Brochures of the Twilight Sleep Association advertised the method as the solution to a wide range of problems: It abolished the need for forceps, shortened the first stage of labor, reduced the time of convalescence and the danger of hemorrhage, and helped the mother produce milk; it was the best method for

women with heart trouble and with "nerves." Above all, it removed the fear of pain, which had kept many women from having
children. Like other new medical techniques, Twilight Sleep was a
panacea for nearly everything.[27]

Many early pioneers in using the method were wealthy society
ladies who could afford to pay their doctors to provide a painless
birth. Such women organized to make the method available to all
women. Mrs. John Jacob Astor's picture appeared in newspaper
articles endorsing Twilight Sleep, along with pictures of well-
dressed mothers and healthy babies. The social standing of such
women made the medical profession take notice. Doctors could
not fail to notice that, if such women once more regarded delivery
as a joyful experience, the Anglo-Saxon race would not "die out,"
and women might rediscover the joys of traditional femininity
and maternity.

Women's testimonials about Twilight Sleep certainly echoed
old ideals, claiming that maternity was delightful once the method
delivered them from bondage. They insisted that they were healthier and more fit than after earlier deliveries, that their children
were more uniformly healthy, beautiful, and intelligent than their
earlier children. Some women celebrated Twilight Sleep for allowing them to lapse into feminine passivity, as they said—into the
great lap of cosmic forces, the unconscious itself—and to enjoy a
birth that earlier, more "natural" women (the Indian squaw again)
had enjoyed, because they were less nervous and self-conscious
creatures of civilization. Since scopolamine was an hallucinogenic,
Twilight Sleep may have impressed women as a return to the
unconscious, not in a Freudian sense but in the sense of discovering in themselves unknown vitalistic powers, which civilization
had denied their knowing.[28]

The campaign for Twilight Sleep was successful, for doctors
and hospitals came to regard it as safe and even useful. Boston
hospitals adopted the method in the early 1920s and, by 1938,
used it in all deliveries. Twilight Sleep not only attracted women
to the hospital, it made them more manageable during labor and
delivery and allowed the routine use of other techniques. In the
language of the 1930s, Twilight Sleep "streamlined maternity's
miracle":

> Two yellow capsules, a jab in the arm, swiftly blot out the scene,
> time, knowledge, and feeling for the woman. . . . When she is not
> aware, sunlight pierces the drapery. And one of the amiable

WOMEN COMBINE TO SPREAD
GOSPEL OF "TWILIGHT SLEEP"

MRS. JOHN JACOB ASTOR.

New York, Dec. 31.—Because they believe the "twilight sleep' child-birth method, originated in Frieberg, Germany, will insure painless birth, a a group of far-sighted women, among them Mrs. John Jacob Astor, widow of the multi-millionaire who perished in the Titanic disaster, have organized an association to give the world of mothers authentic information concerning the treatment. "In the first place," said Mrs. Mary W. Dennett, temporary chairman of the new organization, "we shall establish an office with a secretary to answer all sorts of questions about 'twilight sleep.' We shall circulate pamphlets on the subject and arrange lectures. Then we shall further the introduction of the Frieberg method in the exist ing hospitals. It already exists partially in 10 New York hospitals. But our greatest aim shall be to establish a teaching hospital where doctors from all over the country can come and learn this method of obviating pain at child-birth. It is our aim to establish a maternity hospital similar to the clinic at Frieberg, where a skilled group of doctors who have themselves studied at Frieberg will take charge of the work."

Mrs. John Jacob Astor was one of the celebrities whose endorsement of Twilight Sleep helped to popularize the use of this method during delivery.

nurses chirps, "It's all over. You've got your baby." With such
streamlined ease . . . babies are born.[29]

Middle- and upper-class women had been attracted to hospitals
as private patients since the 1890s when they had difficult birth
conditions or when a doctor devised a new method that promised a
less painful delivery. At the turn of the century many maternity
hospitals were building facilities to attract a few private patients
whose fees would help meet the costs of new equipment, larger
staff, and charity care. General hospitals began to build maternity
wards so that attending physicians could more expeditiously meet
their maternity patients. The gradual acceptance of Twilight
Sleep brought more private patients to hospital delivery. Another
major development that turned women's attention to hospitals
was the widespread public concern for improved safety in birth,
for the achievement of lower maternal and infant mortality rates.
The effect of the public outcry about death in birth led many
middle-class women to seek birth specialists in the hospital. They

A room in the private pavilion of Roosevelt Hospital, New York, 1896. The
elegant fittings were obviously intended to make the upper-class patient feel at
home.

learned to define birth safety as a matter of who attended birth and where birth occurred.[30]

Concern for infant and maternal health began in the 1880s and 1890s and led to the founding of the federal Children's Bureau in 1912. The bureau's first investigations were about mortality in birth and revealed that the United States compared very unfavorably with other industrial nations, standing seventeenth of twenty nations in maternal mortality and eleventh in infant mortality in 1918. The number of maternal deaths actually increased from 16,000 in 1916 to 23,000 in 1918. Each year 250,000 infants died. After World War I women came to recognize that maternity was the second highest killer of women aged fifteen to forty-five, after tuberculosis. Childbirth was women's battleground, as Hemingway was to say in *Farewell to Arms*.

The Children's Bureau, in conjunction with the feminist movement and some medical specialists, began a campaign for federal legislation to provide funds to states to educate women about prenatal and postnatal care. The campaign resulted in the passage in 1921 of the Sheppard–Towner Act, which was the first and principal objective of American women after they acquired the franchise. Sheppard–Towner, one of the earliest health acts of the federal government, was meant to benefit poor women and their children. Middle-class women translated its concern into a personal search for the best care they could find and afford, which meant having a specialist and a hospital birth.[31]

A number of social and cultural changes encouraged women to think the hospital was safer, apart from mortality statistics, and hospitals also sought to capitalize on these changes. The popular culture in the form of advertising, for example, had alerted women to the danger of the "household germ" and of their obligation to rid their homes of it with new cleaning products. Women's magazines of the 1920s made a crusade of making women feel embarrassed and worried about germs at home. Germs at home were thought to be unsafe for birth, for most people knew by 1920 that germs somehow caused infection and sickness. At the same time, the hospital began to picture itself as a superclean, germ-free place, safer than the home; the hospital had rooms that were "white gems of purity and up-to-date models of sanitation," with faucets of "distilled sterile water." Patients' bedding was made in "sun-flooded shops"; the operating room featured natural light and "MacBeth daylight," a trade name for artificial light, presumably even safer. The building was fireproof as well. Clearly, many women thought the hospital was more sanitary than the home. Also, going there saved contaminating one's own home with the soils of birth. When the middle-class housewife had to do her own housework, with higher, perhaps even compulsive, standards of cleanliness, birth was an impure and susceptible affair that happened best elsewhere.[32]

Hospitals also provided trained personnel not readily available for home delivery, for the live-in nurse was disappearing; often she had little medical training anyway. "Doctors and nurses in attendance day and night" read one lying-in hospital's advertisement soliciting funds and promising greater safety. In addition to round-the-clock trained care, hospitals provided numerous specialized facilities that contributed toward safety: X-ray machines, laboratories, blood banks, and eventually transfusion equipment. No home could hope to meet emergencies as a hospital with trained staff and equipment could do.[33]

The safety of newborn infants seemed better assured in hospitals, which publicized extensively their advances in caring for premature infants. Newspapers reported that one hospital had constructed a "premature room" that freed infants from incubators: the room was warmed constantly to 80°, the air purified and humidified. No child should be without this best of all possible environments. Other reports told of doctors' success in keeping alive an infant as small as 3½ pounds. Headlines told readers that "Boston Hospitals Perform Scientific Miracles by Restoring 'Dead' Babies to Life," reporting success in resuscitating and sustaining infants who had suffered various forms of fetal distress. Mothers who read of such heroic efforts to save children knew where the safest delivery would be. New technology and skill promised to remove the sting of tragedy from birth.[34]

In addition to safety, the hospital offered comfort. Until World War II led to a shortage of hospital personnel that drastically shortened a woman's stay there, ward patients remained an average of two weeks after birth, and private patients often stayed three. The scarcity of domestic servants after World War I, when more types of employment opened up to women, made lying-in at home nearly impossible unless a family could afford to hire help. Without such help, without the support nineteenth-century women found in groups of female friends and relatives, women during the 1920s and 1930s gained a respite from housework and a time to recuperate in the hospital, where maids, cooks, and nurses cared for them. Young twentieth-century couples often lived in small apartments without servants and without room for relatives. There may have been as well less psychological space in such nuclear families for relatives, such as the mother of the mother-to-be. People appreciated the efficiency of transferring to an institution the whole daily round of care, feeding, and washing that could hardly be done any more in the home.

The new wards and private wings built in the 1920s were designed to be pleasant as well as efficient. They offered some touches of at-homeness in the way of porches and open-air vistas. Care was taken to produce "charming effects" throughout, to disguise the hospital and institutional character, to use bright, cheerful colors, to design rooms and even wards for the maximum privacy. But women were also struck by the provision of private telephones, beds that did "everything but talk," "duplex window shades," and buzzer systems that "silently" summoned nurses. There were thoughtfully "humane touches" as well, such as separate wards, far from the nurseries, for women who had lost their babies, and also special rooms where husbands of women in critical condition might sleep while waiting.

Hospitals in the 1920s were probably rather quiet places in which to rest. The former head nurse of the maternity ward in a New Haven hospital described it as a place that gave peace of mind, "tranquility, cessation from worry and labor." She said that there were, in those years, no "banging elevators, sterilizers, electric dishwashers, radios" and noisy, officious staff. "The wards were truly suburban."[35]

Delivering painlessly, enjoying the hospital's comforts for several weeks, and employing a specialist's services cost more than home delivery, but most women felt that hospital delivery was worth the difference, though they had to weigh having a baby against acquiring consumer goods. During the 1920s and 1930s there were very few prepaid health plans that covered maternity; birth was an out-of-pocket expense. Women's magazines continually discussed the cost of birth care just as they discussed the cost of mass-produced goods and tried to educate young couples about how to make the best birth buy. That seemed to be, in the view of most commentators, choosing an obstetrical specialist and a hospital delivery, for, if a couple decided to have a baby, they should seek a return on their investment. A safe birth also meant a safe investment, which was not so ridiculous a way of thinking, since hospital birth could take from 25 percent to 35 percent of a middle-income man's yearly salary.[36]

Not surprisingly, many couples limited conceptions and regarded birth rather anxiously in the context of other wants and desires. A typical example of then current thinking appeared in a letter to the *Ladies' Home Journal* in 1923:

> The reason for the decrease in American babies is the high cost of obstetrics. My husband is thirty, I am twenty-seven. We have been married three years. I expect my second child within a few weeks. My husband's salary is $25 per month, out of which a small sum is invested and payments made in a course of study to fit him for a better job. I add, by writing, about $20 a month to our income. I do all my own work. Our first baby cost: for layette—with strictest economy—$25; ten days in a maternity hospital, $35; dressings and laundry at hospital, $5; doctor's charge, $25; anaesthetic, $5; total, $95. I nursed my baby, took entire care of her, and did all my own housework. My mother had seven babies and I doubt if they all cost her $100 put together. We have now $46 in the bank to meet expenses for the new baby. This represents arduous economy—no movies, no ball games, plain meals and shoes and clothes worn beyond their use and looks. If I could have my baby for $15 I could have a new dress and hat afterwards and my husband could have his new overcoat this fall. Let the doctors make a more nominal charge, and let the magazines and newspapers quit scaring people into thinking that medical and nursing attention are necessary for weeks afterward. Then you would see an increase in the birth rate. A child's first meals do not need stream pressure cookers, warming plates, thermometers, etc. I have wanted a potato ricer for a year and haven't been able to get it yet. A friend of mine who is in the same circumstances as ourselves had to pay $150 for the care of her baby, and she is still wearing the same suit she married in.

The cost of hospital birth varied from $50 to $300, and a specialist's fee made it much higher.[37]

Most young couples accepted the view that the safety and comfort of birth in a hospital with a specialist's care were worth the expense. "Having the best" was a continuous theme in women's magazines. A 1929 article in *Harper's* called for more maternity beds and more respect for obstetricians because "childbearing is not a purely physiological process." It urged husbands to safeguard the health and lives of their wives and children by paying for the best medical attention.[38] An *Atlantic* article in 1939 argued that, just as no one would have an appendectomy performed on the kitchen table, so no woman should have her delivery there, no matter how far from a hospital she resided, for delivery was also "a surgical procedure."[39]

The hospital thus offered women many attractions. It promised to remove the physicality of birth from the home and to provide nursing care, the chance to rest, a painless delivery, and safe procedures to prevent disastrous results. Women seem to have taken, as well, a kind of aesthetic delight in the efficiencies of the hospital, in its paring away of the economic, social, and psychological aspects of birth in order to focus only on the pelvis as a machine that needed preventive maintenance and, sometimes, repair. The reduction of concern to mechanics may have pleased women who for long had been burdened with social and moral expectations about births. The processing of birth, the smoothing of its rough edges, and the making of all births as predictably similar as possible may have appealed to women who wished an impersonal and speedy delivery. As one of Edith Wharton's characters expressed it, in the novel *Twilight Sleep:*

> "Of course there ought to be no Pain . . . nothing but Beauty. It ought to be one of the loveliest, most poetic things in the world to have a baby," Mrs. Manford declared, in that bright, efficient voice which made loveliness and poetry sound like the attributes of an advanced industrialism, and babies something to be turned out in series like Fords.[40]

Many poor women in the cities turned to hospitals for a very different reason: There was no other way to find care during labor and delivery, for midwives were retiring or being prohibited from practice, and private doctors were often unwilling to attend them. Although some medical schools had conducted "extern" programs, in which medical students attended home deliveries of poor women, the attempt to upgrade obstetrical education meant that students had to be supervised in hospital deliveries. Both the "Americanization" of second-generation immigrant families and the break-up of social networks to support home delivery prompted women to seek hospital delivery.[41]

By the early 1930s between 60 and 75 percent of the births in various cities were in hospitals. Not only was hospital delivery more expensive than home delivery, but its costs were increasing. Medical potentials for protecting women in labor and delivery were multiplying; the number of specialists, such as anesthetists, and the number of hospital workers were growing; women were expecting more from doctors and hospitals in the way of safer and more comfortable births: the costs of drugs and expensive equipment were accelerating. The rising costs of hospital birth, which was supposed to be safer, were one reason for the widespread concern for the results doctors and hospitals were achieving.[42]

Although people had been paying more for, and expecting more from, hospital delivery, there was actually little guarantee that they would receive better treatment, for the medical profession in 1930 was only beginning to sort out those who were qualified to practice special types of medicine. Although professional groups of obstetricians and gynecologists had existed since the mid-nineteenth century, they had no licensing or accrediting function and could not prevent any doctor, however educated or trained, from undertaking the most complex surgery or procedure. Nor did hospitals at that time have mechanisms to prevent any general practitioner from performing obstetrical surgery or any other obstetrical procedure. The encouragement of higher standards of obstetrical care and the elimination of untrained practitioners were objectives that the specialists were eager to pursue. At the same time, there was widespread public concern for maternal and child health. The concern had been vocal since the first White House Conference in 1909 and had led to passage of the Sheppard–Towner Act of 1921. The medical profession had opposed that law, and it had also opposed attempts to upgrade midwives to meet the needs of the poor. Medicine's opposition to Sheppard–Towner forced the federal funding to end in the late 1920s, and midwives were disappearing. Maternal and child health was not improving, however, and the profession was under considerable public and specialist pressure to create qualifications for the practice of obstetrics.[43]

The American Board of Obstetrics and Gynecology was established in 1930, and one of its primary purposes was to provide hospitals with criteria by which to judge the capabilities of staff members and of general practitioners. The coming of the Depression delayed the development of a coherent and uniformly enforced program to protect the public from "the malpractices of mushroom specialists," but a number of steps were taken to increase residency training programs and to protect hospitals from accepting unqualified "specialists."[44]

There was both specialist and public concern about the abilities of doctors and hospitals in the early 1930s. The New York Academy of Medicine issued a landmark study in 1933, *Maternal Mortality in New York City,* which investigated 2,041 maternal deaths between 1930 and 1932. The study concluded that two-thirds could have been prevented had the best medical knowledge been applied. Of the avoidable deaths, the investigators charged 60 percent to some incapacity in the attendant: lack of judgment, lack of skill, or carelessness. The report pointed to the "ignorance and insufficient training of the attendant," whether obstetrician, general practitioner, or surgeon. The report also pointed to careless enforcement of aseptic standards in hospitals. It actually included many favorable comments on the work of midwives and on the advisability of home birth, both of which were, however, diminishing as options.[45]

The White House Conference on Child Health and Protection issued its report in 1933, entitled *Fetal, Newborn, and Maternal Mortality and Morbidity.* It featured the fact that maternal mortality had not declined between 1915 and 1930 despite the increase in hospital delivery, the introduction of prenatal care, and more use of aseptic techniques. The number of infant deaths from birth injuries had actually increased by 40 to 50 percent from 1915 to 1929. Because the statistics covered a much wider area, approximately eleven states, the impact of this report was even greater than that of the New York study.[46]

Both reports found two main reasons for mortality. One was that women either received no prenatal care or received inadequate care that underestimated or overlooked complications. The other reason was excessive intervention, often improperly performed. Nearly half the women died after an operation done unnecessarily, improperly, or with insufficient care for asepsis. This increased interference derived from the false confidence antiseptics and anesthetics gave to the doctor, from the tendency to value the infant's life over the mother's, from the patients' demand for quicker labors, from the inclusion of convenience for patient, doctor, and family as an indication for intervention, and from the fact that the "laity" were educated to paying higher fees for interventions. After the Papal Encyclical *Casti Connubi* (1930), which prohibited the taking of an infant's life to save the mother's,

Maternal Mortality per 10,000 Live Births, 1915-1973

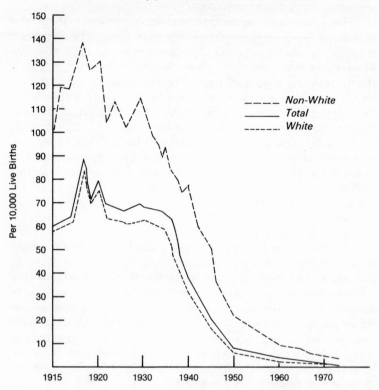

Source: National Center for Health Statistics, *Vital Statistics of the United States,* annual volumes.

many Caesarean sections were done to remove an impacted fetus. Statistics failed to show a saving of infant life, however, and the Conference decried this practice. If unnecessary sections, which the Conference estimated at 75 percent, were eliminated, the maternal mortality rate would have dropped by 10 percent. The Conference also urged a standard fee for all deliveries, regardless of procedures required, in order to discourage unnecessary interventions done to earn higher fees.

The inadequacy of hospital standards represented a cause of death second only to the inadequacy of doctors. Sometimes the surgical operating room doubled as the delivery room, or junior staff members did complex operations without supervision or consultation, or the hospital had no regulations for appropriate procedures. Infection rates remained higher in hospitals than in homes.

The New York Academy urged the profession to educate women to be more intelligent consumers of medical care, to know what a proper prenatal examination and a physical examination involved. But the Academy directed its main emphasis to urging

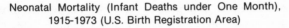

Neonatal Mortality (Infant Deaths under One Month), 1915-1973 (U.S. Birth Registration Area)

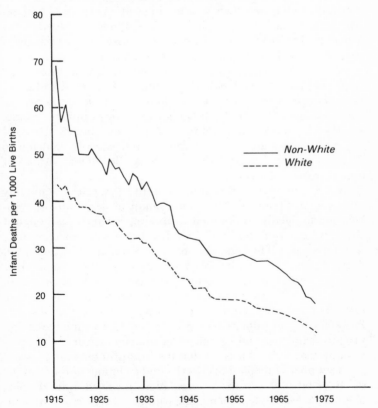

Source: National Center for Health Statistics, *Vital Statistics of the United States,* annual volumes.

better education in obstetrics, prolonged graduate study, and the enforcement of requirements for specialization. The Academy noted that general practitioners were performing 30 percent of deliveries and that legal barriers were required to keep them from doing operative obstetrics. Obstetrical societies, the Academy said, should set up examinations for admission to membership and should distribute lists of qualified obstetricians to the public. Hospitals should honor these lists in making staff appointments.[47]

Doctors and hospitals were deeply embarrassed by the exposure of their ignorance, incompetence, lack of routine, and failure to maintain asepsis. The profession set up hospital committees to investigate each maternal death and assign responsibility for it. In a struggle to improve their results—in what was really a competition with death itself—hospitals instituted rigid regulations for prophylactic procedures in every case. In order to prevent operations by unskilled people, they formed an ordered hierarchy of consultants whose permission was needed for certain procedures. Only doctors who had passed examinations were permitted to perform operations; they were at the top of a hierarchy of residents, interns, medical students, maternity nurses, nurse-anesthetists, nurses in training, and practical nurses. Hospital regulations permitted each person in the chain of command to perform only limited procedures or to handle limited portions of the labor or of the patient.

Starting in 1936, and continuing until 1955, rates of mortality dropped precipitously. The routinization of care and responsibility undoubtedly contributed to the improvement, although it also resulted from new antibiotic drugs that were specific cures for infection. The amount of intervention did not itself decrease—in fact, it probably increased—but the interventions were performed more correctly by more qualified doctors. Birth remained, in the view of doctors, an abnormal, pathogenic process which required routine medical assistance to prevent disaster. Professional and public concern for safety had pruned away improper techniques and egregious incompetence, but not the philosophy that medical arts created the healthful birth.

A number of medical discoveries and techniques improved the safety of birth and of the manipulations involved in it. Hospital bloodbanks were established along with blood typing and transfusion techniques between 1936 and 1945; these removed much of the danger of postpartum hemorrhage. The discovery of oxytocic

drugs to induce or speed up labor meant that doctors could counteract some of the negative effects of anesthetics, which tended to
slow labor and asphyxiate the fetus. X-ray pelvimetry aided in
early detection and diagnosis of pelvic deformities. Conduction
anesthesias left the woman conscious during delivery and were
safer than general anesthesia, which had some danger of as-
phyxiating the woman. High and mid-forceps were no longer
used for impaction; Caesarean sections replaced them. Fetal-
heart-monitoring machines warned of fetal distress caused by
anesthesia or birth movements. Intravenous equipment supplied
the mother with drugs to combat low blood pressure or to slow the
effects of anesthesia.[48]

Medicine continued to emphasize prevention in labor and delivery and therefore treated each woman as though some freak
occurrence might happen in her case. Medicine also continued to
emphasize efficiency and speed in labor and delivery, objectives
that many women shared. The obstetric comparison between the
automobile assembly line and the mother was not without rele-
vance. Nor was the comparison of the mother to a broken-down
automobile and the hospital to an automobile maintenance and
repair shop. During the 1940s, 1950s, and 1960s, birth was the
processing of a machine by machines and skilled technicians.

Labor began in one room. The woman often received
analgesics to reduce pain and scopolamine to remove the memory
of pain. When she was ready to deliver, she was wheeled to the
delivery room and placed on a table with "stirrups." Her arms
were strapped down and her legs were strapped high in the air, in
a bent posture known as the lithotomy position because it was
developed first for the removal of bladder stones (hence *lithos*
[stone] and *temnein* [cut]). She was surrounded by medical
machines; anesthesia equipment, resuscitation equipment for the
baby, blood-transfusion equipment, intravenous equipment,
equipment to counteract the anesthesia, and equipment to
monitor the fetal heart.

Many labors and deliveries alternated between being artificially slowed down and artificially speeded up. Some hospitals had
regulations limiting the amount of time a woman was allowed to
be in the delivery room.[49] Also, one technique could often require
the use of another. Anesthesia was counteracted by oxytocin;
episiotomy required local anesthesia; forceps required anesthesia
and episiotomy; the lithotomy position required episiotomy.

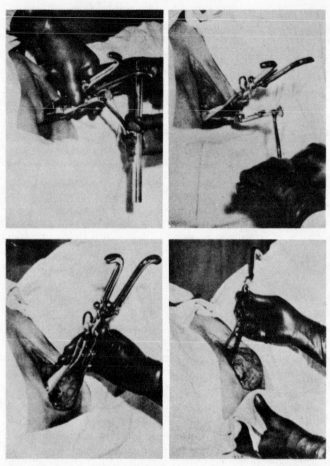

Modern forceps delivery. Note the axis traction bar, which allows the operator to pull in the direction of outlet.

The standardized, production-line methods reflected doctors' belief that birth was best when every precaution was taken to prevent disaster—when it was, in short, as carefully controlled a process as possible. Doctors continued to be on the lookout for trouble, impelled to improve their results, to increase and refine their skills in preventing and curing pathology in birth. They were not unconcerned with the patients as people, but they believed that they did their best for people when they took over the management of birth in order to make it as safe, speedy, and efficient as possible. Doctors also acted in response to social expectations that they improve the safety of birth for both mothers and children. They sensed that they had received a mandate from families and from society to perfect the medical management of birth, that patients shared their view that doctors knew what was best for birth and should manipulate as fully as possible.

This consensus broke down, however, when death became rare; the success of medicine led people to ask whether every birth needed to be treated as if some freak occurrence might threaten the life and health of mother and child. The treatment began to appear to be worse than the threats it prevented.

Hospital delivery was the product not only of medical measures to produce safety, efficiency, and comfort; birth was also conditioned by the social institution of the hospital itself. Between 1900 and 1930 hospitals increased in number; thereafter, they increased in size—that is, in numbers of patients they could accommodate. Many urban hospitals became vast institutions, able to accommodate both private and clinic patients. Maternity care in general hospitals and in maternity hospitals was always divided along the two-class system.

By the 1940s hospitals in urban centers were organized to operate efficiently. Tasks were divided according to skills, and the number of hospital workers and the numbers of tasks were continually multiplying. Like the structure of other large institutions involved in providing a service, hospital organization often reflected the best interests of those who provided the service. Routines were devised for the convenience of the workers rather than of the patients. Thus, the patient had to move from one part of the hospital to another in order to meet staff according to their schedules and where their equipment was located. The patient had to confront many new persons who were interested in only part of her body or behavior. This division of work was convenient for the workers, but it was not comfortable for patients. The facts of organization in a large institution made patients feel like items being processed. That feeling was multiplied because the woman usually went through the procedures without a friend to accompany her and often without understanding what the purpose of the procedures was.

Since the staff members in large hospitals had to repeat many procedures in seeing many patients, they wanted patients to be dependent and trusting so that they might be most easily attended and cared for. The volume of work, particularly in large urban hospitals, prompted the staff to precondition expectant mothers to follow procedures "in their own best interests." Obedient, trusting patients also made the staff's work go more smoothly. Clinics sought to socialize their patients to obey routines and to trust the staff by making weight control a means of obedience training during repeated prenatal visits. The medical rationale was that preventing weight gain prevented "eclampsia," a serious condition often called "toxemia of pregnancy." If untreated, this condition can lead to maternal convulsions and even death for mother or baby. Although for many years some doctors had suspected that eclampsia was related to nutrition, it was not until after World War I that stringent weight restrictions in pregnancy became widely accepted. This occurred because statistics indicated that the incidence of eclampsia was reduced during the war in areas of Europe that had experienced semi-starvation. Doctors reasoned that a similar regime could prevent eclampsia in American women. Subsequently several generations of women were morally judged by their obstetricians or clinics according to the amount of weight they gained between prenatal visits. A woman who managed to gain less than twenty pounds during the entire course of pregnancy was considered a "good patient" for obeying the doctor's orders and exercising self-control. A woman who was unfortunate enough to gain more was lectured at each visit on her laziness, inability to follow orders, or lack of self-restraint and was threatened with dire consequences. If a welfare patient could not afford the diet prescribed, many clinics still treated her noncompliance as a moral problem of self-control rather than as a problem of economics. Doctors found that the scales were a convenient means of social control over the lives of patients and therefore stressed weight control without questioning its medical value. After 1970 medical thinking changed as research indicated that overly severe weight restrictions could lead to underweight babies, and that maternal weight gain and water retention might be symptoms, rather than causes, of the underlying condition called eclampsia. Nutritional authorities suggested that a gain of twenty-five or even thirty pounds was normal. Weight remained a means of socially conditioning patients to obedience, however.[50]

Prenatal examinations themselves taught patients to regard themselves as objects for the impassive and well-meaning medical eye, to accept this unpleasant routine, and by implication all other hospital routines, as meant for their ultimate safety and well-being. Some hospitals sought to isolate patients from one another during the prenatal period and during labor so that they remained dependent upon the staff and no one else for direction and support. Private doctors told their patients during office visits to trust the hospital staff and to cooperate completely with hospital procedures, which were meant for their best interests.

The staff classified patients for the sake of efficient treatment. Private and clinic patients were entitled to different social and medical privileges. Each patient was labeled on her chart according to her economic, marital, and childbearing status, and also according to her degree of cooperation with the staff. This system identified women who had had repeated illegitimate births or who had disturbed routines by asking too many questions, refusing to obey orders, or making too much noise. The labeling system itself encouraged a distancing of feeling and permitted the staff to express moral and social preferences for different types of patient. The "hostile" patient was likely to be treated more roughly and given more drugs to quiet her down; the married woman with few children who was most cooperative gained the most respect.[51]

Classification sometimes affected medical treatment, particularly for pain. Staff persons expected different types of patients to respond differently to pain. A common belief was that women from certain racial or ethnic groups made more noise but suffered less pain and hence needed less analgesia or anesthesia than women from other groups. In *The Bluest Eye,* a black woman spoke bitterly of a doctor's obliviousness to her pain in a big-city labor ward:

> When he got to me he said now these here women you don't have any trouble with. They deliver right away and with no pain. Just like horses—They never said nothing to me. Only one looked at me. Looked at my face, I mean.—
>
> I seed them talking to them white women. "How you feel? Gonna have twins?" Just shucking them, of course, but nice talk. Nice friendly talk.
>
> I moaned something awful. The pains weren't as bad as I let on, but I had to let them people know having a baby was more than a bowel movement. I hurt just like them white women.[52]

The hospital environment unquestionably made birth more difficult. Its impersonality and complexity created fear and anxiety in the patient, emotional conditions that made delivery more

tense and painful.[53] Unfeeling staff often ignored patients, refused to answer their questions, intimidated them or berated
them. Just as the physical environment of the hospital increased
the danger of infection in birth, so the social environment contributed to psychic distress and physical pain. Women have left
many accounts of their unhappy hospital experiences, which confirm how often the assembly-line process was a terrible experience. In 1957 one woman told of her isolation:

> My first child was born in a Chicago suburban hospital. I wonder
> if the people who ran that place were actually human. My lips
> parched and cracked, but the nurses refused to even moisten
> them with a damp cloth. I was left alone all night in a labor room.
> I felt exactly like a trapped animal and I am sure I would have
> committed suicide if I had had the means. Never have I needed
> someone, anyone, as desperately as I did that night.[54]

Another woman told of being frightened by nurses talking
near her labor bed:

> After a while the tone became too extreme for my possible com-
> fort; they described cases of women who had lain in labor for
> unbelievable lengths of time, of one who had screamed solidly for
> three hours. . . . One of them said, *en passant,* "I'll be really glad to
> get out of this ward. I don't really mind the babies, but the
> mothers give me the creeps." Then one of them started to recount
> in vivid detail the story of a woman whose labor she had attended
> a month earlier, who had died because they discovered at the last
> moment that this, that, and the other hadn't been properly dealt
> with; "it was awful," this girl said, "the way they kept on telling her
> it was all fine."[55]

At this point the patient screamed for an anesthetic to block out
the conversation.

One hospital observer has recorded instances in which nurses
told laboring women, "You think this is bad. The hard part hasn't
even started," or "You didn't worry about getting it in there. Now
you can just get it out the same way," or "Bear down, you're lazy,
you're stupid."[56]

In 1957 the *Ladies' Home Journal* printed a letter from a maternity nurse urging an investigation of "cruelty in maternity wards."
In response, the *Journal* received hundreds of letters reporting
experiences of dehumanization and unconcern for mother and
baby. Quite common was the complaint that, when the mother
was ready to deliver, the staff were not ready to attend.

When my baby was ready the delivery room wasn't. I was strapped to a table, my legs tied together, so I would "wait" until a more convenient and "safer" time to deliver. In the meantime my baby's heartbeat started faltering. At this point I was incapable of rational thought and cannot report fairly the following hour. When I regained consciousness I was told my baby would probably not live.

Other women complained that they were tied and trussed to the delivery tables like "trapped animals." Some said they had been left with their feet in the stirrups and their shoulders tied and clamped for as long as eight hours. One reader wrote:

I was strapped to the delivery table on Saturday morning and lay there until I was delivered on Sunday afternoon; with the exception of a period early Sunday morning when they needed the delivery table for an unexpected birth. When I slipped my hand from the strap to wipe sweat from my face (this was in July) I was severely reprimanded by the nurse. If it had not been for a kind old lady who used to be a midwife in Germany, I doubt if I would have come out sane. . . . For thirty-six hours my husband didn't know whether I was living or dead. I would have given anything if I could just have held his hand.

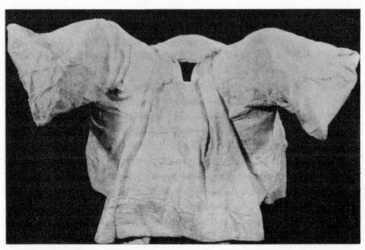

A doctor's eye view of a hospital patient ready for delivery, covered with sterile drapery and with her legs in stirrups. Contrast the impersonality of this scene with the home delivery shown on page 184.

Others were left entirely alone for sixteen hours of labor, had episiotomies sewn up without novocain, or were literally battered by the nursing staff when they did not obey orders:

> During my second baby's arrival, I was strapped to a table, hands down, knees up. I remember screaming, "Help me, help me!" to a nurse who was sitting at a nearby desk. She ignored me. With my third baby, the doctor said at one point, "Stop your crying at me. I'm not the one who made you pregnant!"

Many women felt that their most intimate parts were on public view.

> What about the nameless parade of "interns" who appear unannounced, probe our trapped bodies and "scan" our progress? . . . Since my husband is a veterinarian, I happen to know that even animal maternity cases are treated with a little more grace than is accorded human mothers.
>
> I reached the point where I wouldn't have been surprised if the man who was washing the windows had suddenly laid down the sponge and come over to "take a peek." It seemed that everyone connected with the hospital was doing it!

The need for clinical training had pushed obstetrics to the opposite extreme from the time when students had no clinical experience and doctors proceeded by touch alone.

Many believed the new procedures convenienced the staff but not the patient:

> I have had three children and three different doctors who delivered my children in three different hospitals. The practice of obstetrics is the most modern and medieval, the kindest to mothers and the cruelest. I know of many instances of cruelty, stupidity and harm done to mothers by obstetricians who are callous or completely indifferent to the welfare of their patients. Women are herded like sheep through an obstetrical assembly line, are drugged and strapped on tables while their babies are forceps-delivered. Obstetricians today are businessmen who run baby factories. Modern painkillers and methods are used for the convenience of the doctor, not to spare the mother.

Many readers—about one in seven of those who wrote to the *Journal*—praised the excellent care they had received, and a number of doctors wrote that such practices could not have happened in *their* hospitals. It appeared, however, as if many maternity wards had lost the human element by 1958.[57]

What had begun in the 1920s as a pursuit of safety, comfort and efficiency, a shared effort by doctors and patients to have the "best" for birth, had become by the 1950s and 1960s an unpleasant and alienating experience for many women. Technical routines to control natural processes compounded with social procedures to process the patient no longer seemed warranted by the danger of birth but seemed instead to stand in the way of a humane and meaningful delivery.

Hospital delivery had become for many a time of alienation—from the body, from family and friends, from the community, and even from life itself. The safe efficiencies had become a kind of industrial production far removed from the comforts of social childbirth or the sympathies of the proverbial doctor–patient relation. A woman was powerless in the experience of birth and unable to find meaning in it, for her participation in it and even her consciousness of it were minimal. She was isolated during birth from family and friends, and even from other women having the same experiences. She had to think of herself instrumentally, not as a woman feeling love and fear or sharing in a creative event, but as a body-machine being manipulated by others for her ultimate welfare. She played a social role of passive dependence and obedience.

Hospital birth became a regime against which many women began a critical struggle, questioning the need for such extensive manipulation, questioning the safety of the procedures, and demanding that birth be an experience that permitted them a sense of self-fulfillment. They set out to regain possession of their bodies and of the life they had lost.

Notes

1. Richard Morris, "The Preston Retreat," in Frederick F. Henry, ed., *Founders' Week Memorial Volume* (Philadelphia, 1909), pp. 718–794; W. Reynolds Wilson, "Philadelphia Lying-In Charity," in *ibid.*, pp. 607–608, 757–760; Leonard K. Eaton, *New England Hospitals, 1790–1833* (Ann Arbor, Mich., 1957), pp. 222–226. See also pp. 729, 776–780, 803–807, 834–837 in Henry, ed., *Founder's Week*.
2. Frederick Irving, *Safe Deliverance* (Boston, 1942), pp. 140–167; Rose F. Kennedy, *Times to Remember* (Garden City, N.Y.: Double-

day, 1974), pp. 76–77; Donnell M. Pappenfort, *Journey to Labor* (Chicago, 1964), pp. 9–10, 49.

3. William Goodell, *On the Means Employed at the Preston Retreat for the Prevention and Treatment of Puerperal Diseases* (Philadelphia, 1874).

4. Harold Speert, *The Sloane Hospital Chronicle* (Philadelphia: F. A. Davis, 1963), pp. 82, 108, 168–169, 189–191.

5. Joseph Kucher, *Puerperal Convalescence and the Diseases of the Puerperal Period* (New York, 1886), pp. 8–9.

6. Laurie Crumpacker, "Female Patients in Four Boston Hospitals: Sex, Class and Science in Late Nineteenth-Century Medicine," unpublished paper in the Schlesinger Library, Radcliffe College.

7. Irving, *Safe Deliverance*, p. 255.

8. Speert, *Sloane Hospital Chronicles*, p. 161; Irving, *Safe Deliverance*, pp. 255–262; C. M. Green, "Puerperal Eclampsia . . . ," *American Journal of Obstetrics* 28 (1893):18–44.

9. U.S. Department of Labor, Children's Bureau, *Standards of Child Welfare*, White House Conference Series, No. 1 (Washington, 1919), pp. 149–155, and 14:211.

10. C. A. Ritter, "Why Pre-natal Care," *American Journal of Gynecology* 70 (November, 1919):531.

11. Judson Smith, "The Birth of the Baby," *Boston Evening Transcript*, November 14, 1923, p. 12.

12. Joseph B. DeLee, "The Prophylactic Forceps Operations," *American Journal of Obstetrics and Gynecology* 1 (1920):34–44.

13. Arthur E. Fink, *Causes of Crime: Biological Theories in the United States, 1800–1915* (Philadelphia: University of Pennsylvania Press, 1938).

14. DeLee, "Prophylactic Forceps Operation," pp. 39–41.

15. Kenneth R. Niswander and Myron Gordon, "Safety of the Low-Forceps Operation," *American Journal of Obstetrics and Gynecology* 117 (1973):627.

16. *The Boston Lying-In Hospital Annual Report for 1910*, p. 10, and *Annual Report for 1921*, p. 11.

17. Gerald E. Markowitz and David K. Hosner, "Doctors in Crisis: A Study of the Use of Medical Education Reform to Establish Modern Professional Elitism in Medicine," *American Quarterly* 25 (March, 1973):85–86.

18. Sinclair Lewis, *Arrowsmith* (New York: New American Library edition, 1961), p. 19.

19. J. Whitridge Williams, "Medical Education and the Midwife Problem in the United States," *Journal of the American Medical Association* 58 (January 6, 1912):4, 7.

20. *Ibid.*, p. 7.

21. Abraham Flexner, *Medical Education in the United States and Canada:*

A Report to the Carnegie Foundation for the Advancement of Teaching (New York, 1910).

22. Rosemary Stevens, *American Medicine and the Public Interest* (New Haven: Yale University Press, 1971), pp. 77–148, 188–197.

23. Henry F. May, *The End of American Innocence: A Study of the First Years of Our Own Time, 1912–1917* (New York, 1959), pp. 334–347; James R. McGovern, "The American Woman's Pre–World War I Freedom in Manners and Morals," *Journal of American History* 55 (1968):320–327; David M. Kennedy, *Birth Control in America* (New Haven: Yale University Press, 1970), pp. 50–53.

24. Tom Mahoney and Leonard Sloane, *The Great Merchants* (New York: Harper & Row, 1966), p. 249. Correspondence with Lane Bryant, Inc., provided copies of advertising materials.

25. S. Josephine Baker, *Fighting for Life* (New York, 1939), pp. 58–59, 86; Mary McCarthy, *The Group* (New York, 1954), pp. 227, 247; *Hygeia*, June, 1923, p. 152, November, 1925, pp. 653–654, and June, 1927, pp. 298–299; Ruth Schwartz Cowan, "Household Technology and Social Change," unpublished paper delivered at History of Science Society, San Francisco, 1973.

26. Marguerite Tracy and Mary Boyd, *Painless Childbirth* (New York, 1915); Hannah Rion, *The Truth About Twilight Sleep* (New York, 1915).

27. All quotations and information from the Eliza Taylor Ransom papers, Schlesinger Library, Radcliffe College. Papers are unpaginated.

28. Charlotte Teller, "The Neglected Psychology of Twilight Sleep," *Good Housekeeping* 41 (July, 1915):17–24; Frances W. Wakefield, "Comment," *Overland Monthly* 72 (July, 1919):83–86.

29. Boston Lying-In Hospital, *Annual Report for 1923*, p. 16; *Annual Report for 1934*, p. 10; *Boston Traveller*, February 8, 1938, p. 19.

30. Boston Lying-in Hospital, *Annual Report for 1925*, p. 11; Frederic A. Washburn, *The Massachusetts General Hospital* (Boston, 1937), p. 241; Speert, *Sloane Hospital Chronicle*, pp. 164–165.

31. J. Stanley Lemons, *The Woman Citizen: Social Feminism in the 1920's* (Urbana: University of Illinois Press, 1973), p. 155.

32. Cowan, "Household Technology"; Lillian McCann, "Boston Lying-In Hospital," *North Shore Breeze and Reminder*, July 6, 1923, p. 7.

33. *Boston Evening Transcript*, February 21, 1917; *The Boston Post*, September 7, 1927.

34. *The Boston Herald*, April 5, 1923; *Boston Sunday Post*, n.d. (c. 1927), in Boston Hospital for Women scrapbook.

35. McCann, "Boston Lying-In Hospital," p. 7; A. Kuhkowski, untitled reminiscences by former head nurse in J. Hasbrouck Wallace, *His-*

tory of New Haven Hospital, 1826–1960 (New Haven, 1962), unpaginated.

36. Grace W. Fletcher, "Balancing the Baby Budget," *The Century Illustrated Monthly Magazine* 89 (1925–1926):419–424; Olivia Dunbar, "To the Baby, Debtor," *Good Housekeeping* 67 (November, 1918):35–36.

37. S. Josephine Baker, "Why Do Our Mothers and Babies Die?" *Ladies' Home Journal* 40 (October, 1923):212–213.

38. Dorothy D. Bromley, "What Risk Motherhood?", *Harper's* 159 (June, 1929):20.

39. "I Had a Baby, Too," *Atlantic,* June, 1939, p. 768.

40. Edith Wharton, *Twilight Sleep* (New York, 1927), pp. 14–15.

41. Frances E. Kobrin, "The American Midwife Controversy: A Crisis in Professionalization," *Bulletin of the History of Medicine* 40 (1966):356 ff.

42. Louis S. Reed, *Midwives, Chiropodists, and Optometrists: Their Place in Medical Care.* Committee on the Costs of Medical Care Publication no. 15 (Chicago, 1932), pp. 2–6 and *passim.*

43. G. F. McCleary, *The Early History of the Infant Welfare Movement* (London, 1933): John B. Blake, "Origins of Maternal and Child Health Programs," Yale Department of Public Health, mimeographed, 1953; Harry S. Mustard, *Government in Public Health* (New York, 1945), pp. 71–74; Nathan Sinai and Odin W. Anderson, *Emergency Maternity and Infant Care* (Ann Arbor, Mich., 1948), pp. 7–12; Bernhard J. Stern, *Social Factors in Medical Progress* (New York, 1927), p. 33; Morris Fishbein, *A History of the AMA, 1847–1947* (Philadelphia, 1947), p. 331 and *passim.*

44. Walter T. Dannreuther, "The American Board of Obstetrics and Gynecology: Its Organization, Function and Objectives," *Journal of the American Medical Association* 96 (1931):797–798; Clyde L. Randall, "Responsibility for Excellence," *Transactions of the American Association of Obstetrics and Gynecology,* Vol. 75 (1964).

45. New York Academy of Medicine Committee on Public Health Relations, *Maternal Mortality in New York City: A Study of all Puerperal Deaths, 1930–1932* (New York, 1933), pp. 32, 49, 186, and *passim.*

46. White House Conference on Child Health and Protection, *Fetal, Newborn, and Maternal Mortality and Morbidity* (New York, 1933), pp. 215–217.

47. New York Academy, *Maternal Mortality,* pp. 184–218; White House Conference, *Fetal, Newborn, and Maternal Mortality,* pp. 217–245.

48. Sam Shapiro, Edward R. Schlesinger, and Robert E. L. Nesbitt, *Infant, Perinatal, Maternal and Childhood Mortality in the United States* (Cambridge, Mass.: Harvard University Press, 1968), pp. 145–159 and *passim.*

49. William R. Rosengren and Spencer DeVault, "The Sociology of Time and Space in an Obstetrical Hospital," in Eliot Freidson, ed., *The Hospital in Modern Society* (New York: Free Press, 1963), pp. 282–283.

50. "Symposium on Maternal Nutrition," *Journal of Reproductive Medicine* 7, No. 5 (November, 1971):201–224; National Research Council, Committee on Maternal Nutrition, National Academy of Sciences, *Maternal Nutrition and the Course of Pregnancy* (Washington, 1970).

51. Nancy Stoller Shaw, *Forced Labor: Maternity Care in the United States* (Elmsford, N.Y.: Pergamon Press, 1974).

52. Toni Morrison, *The Bluest Eye* (New York, 1970), p. 97.

53. J. Kelly, "Effect of Fear upon Uterine Motility," *American Journal of Obstetrics and Gynecology* 83 (1962):576–581.

54. "Somewhere in Georgia," *Ladies' Home Journal,* May, 1958.

55. Margaret Drabble, *The Millstone* (New York, 1966), p. 112.

56. Gretchen Walker, R.N., "Nursing, Feminism, and Maternity Care," *Proceedings of the First International Childbirth Conference* (Stamford, Conn.: New Moon Publications, 1973), p. 24.

57. Letters, *Ladies' Home Journal,* May, 1958.

6

"Natural Childbirth"

Mme. Cohen will also be with you at the time of your delivery, and she and I together will assist you while you do the work of bringing your child into the world. We will act together as a team. It is a very beautiful thing to bring a child into the world, n'est ce pas, madame? C'est belle. C'est la plus belle chose du monde!

Marjorie Karmel, Thank You, Dr. Lamaze,

1959

BEGINNING AROUND 1940, a challenge appeared to the medical dominance of birth, initiating important and continuing changes in the understanding and the rituals of birth. Its advocates called it "natural childbirth," signifying that they wished to rely more upon nature and less upon the arts of medicine in childbirth. They saw nature as an orderly, benevolent process rather than a painful, destructive, and possibly catastrophic occurrence. They wanted to face the fact of birth consciously and with less unnecessary protection. This new and joyful attitude about birth was possible not only because women had new aspirations but also because medicine itself had tamed birth's dangers.

Once the fear of death traditionally associated with childbirth was removed by medical advances, women began to regard birth more positively. Now that medicine could anticipate abnormality, prevent it, and usually overcome it, fewer women and children died in birth; women regarded nature itself, therefore, as more reliable and began to wonder whether medical treatment was necessary and safe. As the birth-control movement encouraged voluntary motherhood, for example, women became more eager to protect each child from damage in its beginnings; they questioned the safety of drugs during delivery. They wondered whether obliviousness, for which their mothers had campaigned, was best for the child and for their own experience of birth. After

World War II both popular psychology and a reemphasis on domesticity encouraged women to believe once again that motherhood was a woman's fundamental purpose; she therefore should be awake to experience its sublime beginning. During the 1960s, then, a desire for greater autonomy, for more control over one's own body during birth, was added to the motives of safety and experience. Medicine's part in this development was curious; in their struggle to alter American birth practices, women adopted foreign medical advice and techniques.

American women succeeded to a large extent because their desire for greater safety and enhanced experience gradually won American doctors' approval. But their desire for more autonomy threatened doctors' and hospitals' control and procedures and met with resistance and compromise. By the 1970s the thrust for natural childbirth, which had been a loosely organized cultural movement among middle-class women, aimed at enhancing their experience in birth, acquired a social and political cast; women of all classes began to organize, to educate one another, and to try to change or avoid the professional and institutional structures that exerted such dominance over birth.

This chapter will describe the evolution of the motives and cultural influences that led women to desire natural birth and the responses of the medical profession.

Occasional hints of dissatisfaction with hospital birth, particularly heavy anesthesia, began to appear in the late 1930s. The beginnings of popular knowledge of Sigmund Freud's theories may have initiated this. In 1936 a woman pediatrician declared childbearing to be so essential an experience for a woman that anything that deprived her of the normal, conscious birth experience might "damage her personality." She would "pay for this escape from reality by nervous disorders."[1] In response, *The Nation* remarked satirically that now, if mothers did not suffer, it was "not God, but Dr. Freud" who would be outraged.[2]

In 1939 *The Atlantic* carried the story of a woman so disenchanted with the unavoidable routine of anesthetized birth that she went to Switzerland for what she considered a more humane form of delivery. It was also less expensive than the usual American delivery. Fascinated by accounts from European women who told that birth was "like a mighty thunderstorm" that made one "a complete person," she felt herself "undeveloped, virginal," even after bearing three children.

> Then came the birth—and, of all the exciting experiences I ever read or imagined, it was the most exhilarating. They shouted and I shouted—not because it was painful but because something elemental and stupendous was happening and I was in on it. And then she was there and I saw her, rosy and perfect. I felt as if I could move mountains. It was early on a Sunday morning; the sun was just rising, birds were singing, and bells ringing for Mass. Words cannot recreate this moment. It was one of ecstasy.

The Swiss had done nothing to educate her about birth; they simply proceeded informally and with a minimum of intervention. She compared this ecstatic birth with her dehumanizing experiences under anesthesia in earlier deliveries, her feelings of

> . . . going down into blackness, coming up only to know that something big and dreadful is happening, to feel fear, to hear myself moaning, to sense strange people, with offensive professional voices; then to go way under and to revive hours later, clean and dizzy, in a strange bed, and to be told that one is all right and a boy has been born.[3]

Most women readers reacted unfavorably. One, claiming that having been without anesthesia had done nothing for her self-respect, wondered whether wounded men "enlarge their personalities" by undergoing amputations on the battlefield. Another, repeating the predominant medical view, said that "the actual delivery is a mechanical, inevitable process over which I have not the slighest control," and urged women to submit to anesthesia rather than waste their strength.[4] A woman had to be daring and avant-garde to risk consciousness at birth in 1939.

In that same year Margaret Mead, using knowledge gained in her anthropological researches, demanded and gained the conditions for an unanesthetized delivery in a New York hospital. In her writings she urged other women to overcome the "male myth" of pain in birth, for, as she remarked in her autobiography,

> I have never heard primitive women describe the pains of childbirth. But in societies in which men were forbidden to see birth, I have seen men writhing on the floor, acting out their conception of what birth pangs were like.

She believed that American women "for generations had been muffled in male myths instead of learning about a carefully observed actuality."

Mead had the "money, knowledge, reputation and prestige" to arrange a birth the way she wanted it, or so she thought. She started with the pediatrician, young Benjamin Spock, who found her an obstetrician open-minded enough not to give her anesthetics. She showed the nurses a film of childbirth and breastfeeding in New Guinea. For all this she was nonetheless unable to change hospital routine, which proceeded the same for her as for others, including separation of mother and baby after birth in the interests of sterility. To gain even the autonomy she did, which meant not receiving anesthesia, required enormous force.[5]

Doctors had begun, however, to recognize that anesthesia could be dangerous to both mother and child. By 1942 they had found what seemed a less dangerous substance than ether or chloroform: the spinal anesthesia that allowed a woman to remain conscious while feeling nothing from the waist down. This new drug technique satisfied both safety requirements and the desire for consciousness, although it did not resolve the issue of whether women could endure delivery. The technique became routine in many hospitals. It required routine use of forceps, since the mother could not push. In many ways, however, the spinal anesthesia and its later refinements, the "caudal" and "epidural," seemed ideal: It offered comfort, safety, and experience to the mother; it necessitated skill and intervention by anesthetist and obstetrician and justified their fees. For many decades doctors would hold forth this technique as the answer for women who desired "natural childbirth."

Some women, however, wanted more than consciousness; they wanted to "feel everything," in direct contrast to the Twilight Sleep campaigners, who had wanted to feel nothing at all. The impetus for this new desire seems to have come from a redefinition of womanhood after World War II that Betty Friedan has called "The Feminine Mystique." Friedan remarked that, once the feminist movement had achieved its goal of suffrage, it splintered and failed to reorganize around other goals; after it had declined during the 1930s and had been submerged in the war effort, the way was open for a resurgence of essentially Victorian ideals about femininity. The women who went to work in war plants, wearing overalls and doing men's jobs as a matter of necessity, happily left the factories to return home and resume a life of domesticity at war's end. Nothing since Victorian literature equaled the reverence with which women's magazines of the 1940s and 1950s extolled home and maternity.

Friedan says the postwar years produced a "privatization of life," as Americans turned away from objective concerns and sought a "return to normalcy." Women's concern for home and family was part of this turning inward. A women's magazine could publish an article on "How to Have a Baby in an Atomic Bomb Shelter" in the 1950s in the belief that women might be entertained with the thought of an unaided birth, but uninterested in the bomb's power to destroy the human race.[6] Magazine articles of the 1950s and 1960s read like a replay of Mrs. Sigourney's advice to "true women" during the 1840s. Women's role in politics, for instance, was, according to Adlai Stevenson, to

... inspire in her home a vision of the meaning of life and freedom ... and to help her husband find values that will give purpose to his specialized daily chores. This assignment for you, as wives and mothers, you can do in the living room with a baby on your lap or in the kitchen with a can opener in your hand.[7]

Motherhood was becoming, once again, a total way of life. *Life, Look, Redbook, Ladies' Home Journal,* and other national magazines proclaimed that the college-educated woman, the woman best qualified for a career, was now miraculously turning to nurturing and homemaking. The magazines rejoiced that American women had now "matured" into the recognition that feminism was a "disruptive trend." American women were finally "growing up" and conceding the top jobs to men. The women who made "the old-fashioned choice" of tending a garden and "a bumper crop of children" rated the applause. Partly because they wished to, and partly because other avenues were closed to them, American women turned with considerable intensity to the task of producing more babies. Friedan recounts how the U.S. birthrate by the end of the 1950s was overtaking India's, how statisticians were astonished by the fantastic increase in fertility among college women, who were now having four, five, and six children. "Women who had once wanted careers were now making careers out of having babies."[8]

Childbirth became both symbol and reality of a woman's fulfillment, and women began to savor the moment of birth as epitomizing their uniquely creative potential and value. Breastfeeding heightened this sense of uniquely nourishing creativity.[9]

It is not surprising, therefore, that a book written in the 1930s by a British obstetrician, Dr. Grantly Dick-Read, attained enormous popularity in America. *Childbirth Without Fear* argued that birth was a natural, joyous process that was never meant to be painful. Moreover, Read glorified motherhood as woman's true fulfillment in panegyrics that mixed Victorianism, sentimentality, mysticism, nature philosophy, and religion.

Read began his crusade for fearless birth after attending a delivery in a poor home, where, for the first time in his obstetrical experience, the woman refused chloroform and had her baby without fuss or noise. After the birth she said, "It didn't hurt. It wasn't meant to, was it, doctor?"[10] Read eventually concluded that a woman suffered pain in birth to the extent that she was afraid; relaxed women experienced little pain. Thus he formulated the "fear-tension-pain syndrome": If a woman's fear could be removed by some preparation for birth as a natural event, she would become relaxed and would not suffer. Read could not imagine that God or Nature had ever intended the culmination of human love to occasion pain. The solution to pain lay in re-educating women about their bodies and about the natural process of birth; they should also learn exercises that would strengthen the muscles used in bearing down and should learn deep breathing that would maintain oxygen in the body during contractions. Properly taught how to do the work of labor, 95 percent of women should be able to give birth with little or no anesthesia and thus with greater safety for babies.

Read was misunderstood by many. He never said that natural childbirth meant going "cold turkey" if a woman had pain. He stressed that it was sometimes impossible in modern culture to overcome all fears, and that anesthesia and analgesia should never be withheld from a woman who wanted or needed them.[11] In his own cases, nine of ten women, properly prepared, had been able to deliver without anesthesia. He regarded the routine American usage of outlet forceps and episiotomy as unnecessary and as causative of cerebral palsy and mental defects in babies. A relaxed

woman would need no anesthesia that prolonged labor and required forceps, and her perineal muscles would relax enough to
let the baby through without damage to mother or child.

Read believed that his method brought not only less pain but
an exultation in the experience of motherhood that was itself
religious, "a spiritual uplifting, the power of which they have
never been aware." Read always associated motherhood with essential femininity, with purity, piety, and submissiveness; he was
deeply Victorian in that regard. He believed the moment of birth
was woman's supreme triumph, a moment of ecstatic fulfillment
that the doctor should not take away from her. In fact, he should
envy woman her experience, which was the highest experience of
love. He deplored the obstetrical attitude that told women: "We
are producing this baby for you; what we do is not your business,
and what you want does not concern us." Instead, he said,
motherhood should be given back to women, for "natural" birth
was woman's "personal triumph," her "successful achievement."[12]

The baby's first cry was a moment that no woman should miss
by being unconscious; it marked the fulfillment of her whole evolutionary purpose:

Read believed that childbirth could and should be an ecstatic experience for the
mother. In the home birth shown here, the doctor has delivered the child, and
the mother is supported by a woman friend.

The sight and touch of her child provide the natural thrill that accompanies the reality of possessing a coveted prize; its greeting cry imprints such joy on her consciousness that for all time she can return to that sweet music and live again the crowning moment of her life. No woman ever forgets the first scream. . . . Women long for this moment. "I will have another baby. . . . I must live that divine moment again and again."[13]

Read's method also corresponded to the feminine mystique proper mothering, "a nation of gladiators can arise"; had natural childbirth and breastfeeding aroused natural mother-love, he said, there would not have been two world wars.[14] His philosophy, he believed, could also prevent the race from dying out through birth control inspired by fear of birth; women would want large families, a great social blessing: "Give us back the Victorian mothers of seven and ten children, and we shall again be swayed by the quiet but irresistible goodness of true motherhood."[15] Read wished to free women from fear, but not from family and home. And American women of the 1950s largely agreed.

Read's Victorianism allowed an antifeminist interpretation, one that many doctors, interested in maintaining their control of birth, early adopted. In other words, Read could be interpreted to mean that painless birth followed upon a woman's being more "feminine" or more submissive. As recently as 1970 one manual frequently dispensed by doctors explained that natural childbirth essentially meant having complete confidence in one's doctor:

The transcendent prerequisite [of natural childbirth] is that you have complete confidence in your doctor—confidence that he is your friend, a medically wise friend who is sincerely desirous of sparing you all the pain possible, provided that this is compatible with your welfare and that of your child. The very presence of such a friendly doctor, and the realization that he is competent to handle any situation is in itself the most effective and welcome of obstetric anodynes.[16]

Read's method also corresponded to the Feminine Mystique in urging that the experience of birth be shared by husband and wife. "Togetherness" in household activities was prized by postwar American families. Women's magazines claimed that the husband's helping with the dishes strengthened the family, for example. Thus, when Read stressed the importance of emotional "support" during labor and hoped that husbands would attend childbirth classes and would stay with their wives during labor and delivery, many middle-class families totally agreed. The most popular aspect of early prepared-childbirth programs in the 1950s was the opportunity for wives to have their husbands with them in the early stages of labor.[17] Read believed that the attendance of one emotionally comforting person throughout the birth was necessary to alleviate anxiety and to humanize the impersonal hospital environment. This could be the doctor or nurse, but Read, and most patients, preferred the husband to be the one.

American hospitals, however, were reluctant to admit men who might disturb routine or, worse, compromise the doctor's authority. Hospitals' reluctance was usually couched in terms of "contamination of the sterile environment," and husbands were excluded from the delivery room, and often even from the labor room. Not until the 1970s would husbands gain entrance to the birth scene itself.

That the husband was until recently the only outsider allowed to be present during labor or birth bears witness to the early relationship between natural childbirth and the Feminine Mystique. "Togetherness" was for husband and wife only; it did not include female friends and relatives, not even the woman's mother, who had traditionally helped in birth. The presence of an unmarried father was unthinkable. Natural childbirth was thus a means of strengthening the middle-class marriage.

Other cultural conditions also made the Read method attractive to postwar middle-class women. One was the religious revival of the 1940s and 1950s, which raised church attendance and interest in theology. Read's book was perhaps the most religious work on childbirth to be published in America since Cotton Mather's sermon, "Elizabeth in Her Holy Retirement." Read believed that, since childbirth was as much a spiritual as a physical achievement, women needed "a sound and stable philosophy." To approach birth without fear, he said, a woman had to be a believer; there was no place "in the make-up of motherhood" for materialism or atheism.[18] Read's conception of God was very different from Mather's, of course, for Read saw childbirth as part of an evolutionary movement toward perfection in *this* life, or, as he put it, in motherhood "the fearless woman advances to the dais of the Almighty to receive the prize of her accomplishment."[19]

Just as death was without a place in Read's version of Christian birth, so also there was no place for pain. He reinterpreted the curse of Eve, expressed in Genesis 3:16, to read "in *hard work* shalt thou bring forth children" rather than "in *sorrow*." In fact, he rewrote the Anglican service of Thanksgiving after Childbirth so as to remove phrases like "great danger," "the snares of death," "trouble and heaviness," and "the pains of hell," arguing that not only was birth no longer an occasion to meditate upon death, but a benevolent God had never meant it to be fearsome or painful.[20]

Read's philosophy harmonized well with the religious revival. In a popular book entitled *Natural Childbirth and the Christian Family* Helen Wessel carried Read's Biblical interpretations further and gave the family pastor a role at least equal to the doctor's in preparation for birth.[21] In the 1950s, when Christian ethics were interpreted mostly as personal or family ethics, in tune with the "privitization of life" described by Friedan, natural childbirth, which avoided potential damage to the baby's brain by anesthesia, appeared to some women as a "heroic" Christian act. In the days before the civil-rights movement made social action a viable choice for Christians, having a natural birth was perhaps the only ethical action, Christian or otherwise, that many women could take.

Another important cultural influence encouraging women's interest in natural birth was the flood of popular books on psychoanalysis that appeared after the war, concomitant with the feminine mystique. In accord with the nineteenth-century medical tradition from which it arose, psychoanalytic theory defined physical and mental normality in male terms; the male body and psyche provided the norms, the female represented the aberrant. Likewise, psychoanalytic theory believed that a woman's energies, unlike a man's, were bound up with her physiology. A woman who tried to emulate male interests risked mental illness; woman derived her mental health from accepting the peculiarities of her anatomy as determinative of her life-style. As in Victorian medical theory, motherhood was woman's fulfillment, the means to mental health for her and for the whole society. According to Joseph Rheingold, in a book entitled *The Fear of Being a Woman:*

> When women grow up without dread of their biological functions and without subversion by feminist doctrine and therefore enter upon motherhood with a sense of fulfillment and altruistic sentiment, we shall attain the goal of a good life and a secure world in which to live.[22]

This sounds remarkably like Read's remark that, without good mothering, "a nation of gladiators can arise" and more wars occur.

At any rate, anything a woman did aside from motherhood potentially endangered her childbearing capacity. *Modern Woman, the Lost Sex* (1947), a popular work on properly passive, healthy femininity, essentially repeated the argument of Dr. Edward Clarke's *Sex in Education* (1873): Brainwork would exhaust the reproductive organs and make healthy birth impossible:

> The psychosocial rule that begins to take form, then, is this: the more educated the woman is, the greater chance there is of sexual disorder, more or less severe. The greater the disordered sexuality in a given group of women, the fewer children do they have.

The authors of the *Lost Sex* said, moreover, that women had no excuse for not wanting children, for anesthesia had obliterated most of the pain. Furthermore, such pain as they did feel should be deeply meaningful and satisfying to the psychologically healthy woman.[23] Helene Deutsch, a noted interpreter of feminine psychology, said that woman's "tendency to passivity... inherent in her biology and anatomy," made her an unconscious masochist who obtained pleasure from suffering, as in birth. Deutsch amplified: "She passively awaits fecundation; her life is fully active and rooted in reality only when she becomes a mother. Until then everything that is feminine in the woman, physiology and psychology, is passive, receptive."[24]

The woman who took those theories seriously was advised that the manner of birth would have lifelong effects upon her infant's mental health and upon her own ability to mother. Thus, Margaret Ribble's *The Rights of Infants* (1943) urged the prospective mother to avoid "mental activity" during pregnancy, lest she produce a "nervous" infant.[25] One woman who had somewhat reluctantly left her job at a war plant in 1945 and whose baby subsequently refused to accept the breast felt guilty for having marred his personality while in the womb:

> I cannot deny that during my pregnancy I did an inordinate amount of reading and thinking and that my mental activity could have resulted in the present feeding problem. My son who rejected my milk was somehow aware that during my pregnancy my interest was diverted, thus depriving him of unrestricted at-

> tention.... I read too much, thought too much and during
> pregnancy even became bored and yearned for the challenge of
> a job and the automatic multiple-spindle screw machine![26]

In order to prevent this sort of post-delivery complication
and to make pregnancy itself most positive, the psychoanalysts
urged women to concentrate their energies on the physicalities of
pregnancy and birth. During pregnancy, they were told, they
should be narcissistic, and their "passive needs" or cravings should
be fulfilled, so that they could develop motherliness.[27] In labor,
which psychoanalysts regarded as analogous to coitus, the woman
should also be passive and should "entirely subordinate herself to
the inner forces." According to Deutsch, a woman who wanted
autonomy, who desired "her delivery to be an active accomplishment on her part," had distorted her femininity into masculinity
and would have birth complications.[28] The woman who could not
be passively feminine before birth harmed her child and, after
birth, could not mother it.

The popular psychoanalytic literature urged, however, that
the mother be conscious during birth and also *feel* the birth, in
order to ensure proper love for her child. Deutsch agreed with
Read that women often asked for anesthesia because of fear
rather than because of actual pain, but she believed that hospitals
routinely drugged women so heavily that it was "impossible in the
case of many ... women to speak of an act of childbirth at all."
When such women awaken they feel no love for the child, sometimes even declaring "that the children presented to them were
not theirs," because they had not felt the birth. Spinal anesthesias,
which left a woman conscious but with no pelvic sensations, also
dissociated the woman from the birth. One patient compared her
delivery to a scene at a railroad station where the workers were
trying to make sure the train arrived on schedule. Numb from the
waist down, she concentrated her attention objectively on other
people's activity.[29]

What differentiated the analysts' view from the Victorian belief that the mother's pain was necessary to make her love the
child was the analysts' comparison of labor to coitus, which could
result in orgasm. One analyst made the following explicit comparison:

> In labor, the descending baby can be considered the equivalent
> of the penis in intercourse.... To continue the analogy, as the

climax is reached in both situations, the woman utters involuntary sounds and performs involuntary pelvic movements. With the expulsion of the child, as in reaching the climax of the orgasm, the woman suddenly relaxes and there appears a calm ecstatic look on her face.[30]

In a period when popular psychology interpreted everything as having a sexual aspect, from the shape of cars to eating, it seemed logical also to describe birth as a sexual experience.

Read's "mystical ecstasy" in childbirth became for some American women a "birth climax" or "birth orgasm." "We feel a great deal," said one woman, "but what we feel doesn't hurt." The "crying out" of labor and delivery was not a cry of pain but the involuntary gasp as birth-intercourse reached toward its climax. The delivered woman was left with a "dazed and happy expression," a euphoric excitement that subsided slowly like the excitement of coitus.[31] One woman described her experience:

> Then on the next contraction I started to pull, and was suddenly swept away with primitive strength. Everything went blank and lightning-like streaks flashed, it seemed. It was ecstatic, wonderful, thrilling! I heard myself moaning—in triumph, not in pain! There was no pain whatsoever, only a primitive and sexual elation. From my grimace, the nurse thought I was in pain and started to put the mask over my face. How annoying! In the middle of a push, I gasped, "Go away! It doesn't hurt. . . ." I felt as if I had enough strength to pull the world apart—everything was bright, illuminated. In between contractions, I shouted deliriously, "This is wonderful! My husband only wants two babies, but I want a thousand."[32]

Women who wished to extend this ecstatic sexual experience often chose to breastfeed, as urged by Read and the analysts. A practice doctors had advocated at the beginning of the century in the interests of babies' health now found a middle-class revival, largely for the mother's satisfaction.[33]

Women in the 1940s, 1950s, and 1960s thus had a whole variety of motives for employing the Read method: glorification of motherhood, safety for the child, mystical experience, sexual experience, heroism. Common to all was the stress on individual experience. But to realize that experience, women had to enlist the cooperation of the medical profession, or at least of their personal physicians.

The medical profession's response to natural childbirth was

largely negative. Until the 1970s a certain way for a clinic patient to gain the classification of "hostile patient" in large maternity hospitals was to insist upon some form of natural childbirth. It took too much of the doctor's and staff's valuable time. One doctor compared it to "making a Rolls-Royce" and claimed that "a man would be hard put to make three such deliveries in a single night." Unless patients were paying Rolls-Royce prices for the extra attention, most doctors were not interested. An opponent of the Read method compared it to the "do-it-yourself craze" then popular among Americans; it was like rejecting a totally prepared cake mix in favor of adding a few ingredients yourself—in other words, it was a triviality. It was better to leave the whole process to the doctor and be sure of the result.[34]

Along with these considerations, doctors argued that women who had been exposed to the Read philosophy often felt considerable pain but thought they had to endure it because the use of anesthetics meant failure for themselves and harm to their children. A major drawback of Read's book, in fact, was that he had described birth as an athletic contest at which one either succeeds or fails. Read made the obstetrician into a judge, not only of a woman's success but of "her true nature and the environment from which she comes," which her actions at birth would reveal. Not surprisingly, some women who felt pain pretended that they did not, hoping that eventually they could replace their real memories with textbook memories of "what it should be like." Some, expecting but failing to have an ecstatic experience, got postpartum psychosis, an ailment that appeared to some observers to have increased sharply in the 1950s. Friedan, for example, found that, in one suburban New Jersey area, according to records compiled by a local psychiatrist,

> ... during the 1950s approximately one out of three young mothers suffered depression or psychotic breakdown over childbirth. This compared to previous medical estimates of psychotic breakdown in one out of 400 pregnancies, and less severe depressions in one out of 80.[35]

This meant that "in Bergen County during 1953–57 one out of ten of the 746 adult psychiatric patients were young wives who broke down over childbirth."[36]

Opponents of natural birth were quick to blame this increase on the new method, which they said intensified anxiety; Friedan was perhaps more accurate in attributing it to the emptiness of women's lives, for which birth was no compensation. Apart from that issue, however, the Read method as attempted during the 1950s did not prove adequate for controlling pain, for the simple absence of fear was not enough.[37]

A few doctors were willing to experiment, nonetheless, for a reduction in both anxiety and anesthesia meant greater safety and also might make patients easier to manage. Dr. Herbert Thoms brought the Read method to the Yale Hospital clinic in 1946, one of the few instances where it was not restricted to private patients. Thoms preferred the term "prepared childbirth," for he was aware that many "natural" labors among primitive peoples were not painless. His early results were encouraging, for prepared patients needed far fewer drugs and instrumental aids. More of his patients needed anesthesia or analgesia than Read would have predicted, however; instead of nine out of ten births being drugless, Thoms averaged only five.

One reason Americans needed more medication may have been that they delivered in hospitals—not an atmosphere conducive to relaxation—while most of Read's English births took place in homes. Furthermore, American physicians, while willing to give up the outlet forceps in some instances, never gave up episiotomy, which required local anesthesia. Cutting and stitching had become so routine by the 1950s that prepared-childbirth literature never questioned its necessity. Thus Read's methods were compromised from the beginning. As time went on, the enthusiasm of its professional proponents waned, for the statistics of prepared-childbirth mothers became increasingly similar to those of the nonprepared. Thoms's earlier success may have come from the "newness" of the technique, since patients desiring prepared birth received extra attention and were welcomed with open arms as subjects for research. Once the newness and special attention lessened, so did the favorable results.[38]

The next advance in natural-childbirth methods came from empirical psychology. Although some doctors had experimented with hypnosis and autohypnosis for more than a century, neither method ever gained a large following.[39] Instead, it was the Pavlovian theory of conditioned reflexes that became the foundation for the "Lamaze" method that superseded Read in the 1960s and 1970s. Pain, according to Pavlov's theory, seemed to depend upon how the cerebral cortex of the brain interpreted certain physiologic stimuli. If the experimenter could condition the cerebral cortex not to interpret certain signals as pain, the subject would indeed feel no pain.

After World War II Russian doctors applied Pavlovian theory to labor pains, calling their method "psychoprophylaxis." The object was to send counter-signals to the cortex that would be stronger than the "pain" signals. The Russian doctors derived some counter-signals from midwives' folk practices—these included deep breathing, stroking the abdomen, and a host of other motions, for simple concentration on a bodily movement could suffice to block the pain signals from the uterus. Psychoprophylaxis became the official system of obstetrical pain prevention in Russia in 1951.

In that year two French doctors from the Paris metalworkers' clinic, Ferdinand Lamaze and Pierre Vellay, traveled to Russia to study the new methods. Lamaze simplified and limited the Pavlovian techniques and added one of his own: the rapid shallow breathing, or "panting," that became the hallmark of the "Lamaze method" developed in Paris. In 1959, Marjorie Karmel, an American living in Paris, wrote of her experiences in delivery in a book called *Thank You, Dr. Lamaze,* which quickly went through seven printings in America. Unlike Read, who wrote of childbirth without fear, Lamaze promised childbirth without pain. He did not call his system natural childbirth, however, for "the final result should be better than nature."[40]

Like other new obstetrical techniques, the new method was to be an "improvement" upon nature. Women had to learn how to give birth just as they learned to read. Birth was a "performance" for which one "rehearsed," or a "competition that you are going to win." Early French reports presented the method as a series of challenges to be met with courage and skill, as in the story of the woman who drove for two hours in a truck over country roads to reach the hospital, all the time controlling her contractions. The method shifted emphasis from the doctor to the woman, who was to control her own labor. Childbirth "is not something that you simply let happen to you . . . it is something that you *do.*"[41]

Under the Lamaze method, a woman did not need to be religious to succeed; she did not have to subscribe to the feminine mystique or to psychoanalysis; she did not need an ecstatic or orgasmic experience to prove her success. Above all, she did not need to be passive; autonomy was the key to the new method. The woman regained control of birth; the doctor was there simply to assist. The woman was the star and would deliver the baby, though she cooperated with the doctor and his assistant so that the three became a team. As Karmel described it, birth was a team sport in which the doctor called the signals but the mother carried the ball and gained the applause:

> Dr. Lamaze called the signals . . . and I performed automatically . . . now there was a wild encouraging cheering section, dedicated to spurring me on. I felt like a football star, headed for a touchdown. My fans on the sidelines. Dr. Lamaze . . . the midwife, the nurse, all exhorted me. "POUSSEZ! POUSSEZ! POUSSEZ! CONTINUEZ! ENCORE! ENCORE!"[42]

The idea of regaining control over one's own body became popular among educated, middle-class women and ultimately became a major tenet of the women's liberation movement. Adoption of the new method was slow, however, for doctors advanced the same objections to it as they had to Read's method, plus several new objections. One doctor claimed that Lamaze was part of the "mass application of Pavlovian principles by [the Soviet] government to reshape the behavior of its citizens." It was a method used to produce the ideal dog. Because the Lamaze method stressed autonomy, a psychoanalyst argued that only the "dissatisfied woman . . . wants it to complete her drive for masculine powers," for she believes that "the wound of womanhood, of not having been a boy, will be healed by giving birth, and she wishes to consciously establish her psychic virility." The Lamaze method was clearly not in tune with psychoanalysis or the feminine mystique.[43]

Despite these objections, many doctors came to accept, or at least pay lip service to, variations of the new method. A reduction in the amount of anesthesia necessary for comfort was, after all, a gain for safety. Except for the occasional doctor who preferred to have his patients anesthetized for his *own* comfort, most doctors were willing to allow at least some consciousness. Childbirth education could work for the doctor's convenience as well as the patient's. As one doctor remarked, "It makes the delivery floor run more smoothly." What was at issue was not the patient's consciousness or the degree of anesthetization but control of birth. When doctors realized that their control was intact as long as birth was in the hospital, they listened more willingly to requests for "natural childbirth," for they had the power to define its meaning. The decline in the birthrate may have increased doctors' willingness to meet patients' requests.

By the 1970s many doctors were prepared to offer a more natural childbirth. Most often, however, it was a peculiarly American "natural birth" they provided, for they drew routinely upon the arts of medicine. Episiotomy, outlet forceps, Demerol, and even epidural anesthesia were combined with the Lamaze method. Doctors were satisfied with Lamaze only if they could adjust it to keep birth from being overly time-consuming and to permit them enough activity to justify their professional presence and fees. Anesthetists accepted Lamaze so long as enough drugs were given to require their presence or the hospital ruled that even a nonanesthetized mother must pay for their services. Many women accepted the assurance that they had had a natural delivery when, in fact, many interventions were made. Probably only a Caesarean section or Twilight Sleep would not have qualified for natural birth in American practice.

There was little agreement in the profession about what natural childbirth was. Some doctors spoke of a birth that required no operation not as a natural birth, but as a "spontaneous birth." Others considered a birth "natural" if they did not perform an episiotomy, whether or not the woman had anesthesia or was conscious. Others used the term "natural" to describe the woman who delivered on the way to the hospital. Many doctors told a woman desiring natural childbirth that she had done well during the first stage of labor but that they were slipping in a spinal anesthesia to help her with the second stage, which as a result usually required oxytocin and forceps. The doctor nevertheless told his patient that she had suceded at natural birth, and she probably wanted to believe him. Both Read and Lamaze claimed, of course, that a woman was not a failure if she should ask for analgesics and anesthetics, but the choice rested with her, not the doctor. Doctors usually decided to give such drugs when the woman was having the strongest contractions and least likely or able to protest. The doctor would subsequently tell the woman she had had a natural birth. Natural childbirth thus came to have many meanings, adjusted to consumer demand, individual preference, and doctors' convenience.

Doctors could trim the purposes of natural childbirth because birth remained in the hospital, and the movement for new childbirth practices centered on the wishes of unorganized, medically naïve middle-class women. Most of those women believed that they could achieve their wishes for a different birth experience by persuading their doctors to make changes. Change centered in the doctor–patient relation. The privatization of life, and the feminine mystique itself, kept women from organizing to make demands; rather, individual women shopped for a solution for themselves.

During the 1970s the renewed feminist movement began to explore the behavior of the medical profession and the workings of medical institutions in the treatment of women. In educational groups and in political actions, women sought to extend their control of their bodies in myriad challenges to medical practice. It appeared that the Progressive Era's feminist concern for everyone's safety might be reborn. At the same time, the decline in fertility had encouraged obstetricians to be more responsive to women's wishes, particularly in private practice. Yet traditional attitudes and practices continued to thwart the expectations of many women.

The hospital continued to frustrate the natural childbirth patient in myriad ways. Unlike Lamaze's informal, homelike clinic, where labor and delivery took place in what appeared to be a bedroom, the American hospital frightened patients with an array of personnel and emergency equipment. The hospital operated according to routines that represented its attempt to prevent difficulties and process maternity cases as easily as possible. For example, hospitals often did not feed a laboring woman, which might maintain her strength, for they reasoned that she might develop difficulties and require general anesthesia. Under general anesthesia there was the danger of asphyxiation from inhaling stomach contents. Some of the problems were simply spatial: Lacking room, many hospitals placed a laboring woman in a group labor room, where she was demoralized by the discomfort of other women.

In a novel centering on her own pregnancy and delivery, Charlotte Painter described the sobering effects of her tour through a hospital as part of her prepared childbirth course. The teacher had instructed the class in exercises and rhythmic breathing, and all were full of a "giggly and girly" self-confidence before the tour. The instructor had not, however, prepared them for the hospital realities:

As it happened, our tour showed us that the hospital cracked a whip over [the teacher's] pretty little individuals, and snapped them smartly into line. The labor room had to be entered two by two, in initiate style, because it was too small to hold more.... The beds were narrow and enclosed with bars—like cribs for the insane.... The delivery room took us further back in time than those Bedlam relics. It looked like an underground dungeon. We were shown the delivery table, a narrow slab, to which the mother is transferred in the final stage of birth.... A flat leather-and-metal trap, with plates to strap down legs and leather wrist thongs to hold down hands. I have been unable to lie flat for some weeks, but doubtless the equipment is effective. No longer giggly and girly, the initiates filed out, grimly refreshed by truth.[44]

Forced immobility in one position could almost completely negate the pain-reducing attempts of the Lamaze method. Pain seems to be greatly reducible when persons are free to move their bodies to find a more comfortable position. For the restrained, body pain can be excruciating. Yet the modern delivery table prevented women from adjusting their position. Furthermore, "natural childbirth" as taught in America often put a premium on silence during labor; the "successful" patient was the silent one, who thereby demonstrated relaxation. Screaming, which acts partly to distract the mind from pain, was forbidden, by use of anesthesia if necessary. But, as Painter suggested, "silence is undoubtedly more comfortable to the attendant, but a body needs to release its vocal energy to make room for new stamina. What else is a battle cry?"[45] Unlike the home, the hospital could not tolerate such noise; screams disturbed and frightened other patients. Even if women could tolerate pain, the hospital could not permit its vocal expression; noise was a nuisance that technology, in the form of analgesia, had to flush away.

Prepared childbirth in America has undergone extensive redefinition and adaptation, yet it has made some valuable contributions to birth. Twilight Sleep and general anesthesia are losing popularity as more women desire consciousness and as doctors and hospitals gradually accommodate them. Most hospitals now provide some form of childbirth education, though sometimes the classes become avenues for socializing patients to submit to hospital routines. Many hospitals have dramatically reduced the quantities of analgesia and anesthetics administered. More women are aware of the workings of their own bodies. Most important, perhaps, has been the increased sense of dignity and worth felt by mothers who have shared actively in the birth. The presence of the husband, and occasionally a relative or friend, in the delivery room has helped establish this sense of dignity. Nonetheless, "natural" birth still struggles against the predispositions of the profession and the routines of a hospital, which find their purpose in controlling patients in order to treat abnormality.

Notes

1. Gertrude Siegmond, M.D., quoted in *Time,* May 25, 1936.
2. "From Genesis to Freud," *Nation,* June, 1936, p. 699.
3. Leonore Pelham Friedriech, "I Had a Baby," *The Atlantic* 163 (1939):461.
4. "I Had a Baby Too," Readers' Letters to *The Atlantic* 163 (1939): 765, 768.
5. Margaret Mead, *Blackberry Winter: My Earlier Years* (New York: William Morrow, 1972), p. 51.
6. Betty Friedan, *The Feminine Mystique* (New York: Norton, 1963), p. 51.
7. Adlai Stevenson, Commencement Address at Smith College, 1955, quoted in *ibid.,* p. 61.
8. *Ibid.,* pp. 59, 17.
9. *Ibid.,* pp. 62, 58.
10. Grantly Dick-Read, *Childbirth Without Fear,* 2d rev. ed (New York: Harper & Row, 1959), p. 18.
11. *Ibid.,* p. 170.
12. *Ibid.,* pp. 27, 173, 74.
13. *Ibid.,* p. 74.
14. *Ibid.,* p. 28.
15. *Ibid.,* p. 346.
16. Nicholson J. Eastman and Keith P. Russell, *Expectant Motherhood,* 5th ed., revised (Boston: Little, Brown, 1970), pp. 166–167.
17. Joseph Curi, "A Comparative Study of the Yale Prepared Childbirth Program," M.D. thesis, Yale University, 1964, p. 27.
18. Dick-Read, *Childbirth Without Fear,* pp. xvi–xvii.
19. *Ibid.,* pp. 24–25.
20. *Ibid.,* pp. 96–101.
21. Helen Wessel, *Natural Childbirth and the Christian Family* (New York: Harper & Row, 1963).
22. Joseph Rheingold, *The Fear of Being a Woman* (New York, 1964);

quoted in Phyllis Chesler, *Women and Madness* (Garden City, N.Y.: Doubleday, 1972), p. 93.

23. Ferdinand Lundberg and Marynia Farnham, *Modern Woman, the Lost Sex* (New York, 1947), pp. 270–271, 291–294.

24. Helene Deutsch, *The Psychology of Women: A Psychoanalytic Interpretation* (New York: Grune, 1944), 1:140.

25. Margaret A. Ribble, M.D. *The Rights of Infants* (New York, 1943), p. 107.

26. Florence Rush, "Who's Afraid of Margaret Ribble?" (Pittsburgh: KNOW Publications, 1972), p. 5.

27. Therese Benedek, M.D., *Studies in Psychosomatic Medicine: Psychosexual Functions in Women* (New York, 1952), p. 342.

28. Deutsch, *Psychology of Women*, 2:238, 253.

29. *Ibid.*, pp. 257, 247, 263–264, 266.

30. Wessel, *Natural Childbirth*, pp. 256–257.

31. *Ibid.*, pp. 255–256.

32. *Ibid.*, p. 257.

33. Barbara Seaman, *Free and Female* (New York: Coward, 1972), p. 285.

34. Charlotte Painter, *Who Made the Lamb* (New York, 1965), pp. 52–53; Waldo O. Fielding, M.D., and Lois Benjamin, *The Childbirth Challenge: Commonsense Versus "Natural" Methods* (New York, 1962), p. 59.

35. Friedan, *Feminine Mystique*, p. 293.

36. Richard E. Gordon and Katherine K. Gordon, "Social Factors in the Prediction and Treatment of Emotional Disorders of Pregnancy," *American Journal of Obstetrics and Gynecology* 77, No. 5 (1959):1074–1083.

37. Dick-Read, *Childbirth Without Fear*, pp. 155, 213; Fielding and Benjamin, *Childbirth Challenge*, p. 62; Friedan, *Feminine Mystique*, p. 293.

38. Margaret Mead and Niles Newton, "Cultural Patterning of Perinatal Behavior," in Stephen A. Richardson and Alan S. Guttmacher, eds., *Childbearing: Its Social and Psychological Aspects* (Baltimore: Williams and Wilkins, 1963), pp. 170–171; H. Thoms and F. W. Goodrich, Jr., "A Clinical Study of Natural Childbirth," *American Journal of Obstetrics and Gynecology* 56 (1948):875; L. G. Roth, "Natural Childbirth in a General Hospital," *ibid.*, 61 (1951):167; Van Auken and Tomlinson, "An Appraisal of Patient Training for Childbirth," *ibid.*, 66 (1953):100; H. Thoms and E. Karlovsky, "2,000 Deliveries under a Training for Childbirth Program," *ibid.*, 68 (1954):279; Curi, "Comparative Study," p. 10.

39. K. S. Tom, "Hypnosis in Obstetrics and Gynecology," *Obstetrics and Gynecology* 16 (1969):222; R. V. August, "Obstetric Hypnoanesthesia," *American Journal of Obstetrics and Gynecology* 79 (1970):1131.

40. J. Velvovsky *et al., Painless Childbirth Through Psychoprophylaxis* (Moscow, 1970), pp. 251–253; Marjorie Karmel, *Thank You, Dr. Lamaze: A Mother's Experience in Painless Childbirth* (Philadelphia: Lippincott, 1959), p. 42.

41. *Ibid.,* pp. 45, 65, 72, 42.

42. *Ibid.,* pp. 89–90.

43. Fielding and Benjamin, *Childbirth Challenge,* pp. 17, 52.

44. Painter, *Who Made the Lamb,* pp. 99–101.

45. *Ibid.,* p. 89.

7

Government Involvement

No Mother's Baby Is Safe Until Every Mother's Baby Is Safe.
Poster Distributed by the National Child Welfare
Association during World War I

DURING THE FIRST QUARTER of the twentieth century, the federal government and the states became increasingly involved in financing and overseeing maternity care. Although their involvement has not always been visible to the patient, it has continued and increased. Today, governmental policies determine to a considerable degree the priorities of research, the types of patients receiving special care, and differences in the treatment available. Government did not enter the field of maternity care unopposed; the peculiar alignment of groups favoring and opposing federal involvement in the first twenty years of this century created a unique structure for the provision of health care for mothers and children, a structure in which the medical profession became and remained the dominant force. The concept that the government has a particular obligation toward pregnant women and their unborn children has always been limited in significant ways.

There were three basic currents that swept the federal government into involvement with maternity care: a growing concern for child health; the development of professional philanthropy; and the awareness of public-health officials that maternal and infant care for the poor needed improvement.

The concern for child health became prominent among the middle classes in the 1880s as they began deliberately to limit the number of their children and conversely to expect more achievement from each child. Peter Filene has described the "professionalization of motherhood" at that time: the publication of large numbers of books on child care and of regular columns of advice

201

in newspapers and magazines, and the organizing of women's groups, such as "The Society for the Study of Child Nature," which elevated parenthood from a "natural" to a "scientific" matter. By 1912 there were at least fifty major child-care associations, coordinated by the Federation for Child Study. According to Filene, "parenthood has become a national concern—a problem that required no less deliberate reform than did forest conservation or railroad rates."[1]

These advocates of child care realized that child health began with a healthy pregnancy and birth. Their overriding concern for child care and child health, rather than for maternal health, led to increased scrutiny of birth practices at a time when, with the exception of a few obstetrical specialists, doctors gave little priority to maternity care.

Public awareness of the child-health problem was increased by studies of the urban industrial poor in the late nineteenth century, which revealed that most poor people were poor, not because of their moral negligence, but because of the structure of the industrial system. The studies made apparent that poverty produced ill health and that its effects were worst on women and child laborers, many of whom spent twelve hours a day in factories under the most unhealthy conditions. Infant mortality among the poor seemed much higher than it should have been, but in the absence of reliable statistics about causes of death policy to improve the health of women and children was difficult to form.[2]

Private philanthropies paved the way for some endeavors later taken over by local, state, and federal governments. "Milk stations," which provided clean, fresh, tuberculosis-free milk for urban infants, began in New York City in 1892 under the sponsorship of Nathan Straus, the owner of Macy's, and continued in expanded numbers under the direction of a citywide committee. The committee then began to provide food for infants as well, to educate mothers in child care, and, finally (in 1918), to sponsor a new organization to provide more complete maternity care, the Maternity Center Association of New York.[3]

Philanthropy had played a part in maternity care throughout the nineteenth century, notably in lying-in hospitals. After the Civil War, it acquired a more professional flavor as educated young women working in settlement houses, such as Hull House in Chicago, saw health conditions among the poor at closer view. It was, in fact, from Hull House that most of the early advocates for the reform of child health came. They included Florence Kelley, a factory inspector in Illinois and founder of the National Consumers' League; Grace Abbott, head of the Immigrants' Protective League; and Julia Lathrop, who was to become head of the Children's Bureau.

Those three were joined by Lillian Wald, a professional nurse and founder of the Henry Street Settlement in New York, in forming the National Child Labor Committee in 1904. The Committee pointed to the lack of any national statistics about children's health and urged the formation of a national children's bureau to investigate the welfare of children and to gather statistics about infant mortality. It pointed out that the federal government had better statistics about the boll weevil, young lobsters in Maine, and young trout in Wisconsin than about the numbers of children who were born or died, for no government agency kept such statistics. In 1906 a bill to create a Children's Bureau for this purpose was introduced to Congress; it generated opposition from states' rights advocates, from mill owners who feared a new deluge of factory inspectors, and from those who believed that a federal bureau would "usurp the power of the family." The bill received strong support, however, from middle-class women through national organizations of women's clubs, which were to be active in maternal and child-health issues into the 1920s.

In 1909 Wald and Kelley appealed directly to President Theodore Roosevelt, who lent support to the bill and convened the first White House Conference on Dependent Children. Similar conferences have been called at ten-year intervals ever since. Not until 1912, however, was legislation finally passed creating the Children's Bureau within the Department of Labor. Julia Lathrop became its chief; in 1921 another Hull House alumna, Grace Abbott, replaced her. The philanthropist-reformers had succeeded in institutionalizing their concerns.[4]

Lathrop quickly set about to promote birth registration as a means of attacking infant mortality. The Census Bureau had been authorized in 1902 to issue statistics on birth and death, but the accuracy of these data depended on local compliance, and many states had no birth-registration laws. Some of those that had the laws enforced them laxly. In order to encourage registration, the Children's Bureau mobilized the resources of the national women's clubs, which formed hundreds of committees to urge physicians and mothers to be certain that births were registered. The campaign evolved into National Baby Week, in which the Bureau and women's clubs sought to educate prospective mothers in maternity care. The Bureau also suggested that each state encourage registration by paying local registrars 25 cents per birth.[5]

By 1915 the campaign for birth registration brought results. Thirty-two states had enacted laws, and the Census Bureau had formed a birth-registration area embracing the New England states, Pennsylvania, Michigan, New York City, and the District of Columbia; these areas had laws and procedures ensuring reasonably complete records. By 1929 only two states remained outside the registration area for birth; at the same time, the death-registration area became nearly complete, and for the first time it was possible to make longitudinal comparisons of rates of maternal and infant mortality and to determine whether progress was being made. The results were not encouraging. Since 1915 the United States had lagged behind other industrialized nations, and it continued to do so.

Lathrop's second objective was to have the Children's Bureau investigate in detail infant mortality in certain industrial towns. A 1911 study of Johnstown, Pennsylvania, involved interviewing the mother of every child born in that year, whether the child was living or dead. Investigators found that infant mortality was lower when physicians rather than midwives or neighbors attended, when the mothers were literate and English-speaking, or when the families had been in the United States a relatively long time. The most striking correlation was between infant morality and father's income; the more the father earned, the less likely was his child to die. Studies in Brockton, Massachusetts; Manchester, New Hampshire; Waterbury, Connecticut; Baltimore, and Pittsburgh all produced similar results: Low income was the underlying factor in high infant mortality.[6]

Investigators suspected, however, that mothers in low-income families worked outside the home while pregnant, and that factory work contributed to miscarriages, stillbirths, and prematurities, though such a correlation was hard to prove. Clearer was the relation between a new mother's return to work and her infant's death from diarrhea caused by unsterile bottle-feeding. Education in proper techniques of infant feeding seemed necessary to reduce mortality.

The Bureau also concluded that child health would be improved if women were taught to care for themselves more effectively during pregnancy. Prenatal care first took on substantive meaning after 1900, for by then new medical discoveries made regular checkups during pregnancy truly preventive of birth complications that resulted in the death of infants. The Children's Bureau learned, however, that most urban poor, especially the immigrant poor, received no prenatal care whatever.[7]

The rural poor and sometimes even the rural middle classes were often more desperately lacking in medical care in maternity than the urban poor, for their isolation virtually precluded prenatal care and the attendance of a doctor during delivery. A Bureau study in rural Montana found that most women delivered without any trained attendant. Wealthy rural families sometimes paid hundreds of dollars to board a woman member in a distant city for weeks before a birth. But few could afford that means of ensuring adequate care; most were in the situation of the woman who wrote to Julia Lathrop from Burntfork, Wyoming, in 1916, asking for publications about delivery.

> I live sixty-five miles from a Dr. and my other babies (two) were very large at birth—one 12 lbs., and the other 10½ lbs. I have been very badly torn each time through the rectum. . . . I am 37 years old and I am so worried and filled with perfect horror at the prospects ahead. So many of my neighbors die at giving birth. . . . I have a baby 11 months old in my keeping now, whose mother died. When I reached their cabin last Nov. it was 22 below zero, and I had to ride 7 miles horseback. She was nearly dead when I got there, and died after giving birth to a 14 lb. boy—Will you please send me all the information for care of myself before and after and at the time of delivery. I am far from a doctor, and we have no means.[8]

Such pleas persuaded Lathrop to seek federal funds to provide maternity care for rural people. Congressmen who supported federal involvement in maternal and child health thought of such rural constituents rather than of urban immigrants, who could, at least in theory, avail themselves of the facilities of clinics and dispensaries run by urban hospitals. The Bureau realized that economics and race could make a doctor as unavailable as geography did. Studies of rural Mississippi mentioned white families living only three miles from a town with six physicians who were unable to get a doctor to attend their deliveries. Black families throughout the rural South were known to have severe maternal and child-health problems, for their mortality rates were usually double those of whites in the same areas. Even the mortality rates for whites were not good. Some 15,000 women died in childbirth in 1913, half of them from puerperal fever. Childbirth, in fact, killed more women aged fifteen to forty-four than any condition except tuberculosis and showed no evidence of decrease in mortality between 1900 and 1913.[9]

The Children's Bureau attributed that appalling situation to "general ignorance of the dangers connected with childbirth and of the need for skilled care" and to the "difficulty in the provision of adequate care" in certain sections. In view of those facts, Julia Lathrop proposed in 1917 that the federal government appropriate funds to promote "the welfare and hygiene of maternity and infancy" through matching grants to states. The Smith–Lever Act of 1914, which funded agricultural extension agents, served as a model for her legislation. The first bill for "the protection of maternity and infancy" was introduced in 1918 by Representative Jeanette Rankin of Montana, the first woman elected to Congress. She proposed to grant for a period of five years sums approaching $2 million annually, particularly to benefit rural areas by educating women about prenatal and infant care through extension courses. Some medical and nursing care in outlying areas was permitted, though its use was left to the states to decide. Significantly, Rankin's bill construed maternity care as a woman's right regardless of her income, not as a matter of charity. Although supported by the Bureau, the Department of Agriculture, and the American Federation of Labor, the proposal died in committee.

In 1919 Senator Morris Sheppard (D.-Tex.) and Representative Horace Mann Towner (R.-Iowa) reintroduced the measure. By then its proponents could use battle death in World War I as a standard of comparison, arguing that childbirth was woman's battleground: "During the nineteen months we were at war, for every soldier who died as a result of wounds, one mother in the United States went down into the valley of the shadow and did not return."[10] Although that was not exactly accurate, it was widely believed. Others said that, while Congress dallied, children were dying at the rate of 20,000 a month. Rep. Alben Barkley (D.-Ky.) said the Constitution gave Congress the "power to provide for the general welfare"; he interpreted this to mean that those born into the world have "a right to expect that they will have an equal chance with every other child in the world, not only to be born in health . . . but . . . to survive." Children were future citizens, a val-

Cartoons of this sort were published in support of the Sheppard–Towner Act. The AMA at first favored government aid for maternal and child care but soon reversed itself.

uable resource. Maternal care was largely adjunct to child health, which began in the womb. The Sheppard–Towner bill provoked the first public claims that health care should be the right of every citizen regardless of background.[11]

Opponents tried to laugh the bill down. Senator James Reed (D.-Mo.) ridiculed the Bureau, which was to administer the funds, by reading the names of thirty-three of its principal researchers, all unmarried. He asked if Congress wished to approve the doctrine that only those ladies who have never had babies were capable of caring for them. "Female celibates" who were "too refined to have a husband" should not try to take care of other women's babies when those women wanted to care for their own babies. Billions of babies had survived with only the loving care of their mothers and the family doctor. Perhaps a committee of mothers was needed, Reed said, to teach "old maids" to marry and have children of their own.

In a more serious vein, Reed opposed the bill as a socialist invasion of family privacy. In Russia the state pensioned the mother in order to make the child a ward of the state, and Germany was little better, for there "socialistic doctrinaires" had established maternity benefit systems and compulsory health insurance, implying "the right of State visitation and espionage." He envisioned American mothers having to register with the state when becoming pregnant and having to endure a visit from a woman official who would demand, "in the name of the law," answers to inquisitorial questions:

> When is it going to happen? How did it come to happen? Is the husband healthy? Is the Wasserman indicated? Has it been applied? Will a doctor or midwife be employed? Are they competent? Has the midwife been approved by the Children's Bureau? Have you read the regulations of the Children's Bureau? Are you obeying them? What food do you eat? When do you eat?

Reed concluded that, if the government wished to aid the poor, it should pay physicians' fees.[12]

These arguments were echoed by a powerful coalition, including antisuffragist and antibolshevist groups, but the American Medical Association's opposition was most effective. Having just rejected national health insurance as a socialistic scheme unsuited to American government, the AMA orchestrated nationwide criticism of the bill. An article in the *Illinois Medical Journal* declared that the bill was "a piece of destructive legislation sponsored by *endocrine perverts, derailed menopausics* and a lot of other men and women working overtime to devise means to destroy the country."[13]

Supporters were more formidable, however. The Bureau enlisted the General Federation of Women's Clubs and the League of Women Voters to form a lobbying organization for women's groups. Some congressmen thought this was the most powerful lobby seen in Washington for years. But, finally, it was women's achievement of suffrage that swayed Congress to pass the bill, for Congress felt it could not neglect 20 million organized voters.

There is little doubt that the bill was enfranchised women's first public act. *Good Housekeeping* compared dilatory congressmen with Herod and urged women to telegraph Washington. Florence Kelley, in testifying for the bill, asked congressmen how they would answer women who asked if the legislature wanted infants and mothers to die. She pointed out that, during the two and a half years that Congress had been deliberating the bill, 625,000 babies had died from causes connected with birth or with lack of prenatal care, and that the United States had fallen to seventeenth place among nations in maternal mortality. Posters appeared throughout the country proclaiming "A Baby Saved is a Citizen Gained," "The Nation that Has Babies Has the Future," and "Save the Mother." Middle-class women, with their organizations and their influence upon newspapers and magazines, constituted a powerful group. They carried along some public-health doctors and the specialist section of the AMA devoted to maternal and child health.

The bill was passed in 1921, but with reduced appropriations: $1,480,000 the first year and $1,240,000 in five subsequent years, in matching grants to states. The states were quick to accept the bill, also fearing women's new political power. In New York Governor Miller, who rejected the federal grant but spent a similar amount of money for a new hog barn on the state fair grounds, was defeated in his next election bid when women's organizations publicized his preference for the health of swine over that of children. Every state accepted the bill's grant except Massachusetts, where the organized medical lobby was strongest.

Grace Abbott, the new head of the Children's Bureau, said federal funds should serve two basic purposes: first, to improve women's understanding of what constitutes good prenatal and obstetrical care, and second, to make available adequate community resources for such care. The public health authorities in the states determined how to spend the money. Fourteen states decided that licensing, supervising, and instructing midwives was the most needed service; some states had public health nurses conduct prenatal examinations, including blood pressure readings and urinalyses, in the homes of expectant mothers, while also instructing mothers about birth and infant care. In some areas prenatal clinics, staffed by doctors and nurses, were established. Other states researched the causes of mortality, trying to improve their statistics' accuracy; provided instruction sessions to upgrade general practitioners' knowledge of obstetrics; inspected hospitals; and provided laboratory services. The principal efforts, however, were devoted to promoting birth registration and establishing infant welfare centers and maternity centers—that is, educational efforts for mothers, midwives, and household helpers. Twenty-two million pamphlets were printed to encourage women to get prenatal care and to inform them of the signs of an abnormal pregnancy.

Between 1921 and 1929 Sheppard–Towner money supported 183,000 health conferences, almost 3,000 centers for prenatal care, and more than 3 million home visits by nurses. In its final years the money reached more than 4 million persons. Mortality for infants under one year fell from 75 per 1,000 in 1921 to 64 in 1929. Some doctors disputed those figures, but most public health authorities agreed that the maternal death rate from eclampsia had fallen because of Sheppard–Towner, and eclampsia was precisely the kind of condition good prenatal care could prevent. There was considerable evidence, therefore, that expending federal funds was worthwhile.[14]

Despite such evidence, opponents of the bill forced an end to appropriations in 1929. The AMA had become even more powerful as a lobby against it, but women's groups had also ceased to remain a coherent political lobby in behalf of such maternal and infant matters. Also, the concern of both doctors and the public had begun to shift to chronic and degenerative diseases. The AMA argued that Sheppard–Towner wasted tax money, for it had not reduced mortality or developed a "single new idea"—that is, presumably a new technique to combat birth diseases. The AMA also rejected the Bureau's statistics about U.S. mortality rates in comparison to other countries, saying the rates "compared favorably" and would be improved only by "cooperation between the individual prospective mother and her doctor."[15] On that note, federal involvement in maternity care ended until 1935, when the Social Security Act revived it.

During the years federal involvement developed, states also became concerned for infant and maternal health. As early as the 1890s state public-health departments in New England and New

York studied the high death rates among infants of tenement families. In 1908 Dr. Josephine Baker, after many years' experience as a public-health inspector in New York's slums, persuaded the state health department to form a Bureau of Child Hygiene. New Jersey soon followed suit, and by 1918 twelve states had such departments. Sixteen more were established in 1919 at the urging of the Children's Bureau, and nineteen more appeared while Sheppard–Towner was in force.

The state bureaus dealt primarily with the problem of birth attendants. The issue in regard to maternity that most frequently concerned public health professionals from 1900 to 1925 was what to do with the midwife. Although midwives had ceased attending white middle-class women in the early nineteenth century, they had served rural, and especially black, women continuously. What exacerbated the "midwife problem," however, was the arrival of hordes of immigrants from Southern and Eastern Europe, beginning in the 1880s; these groups brought their own midwives and settled in the major cities. As late as 1920 such midwives attended between 20 and 40 percent of all births in mid-Atlantic cities. Even in Massachusetts, where the practice of midwifery was illegal, they still delivered a sizable number of children.[16] In 1914 they were sufficiently numerous for the state's Commission on Immigration to comment that the medical profession and the state should act to protect immigrant women.[17] In 1935 U.S. Department of Labor Statistics showed only one birth attended by a "midwife" in Massachusetts for that year, but the column headed "other attendant or not reported" listed 36.7 percent of all births, meaning in effect that midwives were continuing to practice illegally.[18]

Midwives were obviously attractive to many people, for they usually charged much less than a doctor and often provided such other services as housecleaning, laundry, and postnatal care of mother and child for several days, while the more expensive doctor usually attended only the birth. For instance, in Detroit in 1917 midwives charged from $7 to $10, a fee that included daily visits for five days or more. Doctors charged from $20 to $30, and the patient had to hire a nurse for all subsequent attention, which in effect doubled the fee. By 1930 the charge for midwives had risen from $25 to $30 but as high as $65 for doctors. Obstetrical specialists charged from $75 up, to which hospital costs had to be added. Women in rural Texas in 1930, when asked why they called a midwife instead of a doctor, answered along the following lines:

> Had midwife because could get her for 75 cents, doctor cost $15.

> Molly was closer and doctor higher. Did my washing and charged only $5. Really worth more.[19]

Immigrant women also thought midwives a "better buy." Many of them disliked clinics, which marked them as charity cases, and most could afford a midwife. Hospital birth was not part of their tradition, nor was the attendance of a man during birth. Italians in particular were sensitive to this issue. Josephine Baker remarked: "If deprived of midwives, these women would rather have amateur assistance from the janitor's wife or the woman across the hall than submit to this outlandish American custom of having a male doctor for a confinement."[20] For these reasons, many public health authorities believed that midwives would be around for many years.

If immigrant midwives had been a trained, educated class of women such as existed at that time in parts of Northern and Western Europe, they would have presented no problem. Baker said that she herself would prefer a competent Scandinavian midwife to an American general practitioner, for the former had more experience than most general practitioners and was less likely to abuse the use of anesthesia or forceps. Unfortunately, however, most immigrant midwives had no such training. Baker had the New York Health Department round up 4,000 midwives for registration and licensing. Baker described these women as clumsy amateurs, often densely ignorant, filthy, superstitious, hidebound—all that a midwife should not be. They supplemented their income by performing "illegal operations under conditions that made you wonder how any of their patients survived." They were unsterile and were inclined to use ergot and abortifacients unwisely. Another telling argument against them was their ignorance of the use of silver nitrate to prevent blindness in infants.

From 1900 on, articles on the "midwife problem" appeared in many medical journals, in the proceedings of the American Association for the Prevention of Infant Mortality, in the White House Conferences, and in the reports of state and local medical societies. The historian Frances Kobrin has divided the discussants of the "problem" into four groups: (1) advocates of immediate abolition of midwives, with legal prosecution of any who continued practice; (2) those who believed in eventual abolition, with careful regulation of existing midwives until enough doctors could be educated to take their places; (3) those who wished to educate the midwife until she reached the status of English and European midwives; and (4) those (mostly Southerners) who believed that, if midwives could be trained to wash their hands and to use silver nitrate drops, no more could be expected. The one thing most discussants agreed upon was that the worst birth attendants were not midwives but the general practitioners who tended to intervene needlessly in normal births. J. Whitridge Williams, Professor of Obstetrics at Johns Hopkins, noted:

> In my experience the average doctor who treats the poor, and sometimes the rich as well, does quite as much harm as the ignorant midwife. Consequently, I do not think that we are justified in trying to abolish her until we can put our own house in order.[21]

State and local public health authorities had no effective powers over doctors' practice, however; it was left to the profession to police itself. Public health authorities had to decide whether to train and license midwives and whether to regard them as permanent features of American life. The experience of Massachusetts indicated that it was useless to abolish them by law, for illegality did not remove them but only made it impossible to supervise them. Yet few people wanted to raise midwives to the professionally trained status they had in Europe. Immigrant midwives were not native-born, middle-class women; had they been, they might have been encouraged toward professionalism. The urban midwives were alien, not only in citizenship, but to American customs. Even the public health doctors who sought to train and license them regarded them as a temporary, though necessary, phenomenon, to be replaced eventually by better-trained doctors who would be willing to attend the poor. The question was not whether midwives should disappear but how rapidly.

The most vociferous opponents of midwives were physicians in private practice or in obstetrical specialization. They wanted midwives eliminated at once, as competitors and as obstacles to obstetric education, for the cases midwives delivered were forever lost to medical knowledge and to the purposes of instructing students. Some doctors contended that educated midwives would be aseptic rather than lethal abortionists, and therefore more women would seek them out for a criminal waste of infant life.[22]

State health authorities took a more moderate view, saying that, since midwives were not about to disappear, it was better to license and supervise them than to try and fail to eliminate them. The worst of them could be eliminated by supervision, and some could be given rudimentary training. State regulations sought, therefore, to compel the midwife to be clean, if not sterile; to know the warning symptoms of abnormal birth; to call a doctor when the warning symptoms appeared; to use no drugs; to administer silver nitrate drops; and to register the birth. Southern states used Sheppard–Towner funds to provide and enforce that kind of training for rural black midwives; they prepared manuals for midwives, stressing that the women were servants of the state who performed invaluable services in attending births.

To instill a spirit of patriotism and camaraderie in such rural midwives, public health nurses organized them into "midwives' clubs," with regular meetings, potluck suppers, instructional talks, and even a "midwives' song." The atmosphere of such meetings was designed to parallel that of a religious meeting, quite appropriate for a region in which midwifery was often considered a religious calling. Public health authorities taught the rural mid-

State departments of public health tried to regulate "granny" midwives by issuing permits. This record card is typical.

wives simple hygienic procedures but made no attempt to upgrade them into anything like professionals. Most were illiterate
and too old for elaborate schooling. The authorities expected doctors, clinics, and perhaps black nursing graduates to replace
them.[23]

Several Northern industrial states with large immigrant populations tried more ambitious social experiments in training and
regulating midwives, often with considerable success. Bellevue
Hospital in New York City began a school for midwives in 1911,
and several hospitals in New Jersey and Philadelphia did the
same. Such schools were meant for practicing midwives who had
had no formal education; they were not for "nurse-midwives."
New Jersey's high standards required a midwife to graduate from
a recognized school for midwifery. New York and Pennsylvania
required only that a midwife have attended twenty births under a
doctor's guidance.

Public health authorities believed that the Bellevue graduates
were better birth attendants than three-quarters of medical
graduates. Trained midwives in the North significantly lowered
maternal and neonatal mortality, a fact that led some public
health officers to think that such midwives might be the answer to
high mortality rates. They pointed to the example of England,
where the Midwives' Act of 1902 had upgraded midwifery and
resulted in a drop in infant mortality from 151 per 1,000 in 1901
to 106 in 1910. New Jersey's experience seemed to confirm that
the same could happen in America. Midwives were more patient
"waiters" than doctors and did less harm because they were less
hurried. The midwife was the better candidate in normal births to
"sit by the bedside until nature takes its course."[24]

Opponents of the Northern experiments challenged the statistics of success, saying that it was unfair to compare the normal
cases attended by midwives to the difficult cases often handled by
doctors. That argument was essentially false, however, for the
statistics were actually biased against the midwife, attributing any
death to her even if a doctor had also attended the delivery. The
New York Academy of Medicine's study of 1930 followed the
same method of attribution, yet found that midwives had a maternal mortality rate of 1.4 per 1,000 while general practitioners
had a rate of 2.5.

By the 1930s, statistics about midwifery were largely irrelevant, however, for the Northern urban midwife was disappearing.

Doctors noted with pleasure that the restriction of immigration in 1919 had prevented new midwives from arriving. While some doctors continued to attack midwives as "relics of the barbaric past," other doctors could look upon their dwindling ranks somewhat wistfully:

> In many instances poorly trained, always inadequately supervised, the object of only faintly disguised and often open antagonism, lack of cooperation, and contempt, the midwife still attends... deliveries... with as good results for both mothers and babies as physicians under similar circumstances. We believe she has proved her value.[25]

Magazines also treated immigrant midwives as curious anachronisms, repeating horror stories replete with racial and ethnic slurs about "rat pie among black midwives" or deformed babies allegedly delivered by Italian or Russian Jewish midwives. Photographs of such older women, attired in the shapeless black clothes frequently worn by European widows, contrasted sharply with the pictures and advertisements showing fashionable women. One article captioned the picture of an elderly black midwife: "A former slave, 98 years old, still actively engages in the work of mid-

Doctors' campaigns against midwives played on ethnic and racial prejudice. The captions of these widely distributed photographs read as follows: "A typical Italian midwife practicing in one of our cities. They bring with them filthy customs and practices.... A 'granny' of the far South. Ignorant and superstitious, a survival of the 'magic doctors' of the West Coast of Africa.... Surely, it might have been this woman of Irish-American parentage who is quoted as having said: 'I am too old to clean, too weak to wash, too blind to sew; but, thank God, I can still put my neighbors to bed.'"

wifery! A direct transplantation into a progressive American city of African voodooism!"[26]

The daughters of immigrants, and even some first-generation women, sought delivery by doctors because it was the American custom. Doctors were gratified at how quickly these women abandoned old-country midwives, overcame their reluctance about male doctors, and flocked to the maternity clinics of city hospitals. Southern blacks migrating to Northern cities did the same. Few second-generation immigrant women became midwives, for better-paying jobs were available, and many states ceased to license midwives after immigration ended. Americanization made midwifery obsolete.

A new and uniquely American practitioner appeared in the 1930s, however: the nurse-midwife, who emerged from the tradition of professional nursing rather than from the tradition of independent midwifery. Nurse-midwives evolved from the activities of two quite different organizations that sought to provide maternity care. The first was the Maternity Center Association (MCA) of New York, founded in 1918 to provide prenatal care in poor neighborhoods and education for mothers. In 1932 the MCA began to train qualified public health nurses in midwifery; the nurses supervised the remaining immigrant midwives and also delivered babies among the urban poor and the rural poor in a MCA rural project. Eventually, after hospital clinics provided prenatal care and delivery services, MCA merged with Kings County Hospital, Brooklyn, in 1958, where nurse-midwives continue today to deliver a significant percentage of clinic patients.[27]

The second organization to foster nurse-midwifery was the Frontier Nursing Service of Hayden, Kentucky, founded by Mary Breckinridge in 1925. Breckinridge was a nurse who had cared for children in devastated postwar France, and she deliberatedly chose, upon her return to America, to work in a remote area of Appalachia, accessible only on horseback, where no doctor or trained midwife practiced. She had acquired midwife's training in England and, until World War II, brought a number of trained English midwives to America or sent Americans to England for training. Only after the war began did the Frontier Nursing Service begin to train its own nurse-midwives. What Breckinridge had originally envisaged as a network of philanthropic services throughout remote areas did not develop, for new roads made access to centralized hospitals possible. Now FNS uses centralized hospitals for delivery, though nurse-midwives retain control of normal births.[28]

Nurse-midwifery filled a gap in American medical care, where patients could not pay for doctors and federal and state health funds were inadequate to do so. This gap became especially apparent from 1930 to 1934, after the repeal of the Sheppard–Towner Act. The nurse-midwife was always intended to serve the poor and not to compete with doctors in attending the middle class; thus she became an adjunct of public health, serving in hospital clinics or rural maternity-care centers. In 1973 the number of nurse-midwives in the United States was estimated at 1,300, mostly in the eastern half of the country, and they attended an estimated total of 4,000 births out of the 3,136,965 that took place that year. The number of nurse-midwives was very small when compared with 20,500 obstetricians and 366,400 physicians as a whole. Nurse-midwives were also outnumbered by the 2,900 licensed lay midwives, clustered in Texas, Alabama, Mississippi, and other Southern states, who delivered 23,024 (0.6 percent) of the babies born in 1969, the last year for which figures are available.

In 1975 twenty-two states and the District of Columbia had licensing laws for lay midwives, and several others issued "permits to practice" in an effort to keep midwives under control. In all those states nurse-midwives functioned under the lay midwife licensing laws. Eleven other states had separate licensure laws or statutory provisions for nurse-midwives. These were Florida, Kentucky, New Mexico, New York, Ohio, Pennsylvania, Utah, Indiana, Louisiana, Maryland, and New Jersey, plus the Virgin Islands and Puerto Rico. According to a self-definition by the American College of Nurse Midwives, "the American nurse-midwife always functions within the framework of a medically directed health service. She is never an independent practitioner."[29] Usually she is affiliated with a hospital or public health service, and her employer's regulations may prevent her from doing home deliveries.

In some other industrialized nations the balance between midwives and obstetricians is very different. In Switzerland in 1961 there were 1,682 professional midwives, no lay midwives, and only 284 obstetricians. In England and Wales there were 17,370 professional midwives (21 per 1,000 births), no lay midwives, 513 obstetricians (0.62 per 1,000 births), and 53,000 other doctors (64.2 per 1,000 births).[30] Thus, even though most births in England now occur in hospitals, the relative proportions of midwives and obstetricians has led to the retention of midwife delivery in the hospital setting. Although there is a resurgence of interest in nurse-midwifery in the United States, the ten nursing schools with nurse-midwife programs graduated a total of only 85 students in 1973. In England there were more than 250 schools for professional midwives. If nurse-midwifery is to become a significant factor in the United States, the numbers will have to increase considerably.

The proportion of women physicians has remained low. In 1973 there were only 30,600 women doctors (including 3,500 inactive), about 8 percent of the total number of physicians in the United States.[31] The proportion may be even lower in obstetrics, for it is a field in which women have had special difficulty in obtaining residencies. There are economic reasons for restricting entry into the field, reasons that are becoming increasingly important as the birth rate falls. In 1973 obstetricians received the highest net income of all physicians practicing in rural areas and in metropolitan areas over 1 million in population, averaging $55,600 and $59,900, respectively. In metropolitan areas between 50,000 and 1 million in population the obstetricians' income ($53,200) was exceeded only by that of surgeons.[32]

Federal involvement in maternity care did not end with the repeal of Sheppard–Towner, though it became less visible as a public issue as it was subsumed in laws with larger health and welfare purposes. During the Depression, at the urging of the U.S. Public Health Service, a national Committee on the Costs of Medical Care, consisting of doctors and economists, was formed; it determined, among other things, that federal support of adequate maternal and child care was needed to ensure the future health of the nation. Consequently, the Social Security Act of 1935 provided grants to the states, even more generously than had Sheppard–Towner, for maternal and child health. The Children's Bureau distributed the money, but state and local authorities determined its use.[33]

The Social Security Act underwent amendments that increased the scope of activities for which Maternal and Infant Care (MIC) money was available. In 1963 funds were authorized to prevent and combat mental retardation through maternity care.

The funds encouraged demonstration projects and research, provided that state and local health authorities had determined that the women and infants involved were from low-income families, were at special risk for mental retardation, and would not otherwise receive the necessary care. One type of project qualifying for the funding was fetal heart-monitoring machines, which gave early warning of fetal oxygen deprivation during labor. In some areas today so many machines are available that nearly every clinic birth is so monitored. In other areas funds were used to provide better prenatal care and sometimes even home deliveries by nurse-midwives working in rural areas. The states who used the MIC funds for nurse-midwifery were usually Southern ones that had earlier used Sheppard–Towner funds to train black midwives. In those states provision of basic care has had first priority.

A striking demonstration project using MIC funds occurred in California in the late 1960s. Nurse-midwives made home visits to give prenatal and postpartum examinations and to instruct mothers on infant care; deliveries occurred in hospitals. The increased home care during the project caused neonatal mortality to decrease; after the project ended, prematurity jumped from 6.6 to 9.8 percent, and neonatal mortality tripled, rising from 10 to 32 per 1,000 live births.[34]

The termination of such beneficial projects points to a basic flaw in the provision of federal funds. The initiative for projects comes from state and local sources. In some states this means that the medical profession initiates projects that interest it by applying through the state health authority for federal funds. This is the pattern of practice in states that have hospital clinics and where the medical profession can argue that basic care for the poor is available. In other states the public health department itself initiates the projects using federal funds. Since 1973 all projects receive basic approval from the state health department, and the federal government simply sets funding limits. This practice of initiation and approval of projects means that there is a great variety in the care available through federal monies, not only from state to state but also among localities within the same state.

A woman who lives where a group of doctors or a local health agency has an ongoing project, whose income meets the requirements, and who satisfies the "high-risk" category of interest to the project may be the recipient of very special care. She may even fit into several special projects and receive several kinds of special care simultaneously. Investigators have found that the same woman was a subject of seven or eight different projects without being aware of it and without the awareness of the separate projects. On the other hand, the woman who lives outside any project area, whose family is slightly over the income limit, or who does not meet the category of medical interest may receive no care backed by federal funds.

Today the federal government provides larger sums for maternity care than ever before, yet the sums go for temporary, experimental programs that affect only selected populations of women. This care is not visible to most women, and it may not include basic care, which many women do not yet receive and which it was the intention of federal involvement, since Sheppard–Towner, to provide. Piecemeal care advances research and experimental medicine, but it presents women with a maze of programs in some localities, none at all in others. In Los Angeles County, for example, a woman in 1968 might have gone to a prenatal clinic established by the county health department with MIC funds, been delivered in a county hospital that had no access to her prenatal record, visited a different clinic for postpartum care, and seen a fourth clinic for family planning. If she fell into the right categories, she might also have received assistance from programs offered by the Departments of Defense; Health, Education, and Welfare; Housing and Urban Development; Agriculture; and by the Office of Economic Opportunity. She might also have received help from California's Health Care Services, and the state Departments of Mental Hygiene, Rehabilitation, and Social Welfare. On the other hand, if she were a Medicaid patient, she might have been left entirely to the private health-care system.

Given the separately funded, temporary, project-oriented pattern of using federal funds, it is not surprising that in 1968, 22 percent of the California women whose deliveries were paid for by Medicaid received no prenatal care until immediately before delivery, and that 26 percent of all women delivering at the largest hospital in Los Angeles County received no prenatal care whatever. But the point is that women in the same county, admittedly an unusual one, received markedly different amounts of federal funds, attention, and medical care in maternity because of the structure of funding.[35]

Adequate prenatal care is usually regarded as the key to reduction of neonatal and maternal mortality. Doctors estimated that in New York City in 1968, if all mothers had received early prenatal care, the neonatal death rate could have been reduced from 21.9 to 18.4 per 1,000 live births.[36] Dr. Louis Hellman, Professor of Obstetrics and Gynecology at SUNY in Brooklyn, estimated that in that year about one quarter of the pregnant women across the nation received no prenatal care at all, largely because the impersonality and bureaucratic structure of the centralized hospital clinic discouraged them from attending.[37]

More women receive prenatal care today than ever before, partly because of attempts to decentralize care through neighborhood health centers. Nevertheless, a study by the National Center for Health Statistics indicated that in 1973, the last year for available statistics, 44,000 women, or 1.5 percent of all pregnant women, received no prenatal care, and 155,000, or 5 percent, received prenatal care only in the last trimester. The percentages of black women receiving inadequate care were more than twice those of whites.[38] "Adequate" prenatal care, however, is now understood by medicine to be care beginning in the first three months of pregnancy, for the great majority of medical and socio-economic risks can be identified at this time and early preventive measures taken. By this standard, 28 percent of all American women, not just low-income women, received inadequate prenatal care.

In recent years the definition of "adequate" prenatal care came to include more than a series of visits to a doctor, for the woman's environment and diet were also considered vitally important. In line with this thinking, Congress authorized a special food-supplement program for Women, Infants and Children (WIC), to be administered by the Department of Agriculture. Like MIC, however, the program depended upon the submission of projects by local agencies or authorities and was limited to target areas and to low-income women.

Federal legislation since Sheppard–Towner has had little effect upon the needs of the middle classes. A series of proposals to provide more adequate medical care, including maternity care, was discussed from the Progressive Era until the present, but all failed largely because the medical profession opposed them. The private practice was normative for most doctors. In 1912 a Pittsburgh physician named Charles E. Ziegler, disturbed by what he considered the "commercialism" of obstetricians who charged more than lower-middle-class families could pay, set up his own maternity service, in connection with a hospital, to serve noncharity patients at reasonable fees. The county medical society suspended Ziegler in 1915 for taking patients who could pay a private physician.[39]

The repeated failure of legislation to establish national health insurance for all classes was the work of the medical profession, mostly general practitioners, who wished no interference in the private doctor–patient relation, fee-for-service treatment, and the largely unregulated and equalitarian practice of medicine, which allowed each doctor the same economic chances as every other one. Although some specialists saw that many people who were not poor were not getting adequate care, specialists, who were a minority in the profession, could not prevent medical lobbying against federal involvement in health.

Most doctors, who were poorly educated in the early decades of the century but continued to dominate medicine until the 1940s, believed that every American could (they really meant should) have a family doctor and therefore have first-class care. They believed, for instance, that every woman could have a doctor rather than a midwife, who provided, by definition, second-class care. Most doctors were unconcerned that a two-class system of maternal care was developing, that while middle- and upper-class women had doctors, other women had midwives or inferior clinic care out of necessity. They refused to believe statistics that showed higher mortality rates in the United States than in other industrialized countries. If a woman or a child died, it was a sign of the patient's ignorance or failure to seek a doctor or a hospital clinic. Blinded by their ideology of private practice as the answer to all health problems, these doctors did not think about the fact that many areas had no doctors or clinics. What medicine should be was largely a reflection of their self-interest. When the AMA's Section on Diseases of Children came out in favor of Sheppard–Towner, the specialists who were members were not allowed to go on record as dissenting from the opposition of the organization as a whole. The AMA in 1922 announced its opposition to all "state medicine," including national health-insurance proposals.[40]

In the Depression the idea of such insurance was revived, for many middle-class families were unable to pay for medical care. But AMA opposition again thwarted federal proposals for health insurance. Private insurance plans began to develop, but they unfortunately failed to provide for maternity care, paying only for complicated deliveries, such as Caesarean sections. Even today most private plans still provide only partial coverage for the costs of birth; full coverage is extremely rare. The insurance companies' philosophy is that birth is voluntary and budgetable, although many pregnancies are clearly not voluntary because of religious beliefs or the failure of contraception. Nor is maternity budgetable when a family has only seven or eight months in which to save for a birth that may cost from $1,000 to $1,500 and when insurance pays as little as $200.[41]

A closely related question, never resolved in American health care, is that of maternity leaves, paid or unpaid, and disability insurance for working women for conditions related to pregnancy and birth. Although most working women around 1900 were single or widowed, some women had to work while pregnant or return to work soon after delivery because of economic necessity. Often such women had physically demanding jobs with long hours. The Children's Bureau early recognized that maternal and infant mortality was correlated with the lack of maternity leaves and benefits or disability insurance, because the Bureau made many studies of working women's health between 1915 and 1925. Many children died from unsterile feedings, for example, because new mothers who worked could not nurse.

Some Progressives believed that states should pass laws to prevent women from working immediately before and after birth, but such laws were not enforced and made no provision for economic support. Forced but unpaid absence from work was a real economic hardship, hardly conducive to health. Moreover, a dismissed worker lost her seniority and often her job. The working mother was an anomaly that middle-class progressive society preferred to ignore. The legal system provided little help to working mothers, for it declared repeatedly that maternity took precedence over all other activities. The belief that motherhood was woman's primary mission could have been used as an argument in support of federal maternity benefits. The same belief, however, was a rationale for ignoring the plight of women who could not take time off from work to recuperate or to nurse, or who feared they would lose their jobs if they did so. Women who were both mothers and workers were not supposed to exist. They were invisible.

The one suggestion for paid maternity leaves, made by the American Association for Labor Legislation, failed to pass. The

AALL suggested in 1916 that federal law provide maternity benefits such as already existed in Northern European countries; that is, they asked that any woman who earned less than $100 a month, which meant most blue-collar women, should receive, from a fund subsidized by employer, employee, and federal government, free medical care and a cash benefit amounting to two-thirds of her wages during the two weeks before and six weeks after delivery, on condition that she abstain from work during that period.[42] Industry argued that such a plan would be too expensive and, moreover, that most women left employment once they became pregnant. Until the 1970s law and industry assumed that motherhood and work were mutually exclusive, and there were no federal or state provisions for maternity benefits for working women.

In the 1970s, however, women came to constitute half the labor force and began to challenge customs and laws that appeared to discriminate against working mothers. Unlike women of seventy years earlier, many of today's working women are married, have small children, and belong to the middle class. To these women, the situation of the woman worker who wishes to be a mother is a key area of sex discrimination.

Many employers refused to hire, or dismissed, pregnant women, claiming that work was a health hazard in pregnancy. Other employers forced pregnant women to take unpaid leaves for some period before and after delivery. But few jobs were so physically demanding that a pregnant woman had to cease working for health reasons for more than a month before and after delivery; even conservative medical opinion said that extended leaves during pregnancy were unnecessary. In some cases dismissal of pregnant women reflected the employer's opinion of what was suitable rather than what was objectively necessary for health reasons: Schoolteachers, for instance, were often thought unsuitable when pregnant.

Employers who dismissed a pregnant worker or forced her to take a leave usually maintained that she was more likely when pregnant to have an accident, but statistics did not substantiate this claim. On the other hand, if medical complications of pregnancy or of birth itself required a woman to leave her job, she could rarely obtain disability benefits or sick leave. During the 1970s women workers sought to have normal birth qualify for disability insurance, arguing that the exclusion of pregnancy and birth from sick-pay coverage violated their constitutional rights. In 1976 the Supreme Court ruled against them, but the issue is probably not closed.

The policy of most employers and insurance companies was that pregnancy and birth should not be covered by disability and sick-leave policies because they were "normal physiological functions" rather than illnesses or diseases. Union contracts frequently ignored maternity benefits for women workers, even though the wives of male workers were covered. A 1966 study of 100 health-insurance plans under collective-bargaining agreements showed that only half provided paid maternity leaves, generally six weeks, at one-half to two-thirds pay. In contrast, many other countries had private or state standards providing far more liberal benefits. A twelve-week program of paid leave applied in fifty countries, and a fourteen-week program in twenty-two others, providing from two-thirds pay to full wages and guaranteed job security if a woman returned at the end of the leave period, which in some cases could be extended, on an unpaid basis, for the care of the infant. Programs in other countries rested on the assumptions that health was the state's responsibility, that a woman's economic security was a prerequisite of her health and her family's health, and that providing medical care was only *part* of health maintenance.[43]

American women workers were caught in a situation where the federal government had no policy about health maintenance; hence they had to deal with private insurers and employers and try to get similar maternity benefits on the basis of disability or sickness.

Although there was little cause to dismiss pregnant women from jobs because of physical strain, there was a virtual ignorance of whether some jobs might be hazardous for pregnant women and their unborn children because of hidden dangers such as radiation, lead poisoning, or toxic chemicals. There was little or no occupational health research on fetal tolerance levels in toxicity. Since the fetus could be susceptible to harm even before the mother knew she was pregnant, some employers moved all women of childbearing age to jobs away from hazards but then found that such a solution could conflict with equal employment opportunity regulations. The alternative would have been to set lower tolerance levels for all workers in order to protect unborn children, but what such levels might be was unknown, and workmen's compensation did not even cover birth defects. The absence of research about dangers to unborn children and the absence of regulation indicated once again that the society preferred to assume that mother and worker were mutually exclusive social roles.[44]

The American government on federal, state, and local levels has been involved in maternity care for half a century. Many American women have remained unaware of this involvement, however, and of how it has influenced their own options for care during maternity. Whether or not a fetal heart-monitoring machine was available, or whether or not a woman might choose a midwife or even a home delivery, depended on where she lived and on what projects state and local governments and the medical profession had initiated. Whether a new baby could "room in" with the mother in the hospital often depended on the type of room she occupied and on the policies determining payment for that room. The mother's ability or willingness to breastfeed could depend upon regulations about maternity leaves from her work, and thus depended upon her employer's or her union's policies. Her baby's health could depend not only upon reducing the amount of drugs used in delivery itself but upon her exposure during pregnancy to environmental hazards at work, in industrial areas, and in consumer products. Options for care, and health itself, were not simply a matter of ability to pay. Middle-class nonworking mothers as well as working women and poor women were alike in confronting birth in terms of haphazard, piecemeal federal policies for maternity.

The need for a comprehensive policy is underscored by mortality figures for 1973. Although the maternal and neonatal death rates have been declining steadily every year, the differential between the census columns headed "White" and "Negro and other" is startling. Whereas the overall maternal death rate was 15.2 per 100,000 live births, the rate for Negro mothers (34.6) was nearly three and one half times that for white mothers (10.6).[45] According to United Nations statistics, the United States ranked behind most of the industrialized nations of Europe and Asia in this respect.[46] The overall death rate for neonates (infants under one month) stood at 13.0 per 1,000 live births, but again was significantly higher for black babies (17.9) than for white babies (11.8). The death rate of infants under one year was 17.7 per 1,000 live births overall, but was almost twice as high for blacks (26.2) as for whites (15.2). The National Center for Health Statistics ranked the United States fifteenth in the world in infant mortality, behind most nations of Europe.[47]

What accounts for the more favorable rates in those nations are comprehensive systems of health care and an emphasis on prevention. Even if the United States were immediately to institute a perfect system of health-care delivery and preventive nutritional supplements, however, the effects of long-term poverty would not be eradicated overnight. Evidence from Britain indicates that women who grew up in the Depression and were themselves malnourished as children had a significantly higher number of birth difficulties and damaged infants than did women who grew up in economically comfortable circumstances, in spite of adequate care during pregnancy.[48] Deprivation seems to have long-term physical effects extending to the next generation; if this is the case, it would take at least a generation for preventive measures instituted now to be fully effective. Some argue that the elimination of poverty would do more to promote maternal and infant health than would any specific medical programs.[49]

Women were active from the 1950s in attempts to make maternity a more meaningful and safer experience, and they most often proceeded on the assumption that the individual mother-to-be and her doctor might exert control over birth rituals. They were largely unaware of how the range of possible changes depended upon larger structures and policies influencing birth. Not until the 1970s did women begin to recognize that they needed to organize in order to change federal and state policies for health, that maternity benefits, maternity leaves, the availability of nurse-midwives, improved occupational safety, and better insurance coverage were matters that also affected the experience and safety of birth; that birth safety crossed class lines; and that measures should be taken to improve maternal and infant health for all women. Josephine Baker's slogan from the days of Sheppard–Towner came to have meaning again. "No Mother's Baby is Safe Until Every Mother's Baby is Safe."

Notes

1. Peter Gabriel Filene, *Him/Her/Self: Sex Roles in Modern America* (New York: Harcourt Brace Jovanovich, 1975), p. 46.

2. Robert H. Bremner, *From the Depths: The Discovery of Poverty in the United States* (New York: New York University Press, 1956), pp. 67–86, 204–230; *idem, Children and Youth in America: A Documentary History,* Vol. II, 1866–1932 (Cambridge, Mass: Harvard University Press, 1971), pp. 958–983; *idem, American Philanthropy* (Chicago: University of Chicago Press, 1960), pp. 89 ff.

3. Rosemary Stevens, *American Medicine and the Public Interest* (New Haven: Yale University Press, 1971), p. 200n.; Helen M. Wallace, *Health Services for Mothers and Children* (Philadelphia, 1962), pp. 5–8.

4. James Johnson, "The Role of Women in the Founding of the United States Children's Bureau," in Carol V. R. George, ed., *"Remember the Ladies": New Perspectives on Women in American History* (Syracuse: Syracuse University Press, 1975), pp. 179–196; Lillian Wald, *The House on Henry Street* (New York, 1915), pp. 163–165; Florence Kelley, "The Federal Government and the Working Children," *The Annals of the American Academy of Political and Social Sciences* 27 (1906):289–292; *White House Conference on the Care of Dependent Children* (1909), pp. 6–7; Hearings Before the Committee on Labor, House of Representatives, Sixty-Fifth Congress, on H.R. 12634, pp. 7, 9, 37, 45. See also Bremner, *Children and Youth,* 2:757–776.

5. Bremner, *Children and Youth,* 2:958–965.

6. Emma Duke, *Infant Mortality: Results of a Field Study in Johnstown, Pa.,* U.S. Children's Bureau Publication No. 9 (1915), pp. 11–15, 32–35, 53–54. See also U.S. Department of Labor, Children's Bureau, Infant Mortality Series, especially No. 6, *Infant Mortality: Results of a Field Study in Manchester, New Hampshire,* by Beatrice Sheets Duncan and Emma Duke (Washington, 1917); No. 7, *Infant Mortality: Results of a Field Study in Waterbury, Conn.,* by Estelle Hunter (Washington, 1918); No. 8; *Infant Mortality: Results of a Field Study in Brockton, Mass.,* by Mary V. Dempsey (Washington, 1919).

7. U.S. Department of Labor, Children's Bureau, *Standards of Child Welfare: A Report of the Children's Bureau Conferences, May and June 1919,* White House Conference Series, No. 1, pp. 149–155. See also Bremner, *Children and Youth,* 2:874–880.

8. Mrs. A-C-P to Julia Lathrop, Chief of the U.S. Children's Bureau, October 19, 1916, folder 634, Ethel S. Dummer papers, Schlesinger Library, Radcliffe College, quoted in Bremner, *Children and Youth,* 2:1071. See also U.S. Children's Bureau, Rural Child Welfare Series, No. 3, *Maternity Care and the Welfare of Young Children in a Homesteading County in Montana,* by Viola I. Paradise (Washington, 1919).

9. Helen M. Dart, *Maternity and Child Care in Selected Rural Areas of Mississippi*, U.S. Children's Bureau Publication No. 88 (Washington, 1921), pp. 47–50; Frances Sage Bradley and Margaretta Williamson, *Rural Children in Selected Counties of North Carolina*, U.S. Children's Bureau Rural Child Welfare Series No. 2 (Washington, 1918); J. H. Mason Knox, "Mortality and Morbidity in the Negro Infant," *Transactions of the Maryland Pediatric Society* 36 (1924):46–51; Grace L. Meigs, *Maternal Mortality in All Conditions Connected with Childbirth in the United States*, U.S. Children's Bureau Publication No. 19 (Washington, 1917), pp. 7–8, 24–27.

10. S. Josephine Baker, "Why Do Our Mothers and Babies Die?" *Ladies' Home Journal* 40 (October, 1923):212–213.

11. J. Stanley Lemons, *The Woman Citizen: Social Feminism in the 1920's* (Urbana: University of Illinois Press, 1973), pp. 153–180; Johnson, "Role of Women in Founding Children's Bureau," pp. 190–196; Bremner, *Children and Youth*, 2:1003–1025; *Congressional Record*, 67th Cong., 1st Sess. (1921), LXI, pt. 5, pp. 7932–7933; Hearings Before the Committee on Labor, House of Representatives, 65th Congress, on H.R. 12634.

12. *Congressional Record*, 67th Cong., 1st Sess. (1921), LXI, pt. 9, pp. 8759–8760, 8764–8767, quoted in Bremner, *Children and Youth*, 2:1012–1018.

13. Editorial, *Illinois Medical Journal*, 29 (1921):143.

14. Grace Abbott, "Administration of the Sheppard–Towner Act, Plans for Maternal Care," *Transactions of the American Child Hygiene Association* 13 (1922):194–201; Blanche Harris, "Effect of Antepartum Care on the Mother," *American Journal of Public Health* 20, No. 3 (March, 1930), 273–274.

15. "Government Subsidies and Maternal Health, an Editorial," *Hygeia*, March, 1932, p. 212.

16. Frances E. Kobrin, "The American Midwife Controversy: A Crisis in Professionalization," *Bulletin of the History of Medicine* 40 (1966):350–363.

17. Grace Abbott, "The Midwife in Chicago," *American Journal of Sociology* 20 (March, 1915):684–685. See also R. M. Woodbury, *Maternal Mortality: The Risk of Death in Childbirth* . . . U.S. Children's Bureau Publication No. 158 (Washington: U.S. Government Printing Office, 1926), Table 57, pp. 88–89.

18. U.S. Department of Labor, *Live Births By Race and By Person in Attendance, 1935*, Table BS-4, p. 2.

19. Louis S. Reed, *Midwives, Chiropodists and Optometrists: Their Place in Medical Care*, Publications of the Committee on the Costs of Medical Care, No. 15 (Chicago, 1932), pp. 17–19.

20. S. Josephine Baker, *Fighting for Life* (New York, 1939), pp. 112–

114; See also Elizabeth Crowell, "The Midwives of New York," *Charities* 17 (January 5, 1907):671–677; A. K. Paine, "The Midwife Problem," *Boston Medical and Surgical Journal* 173 (November 18, 1915): 760.

21. Kobrin, "American Midwife Controversy"; J. Whitridge Williams, "Medical Education and the Midwife Problem in the United States," *Journal of the American Medical Association* 58, No. 1 (Jan 6, 1912):6.

22. E. R. Hardin, "The Midwife Problem," *Southern Medical Journal* 18, No. 5 (1925):349; John Van Doren Young, "The Midwife Problem in the State of New York," *New York State Journal of Medicine* 15, No. 8 (1915):301; Linsly R. Williams, "The Position of the New York State Department of Health Relative to the Control of Midwives," *New York State Journal of Medicine* 15, No. 8 (1915):298; James L. Huntington, "The Midwife in Massachusetts: Her Anomalous Position," *Boston Medical and Surgical Journal* 168; No. 12 (March 20, 1913):418–421; A. K. Paine, "The Midwife Problem," *Boston Medical and Surgical Journal* 173 (November 18, 1915):760.

23. Mississippi State Board of Health, *Manual for Midwives*, 1925, pp. 30–31; *White House Conference on Child Health and Protection*, vol. 14, *Obstetric Education*, section 1, "Medical Service" (New York, 1932), pp. 192–194, 200–201, 206, 220.

24. Julius Levy, "Maternal Mortality and Mortality in the First Month of Life in Relation to Attendant at Birth," *American Journal of Public Health* 13 (1923):88–95; *idem*, "The Maternal and Infant Mortality in Midwifery Practice in Newark, New Jersey," *American Journal of Obstetrics* 77 (1918):41–51; Lee K. Frankel, *The Present Status of Maternal and Infant Hygiene in the United States* (New York, 1927), pp. 9–10; J. H. Mason Knox, Jr., and Haven Emerson, "Discussion," in *White House Conference*, pp. 217, 229.

25. New York Academy of Medicine, *Maternal Mortality in New York City: A Study of All Puerperal Deaths, 1930–1932* (New York, 1933), pp. 186, 211; Baker, *Fighting for Life*, pp. 114–115; Charles V. Chapin, "The Control of Midwifery," in Children's Bureau, *Standards of Child Welfare*, p. 157; "Midwives Dwindle Under Immigration Restrictions," *Journal of the American Medical Association* 93, no. 17 (Oct. 26, 1929):1317.

26. Young, "Midwife Problem in New York," p. 291; Charles E. Terry, "The Mother, the Midwife, and the Law," *Delineator* 92 (February, 1918):12–13; *idem*, "Save the Seventh Baby," *Delineator* 92 (October, 1917):15–16; Joseph B. DeLee, "Before the Baby Comes," *Delineator* 109 (October, 1926):35, 84, 86; Caroly Conant Van Blascom, "Rat Pie Among the Black Midwives," *Harper's*, February, 1930, pp. 322–327.

27. Maternity Center Association, *45th Annual Report* (New York, 1963); M. Theophane Shoemaker, "History of Nurse-Midwifery in the United States," M.S. dissertation, Catholic University of America, 1947; Josiah Macy, Jr., Foundation, *The Training and Responsibilities of the Midwife* (New York, 1967), pp. 149–160.

28. Mary Breckinridge, *Wide Neighborhoods: A Story of the Frontier Nursing Service* (New York, 1952), pp. 89–101, 111–147, 157–169, 303–323.

29. National Center for Health Statistics, *Health Resources Statistics 1974* (Washington: U.S. Department of Health, Education and Welfare, 1975), p. 193. See also pp. 194–196.

30. Joint Study Group of the International Federation of Gynaecology and Obstetrics and the International Confederation of Midwives, *Maternity Care in the World* (New York: Pergamon Press, 1966), pp. 315–320.

31. U.S. Department of Commerce, Bureau of the Census, *Statistical Abstract of the United States, 1975* (Washington: U.S. Government Printing Office, 1976), p. 63.

32. National Center for Health Services Research, *Health, United States, 1975* (Rockville, Md.: U.S. DHEW, Public Health Service, National Center for Health Statistics, 1976), p. 87.

33. U.S. Department of Labor, Children's Bureau, *Grants to States for Maternal and Child Welfare Under the Social Security Act, Title V, Parts 1, 2, 3* (Washington, 1935); *idem, Emergency Maternity and Infant Care Program* (Washington, 1943); William M. Schmidt, "The Development of Health Services for Mothers and Children in the United States," *American Journal of Public Health* 63, No. 5 (May, 1973):419–427; Joan Elizabeth Mulligan, "Three Federal Interventions on Behalf of Childbearing Women: The Sheppard–Towner Act, Emergency Maternity and Infant Care, and the Maternal and Child Health and Mental Retardation Planning Amendments of 1963," Ph.D. dissertation, University of Michigan, 1976.

34. B. S. Levy *et al.*, "Reducing Neonatal Mortality Rates with Nurse-Midwives," *American Journal of Gynecology* 109 (January, 1971):50–58. See also U.S. DHEW, Public Health Service, *The Maternity and Infant Care Projects,* (Washington, 1975); *idem, Maternal and Child Health Programs: Legislative Base* (Washington, 1975); Florence A. Wilson and Duncan Neuhauser, *Health Services in the United States* (Cambridge, Mass.: Ballinger, 1975), pp. 114–147, 185, 209.

35. Ruth Roemer, Charles Kramer, Jeanne E. Frink, *Planning Urban Health Services: From Jungle to System* (New York: Springer, 1975), pp. 63–89.

36. National Academy of Sciences, Institute of Medicine, *Infant Death: An Analysis of Maternal Risk* (Washington, 1973).

37. Louis M. Hellman, "The Midwife in the United States," in Josiah Macy, Jr., Foundation, *Training of Midwife,* p. 159.

38. National Center for Health Services Research, *Health, United States, 1975,* p. 365.

39. Charles Edward Ziegler, "The Elimination of the Midwife," *Journal of the American Medical Association* 60, No. 1 (January 4, 1913):32–38.

40. Stevens, *American Medicine and Public Interest,* pp. 143–144.

41. Daniel S. Hirshfield, *The Lost Reform: The Campaign for Compulsory Health Insurance in the United States from 1932 to 1943* (Cambridge, Mass.: Harvard University Press, 1970), pp. 88–96, 136–140; New York State Senate, Task Force on Critical Problems, *Insurance and Women* (Albany, N.Y., 1974).

42. "Maternity Insurance and Childbirth Protection," *American Labor Legislation Review* 74 (1916):1–8.

43. Erica B. Grubb and Margarita McCoy, "Love's Labors Lost: New Conceptions of Maternity Leaves," *Harvard Civil Liberties Law Review* 7 (1972):260–297; W. J. Curran, "Equal Protection of the Law: Pregnant School Teachers," *New England Journal of Medicine* 336 (1971):285.

44. U.S. DHEW, "Occupational Health Problems of Pregnant Women," by Vilma R. Hunt (Washington, 1975).

45. U.S. Department of Commerce, Bureau of the Census, *Statistical Abstract of the United States, 1975,* p. 63.

46. United Nations, *Demographic Yearbook 1974,* 26th issue (New York: 1975), pp. 342–361, 330–339.

47. National Center for Health Services Research, *Health, United States, 1975,* pp. 338, 339, 349.

48. Sir Dugald Baird, "Sociological Considerations of Maternal and Infant Capabilities," in Norman Kretchmer and Eileen G. Hasselmeyer, eds., *Horizons in Perinatal Research* (New York, 1970), p. 11.

49. Peter Isaacson, "Poverty and Health," *New Republic,* December 14, 1974, pp. 15–17.

Epilogue: The Search for the Best

WE BEGAN THIS STUDY in order to explore how America's peculiarly medicalized birth rituals developed: Why, we wondered, was birth in America, unlike birth in England and in European countries, enfolded in doctors' control at so early a date, routinely subjected to medical interventions, and enmeshed in hospital care? We strongly suspected that such extensive and regular medicalization was unnecessary, was often dangerous and dehumanizing, and was primarily the product of a long-term, relentless, and pervasive effort by doctors to control birth, to technologize, institutionalize, and ultimately denaturalize and standardize it.

Our study confirmed some of these hypotheses, but not all of them. In the course of writing and reflecting, we came to have a somewhat different perspective. While we believe that American medicine treats birth inappropriately and inadequately, we would not blame it exclusively for the dehumanized character of the experience. What is interesting about birth is that its faults point in several directions, for it reflects widely held values, and it both mirrors and reinforces our social order.

Birth in America developed in a historically unique manner, which is to say that American society and culture, not merely medical purposes, produced it. The roots of the American view of birth probably lie in seventeenth-century Protestantism, which eschewed magic and priestly intercession and placed its trust in a combination of self-help and God's Providence. By the eighteenth century this tended to become faith in practical science to improve life. American religion placed no great value upon suffering, which was regarded simply as an evil to be overcome by all possible means. Americans greatly admired instrumentalists, people who dared to attempt the impossible. Therefore, it is not surprising that women who could afford it selected doctors, with their inventive manipulative devices and drugs promising a speedier and less painful birth than could be provided by midwives, who waited patiently and sympathetically but could not abbreviate or alleviate suffering.

In England midwives continued in favor during the nineteenth century, and many of them received medical training in the early twentieth century, so that midwives continue to practice there; but most American midwives began to disappear after 1820 except among isolated, poor, and black people. American doctors, on the other hand, using midwifery as their entrance to family practice, increased in unregulated numbers and quickly spread throughout the expanding nation, while their counterparts in the more hierarchical and regulated English medical profession did not. Most American doctors opposed the training of women in medicine during the nineteenth century or in midwifery during the twentieth. That opposition succeeded because doctors and their female patients were largely of one mind in believing that the mechanisms of male midwifery were the "best buy" for safety and health.

This pattern of shared values and cooperation between women and doctors continued through many decades, despite the grumblings of a few because of offenses to modesty or autonomy, for both women and doctors found fresh reasons for intervening in birth in the interests of safety, comfort, and convenience. The move into the hospital illustrates how widespread was faith in the practical science of medicine, how cultural, social, and medical motives interacted to medicalize and institutionalize birth.

Not until the 1940s did women persistently question whether birth was so commonly pathogenic that it needed regular treatment that denied them the birth experience many of them desired. Later, feminism sharpened the questions, asking why women could not have greater responsibility for self-care. These were the first significant diversions of value from the medical consensus, and they have generated some new rituals: birth education, less anesthesia, and a willingness to humanize birth, often by allowing the presence of the husband. Yet doctors retain control of birth, and most patients are rendered powerless in the experience. While women welcome these changes, most still defer to medical judgment about medicalization and would find any other arrangement unthinkable: Women are largely eager and passive consumers of medicine, depending upon doctors, drugs, and hospitals to produce health for themselves and their children rather than depending on themselves and on the innate strength of natural processes. Most women therefore acquiesce in the view of birth as potential disease. This is of course a learned, cultural response that is widely shared by Americans in the face of threats to health or life. Most of us would willingly enslave ourselves to medicine in order to save ourselves or a family member. The natural childbirth movement has improved birth but has not altered it in any fundamental way, and it has done little to lessen the thrall of medicine and its application to birth. Even though many women know that 95 percent of births are "safe," they prefer to trust a medicated, hospitalized birth rather than themselves and natural processes, for they in fact have no experience of themselves in those processes. The women who take childbirth education classes approach their deliveries with far more anatomical and technical knowledge but with less actual experience than their uneducated forebears of the seventeenth, eighteenth, and nineteenth centuries, who had actually witnessed other women's labors and deliveries before their own time came. Studies have shown that women who have had childbirth education have more positive feelings about birth but no less anxiety than women without such education.[1] Only the multipara, the woman having her third or fourth delivery, can draw upon her own experience and relax. Much of our anxiety and the resultant willingness to become passively dependent upon medicine result from the removal of birth from direct human experience. We fear what we do not know. How many children witness birth, even at a distance? Children learn, instead, that birth is a "sickness" that requires the hospital and the doctor.

The question remains, however, whether a medicated, hospitalized birth is necessary and appropriate for most women. Those who doubt it point out that the great majority of births are healthy, safe, natural events, that good medicine can differentiate through prenatal diagnosis between the normal and the abnormal delivery, and that simple logistical rearrangements could handle the rare unexpected difficulty in delivery or in postpartum condition. Advocates of a more humane and less medicalized birth agree that premature or complicated births should occur in hospitals for the sake of the child but do not think that there is convincing scientific evidence that the mental capacity of each newborn is better protected by hospital birth. Rather, these advocates say, most births do not need all the rituals devised for them and might even be not only more humane but also safer without them.

These advocates of home birth express in the most radical fashion the dissatisfaction with medicated, hospitalized birth and the attempts to restore trust to nature and birth to a human environment. Yet the movement has raised the important question of whether the industrial model of centralization is the best model to apply to the handling of birth. The question is similar to the one raised by physical and social scientists about "small-scale technologies" in industry; these have the advantage of greater democracy, greater accessibility to community criticism, inspection, and participation. Except for "capital-intensive" industries, decentralized units of production can be as efficient as centralized units, and they allow a diversity of styles. Some people believe that decentralized birth centers could be as medically efficient, when necessary, and much more humane than large-scale, impersonal hospitals, at least for normal deliveries.

In the Fall of 1975 the Maternity Center Association of New York City, an organization that has worked since the early decades of the century to improve birth practices, opened a childbirth center that offered obstetrical and nurse-midwife care during labor and delivery in a homelike setting, which, however, had "safety equipment" at hand. The MCA experiment is something of a compromise, an attempt to overcome both the inconvenience and danger some women may feel are present in a home birth and the pathological and dehumanized orientation of the hospital. This modest experiment nonetheless created a furor among obstetricians. In January of 1976 the New York chapter of the American College of Obstetricians and Gynecologists issued a strong statement opposing out-of-hospital delivery services as unsafe for mother and child.[2]

Some women and families select home birth, with or without medical attendance, simply because it better suits their life-styles. Authorities estimate that 15 percent of the births in California occur at home. An organization centered at Chapel Hill, North Carolina, and called NAPSAC (National Association of Parents and Professionals for Safe Alternatives in Childbirth) claims that, because pregnancy and parturition are natural events, not the products of disease, and because they have profound emotional significance in the lives of families, they should be the primary

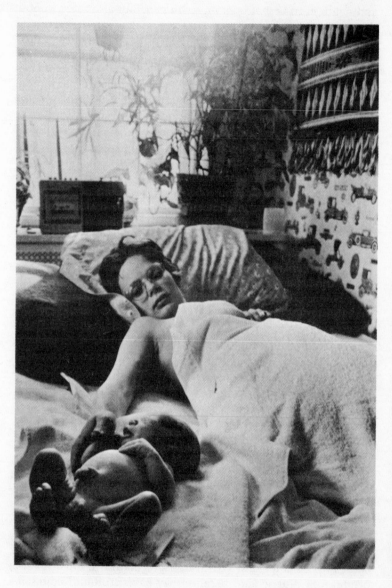

A home birth.

responsibility of families and should occur at home, although NAPSAC advocates having medically trained attendants present.[3]

The home birth question is an economically sensitive matter because the challenge comes at a time of a decreasing rather than an increasing birthrate, when maternity wards are emptier and losing money, when obstetricians are considering consolidating deliveries in regional hospitals, and when each birth, despite concessions to natural childbirth, is more thoroughly monitored by machines than ever before. Obstetricians remain deeply committed to hospital delivery for institutional, professional, economic, and safety reasons, and they recognize that out-of-hospital birth is less amenable to their fundamental purposes than was natural childbirth.

Home birth also challenges the safety of hospital birth more sharply than natural childbirth did. Should significant numbers of middle-class women and families come to believe that home birth is safer, or even as safe, the thrall of medicine and hospital birth will be seriously disrupted.

It is difficult to compare home and hospital birth, since the number of home births is small. Yet one comparative study of 1,000 home births and 1,000 hospital births among groups of women matched in race, parity (number of previous deliveries), age, and socio-economic status, all having low-risk births, reached the guarded conclusion that home birth is as safe as, if not safer than, hospital birth.[4] This study found home births generally required less anesthesia since women apparently refused it. Whether their refusal stemmed from principle, from new learned behavior, or from less tension is not clear. Less anesthesia, of course, reduces the chance of fetal damage. The home births involved fewer forceps maneuvers, such as to turn the fetus so that every child was born in the same presentation, perhaps because doctors felt less peer pressure to use them. Home births also less often employed drugs to speed up delivery. Sociologists of medicine have commented that obstetricians in hospital delivery allot a given amount of time for routine procedures because they feel obliged to manage hospital space economically.[5] Doctors may also be more dismayed by pain in the hospital.

The home births examined in the study also resulted in fewer perineal tears into the fleshy tissues, into the muscles of the vagina, and into the anus, despite the fact that the hospital births routinely involved episiotomies to prevent such tears. Why hospital births caused more tears is uncertain. Perhaps the lithotomy position itself, the use of drugs that secondarily constrict the perineum, and the patient's emotional anxiety contributed to this unexpected situation. The home births also entailed fewer post-partum hemorrhages and resulted in fewer birth injuries to children than did the hospital deliveries.

Although these surprising statistics have been gathered and presented by medical doctors, the advocates of home birth are quite guarded in their conclusions, in part no doubt because of the sensitivity of the issue, in part because of the very limited range of their sample. At any rate, they conclude that home birth is as safe as hospital birth for normal deliveries and that hospitals will nonetheless not disappear, since abnormal births must occur there. Their main point, however, is the important one: the risks of home birth have been greatly overrated.

In fact these advocates are claiming that there is less iatrogenic disease in home birth and that women would be well advised to consider home delivery. The symbol of this is the "blue baby." Doctors who have attended home births report how startled they were to see a newborn child whose hands and feet were not blue as the result of anesthesia given the mother. Perhaps, therefore, home birth produces the more perfect baby.

Those who advise home birth also claim that the value of a family-centered birth may well outweigh what risk there is for the family who chooses it. They speak of the need for maternal bonding, which is difficult in the hospital. Maternal bonding refers to the hypothesis that there exists a biologically determined emotional relationship between mother and child, formed during the first several hours after birth. Hospital birth usually separates mother and child for this period. Even "rooming in" occurs after the first few hours. They speak of the woman's need not to feel herself a patient passive observer, but rather the importance of her becoming, with her husband, primarily responsible for the event of birth.

There is much to be said for increased self-care and responsibility in the event of birth. Like other states of health and sickness, birth has been mystified by medicine, which means that people are not only ignorant about it but excessively dependent upon medicine to control it. Even physicians who do not necessarily favor home birth admit medicine's mistake in having encouraged women to trust medicine magically to rectify the results of poor eating habits and detrimental environmental effects rather than having shared more knowledge and responsibility for correcting these conditions. Many confess that medicine has been too concerned with scientific achievements in saving the rare pathological birth that might have been prevented by better education and prenatal care. Possibly the women who are interested in more decentralized, natural, and family-centered birth, and the physicians who are willing to share knowledge and responsibility may influence the larger groups of women and doctors who believe that medicalization and passive dependency are the only way for birth to happen safely. There seems to be considerable room for safe change.

Most advocates of home birth are not neglectful of safety. They believe attendants should be well-trained and screened for home births. Doctors, for example, who are trained to spot abnormality and to rely upon extensive machinery, might need additional training to attend normal home birth. Back-up equipment would be necessary in a portable form if the birth were to occur more than fifteen or twenty minutes from a hospital, for experience has shown that approximately 5 percent of women attempting home birth need to be transported to hospitals, in spite of careful screening to ensure that only "low-risk" births take place at home.

Although home birth is attracting more attention as an alternative for a small group of people who find that it suits their life styles or who believe that it affords greater safety—the more perfect baby—the dominant trend in obstetrics is in the opposite direction. Obstetricians and public health authorities are placing their faith in greater centralization of care facilities; they are closing maternity services in small hospitals in favor of large regional centers with an elaborate range of equipment and staff. Doctors attribute much of the recent decline in the neonatal death rate to the specialized neonatal care available in such centers, and believe all women should have such care at hand.

Because most women plan to have no more than two children, they are willing to forego delivery in a local hospital in favor of having the best care in a regional facility. Not only the survival, but particularly the mental health of children has become increasingly important to families. Couples are aware that the costs of caring for a defective child can be ruinous to a family and, on the other hand, they want each child of theirs to be as nearly perfect as possible in order to take its place in an achievement-oriented society that makes education and mental ability a prerequisite of social mobility. If couples are going to make the immense economic and emotional outlay necessary to have and rear children, they want "the best" for them so that they may become the best. As psychologists discover increasingly subtle forms of "minimal brain damage" in schoolchildren, damage often attributed to birth trauma, the search for the best delivery is accelerated.

Centralization of hospital birth allows doctors to attempt to eliminate all damage that may occur in birth. In practice this means more operative interventions to terminate labors that threaten to be too long or exhausting for the child. The Caesarean section, formerly an infrequent operation, now accounts for 30 to 40 percent of births in many hospitals. Doctors' rationale for this is that the operation, by preventing fetal oxygen deprivation in labor, will guarantee a better, brighter baby. If a labor deviates from the doctor's idea of what is the optimal process, many obstetricians believe there is no good reason for not operating. They tend to assume that every woman will have only two children anyway. The routine use of fetal heart monitoring machines has contributed to the increase in operations and to doctors' belief that better babies result from more sophisticated techniques. Many doctors are aware that there is a circularity to these techniques, that the need for some exists only because of the use of others, usually drugs. Nevertheless, they rationalize frequent usage of mutually necessary techniques—what they sometimes refer to as a "cascade of interventions"—on the basis that medical art now saves babies once considered hopeless. There are additional reasons, not related to safety, for intervening frequently. Doctors' training emphasizes the abnormalities of birth; the hospital environment makes intervention convenient and sometimes even requires it; and insurance companies offer financial incentives by providing higher payments for operative deliveries.

There is thus little agreement at present about the way to handle birth for the most perfect babies. Most doctors believe safety lies in a fully equipped and staffed hospital. Home birth advocates are likely to think the more perfect baby and more comfortable mother are likely to be found outside the hospital, although not necessarily outside of medical care. Some advocates of home birth, who prize being natural more than being perfect, having dropped out of the struggle for socio-economic achieve-ment, define "the best" in terms of protecting their life-style, and in order to do so are willing to take the risks of home birth.

Doctors and hospitals have responded to new patient demands for a more "natural" and "humane" delivery. In recent years one of the more interesting is Dr. Frederick Leboyer's "birth without violence," a method that uses a quiet, semi-darkened delivery room (no bright overhead lights to frighten mother and baby), and that gently immerses the newborn in a tub of lukewarm water before placing it on the mother's stomach to minimize the trauma of separation and ensure maternal bonding. Such practices are novel only in the context of the modern hospital; midwives deliv-ered babies in this way for centuries. A more typical and irrelevant hospital response has been to redecorate private and semi-private rooms with the trappings of home decor.

Basic agreement does exist, however, about what constitutes the "best" maternity care whether birth occurs at home or hospi-tal. All agree that the underlying factors in maternal and child health are a sound environment, including good nutrition, for the mother and the provision of basic prenatal and postnatal care. It is a sad comment on our medical system that while increasing amounts of money are spent on research, experimentation, and sophisticated treatments for rare and unusual births, the most basic care and the simplest preventive measures are not reaching women of all classes.

If the dominant American form of medicalized birth tells us about our values in regard to medicine, the distribution of health care tells us much about our social order. We think many advo-cates of home birth are as mistaken as most physicians in identify-ing the underlying causes of "imperfect birth." Both those who advocate increased patient responsibility and those who stress ad-vanced "crisis" technology tend to be myopic about the socio-economic and environmental causes of death in birth, which create the continuing critical problem for American birth, the reason why the United States has consistently had higher infant and maternal mortality than other industrial nations.

It is our belief that the definition of what is "best" cannot be left entirely to individual patients and their physicians, that the health of mothers and children is so critically important to our nation that it must participate in birth to ensure that every mother and child has not only the best but the minimal of care.

It is the pride of scientific medicine that its knowledge and capabilities transcend differences of race, sex, and class. This is largely true in theory, but the *practice* of medicine occurs in a social milieu and may be deeply influenced by these differences. Considerable evidence—much of it presented in this history— suggests that those women who are most in need of health care in birth do not receive it. It has been known for many years that the causes of childbirth mortality are largely resistant to sophisticated crisis medicine; these are socio-economic causes associated with being poor and nonwhite: septic abortion, malnutrition, lack of prenatal care. Those factors call for a variety of persistent preventive treatments early in pregnancy (or even earlier), and for caring skills.

Nonwhite women and poor white women are less likely to receive prenatal care than are middle-class women, who need it less because they are healthier. In municipal hospitals in large cities, about half the women have either late prenatal care or none at all, whereas in private hospitals 95 percent of the women have early prenatal care. The biggest cause of neonatal death in the first month is prematurity, measured by low birth weight. The proportion of nonwhite infants' deaths to white infants' deaths (about three to two) has remained nearly the same since 1950, despite the increased sophistication of neonatal medicine. The deaths of nonwhite mothers exceed the deaths of white mothers by 346 percent. It is nonwhite deaths that largely account for America's low standing among industrial nations.[6] Why this continues to be so is a serious matter that should concern all Americans.

In the second decade of this century the Children's Bureau recognized that poor women needed to be educated about prenatal and infant care and sought through the Sheppard–Towner Act to provide the necessary education; the medical profession resisted such federal programs for the next thirty years, arguing that greater safety would come through greater cooperation in the doctor–patient relation. While that arrangement has largely succeeded for middle- and upper-class women, it has not really reached the poor. The poor have access to doctors in hospital clinics. Many poor women do not use clinics because they must spend hours waiting for a 30-second examination, cannot reach the clinic because they work, or have no place to leave their children while visiting it. If given a diet she cannot afford, the poor woman must hassle the welfare office for additional money. Often the clinic treats her impersonally, without respect, and without patience or understanding. So while clinical care is available for the poor, the circumstances surrounding it may be so time-consuming, inconvenient, or degrading that many poor women do not bother with it. The question still exists, therefore, whether medicine can initiate of itself more imaginative and effective programs to provide the poor with minimal care in birth.

Doctors receive their training in such hospital clinics and there they are trained to treat disease, not people. Scientific medicine has decided that it is more convenient to avoid examining the behavioral and environmental problems that may generate pathology, including pathogenic births, for those problems are difficult to resolve and involve complicated social and economic matters. Doctors believe their skills are more readily exercised once the medical problems become apparent. Although this perspective may not have this purpose, it results in a continual flow of pathology for which more sophisticated crisis medicine is required. What is needed, however, is effective preventive medicine, which does relate to the social and economic origins of diseased birth. Many doctors recognize the need and have sought federal funding for experimental projects to provide better prenatal care. But such programs are scattered, short-lived, and not widely accepted by all doctors as worthwhile.

Prenatal care for the poor presents serious problems for doctors, as many are aware. Doctors usually are of a different social class, almost always a different race and sex; they have trouble understanding the patient's beliefs, background, and culture and are inadequately trained to meet poor people as people. Doctors admit to a lack of rapport even with middle-class patients in private practice; the problems of relating meaningfully to the poor are even greater. In a recent discussion, obstetricians said that

> ... prenatal care is provided in a superficial, uninterested, and hurried manner by many obstetricians. Our dietary instructions are minimal or nonexistent and we do not spend enough time with each patient, answering her questions, reassuring her, and gaining her confidence.[7]

Doctors have considered numerous means to overcome their liabilities, such as employing nurse-midwives who would engage poor women in their homes instead of clinics for prenatal care, and follow them through hospital delivery. Where such plans have been tried experimentally, mortality rates have dropped sharply.

If adequate prenatal care is to become realistically available for the urban poor, some consistent federal policy will be needed which will aggregate such successful social experiments and make them available to all. Piecemeal experiments are fine, but their proven benefits should be made as available to the poor as new crisis hardware, such as fetal monitoring devices. Many commentators believe that more than prenatal care is required to correct dietary inadequacies, irregular pelves, and blood-pressure abnormalities, all of which contribute to birth disease. They think a program to improve the general health of potential mothers will be needed. A small start has been made to provide nutritional aid, but this federal program has also been small, scattered, and sporadically funded.

We believe that every woman has the right to the "best," that the health of mothers and children is so fundamentally important for the whole society that the federal government should pay for the "best" even if it pays for nothing else. The cornerstone of any national health insurance program should be an imaginative and thorough prenatal and maternity program. The greatest potential returns to society will come through the prevention rather than the long-term treatment of conditions that begin before or during birth. As the original proponents of Sheppard–Towner proposed, maternity care should be the right of every woman and child.

We believe that this matter cannot be left any longer to the "patient and her private physician," since that ideal does not describe the medical reality for many women, and since medicine has shown that it cannot find the means to distribute basic care to all women.

A detailed policy proposal is beyond our purpose, but we can point to several social programs that might become part of a national responsibility for maternal and child health: encouragement of nurse-midwifery, capitation payments for each woman, maternity leaves, child care. We think it important to stress also that the possibility that a birth may be pathological should not make birth any less a responsibility of parents, but a matter about which they have an important role to play. There is no good reason why centralization of maternity facilities cannot co-exist with home birth, why people cannot have a range of choices for low-risk deliveries, why an adequate medical system can not provide regular emergency transport facilities.

We believe there is still room for the intentions of third parties between "the privie works of God . . . and the prickes of nature," and not only the intentions of parents and physicians. Birth is a political, economic, and cultural concern for all citizens. Class divisions in health care and in the safety of birth reflect our social order only too well, and they also reinforce those differences and contribute to the social disorders that disturb us. To be underprivileged at birth is a terrible fate for individuals and for the society in which they are born.

Notes

1. Melvin Zax, Arnold Sameroff, and Janet E. Farnum, "Childbirth Education, Maternal Attitudes, and Delivery," *American Journal of Obstetrics and Gynecology* 123, No. 2 (September 15, 1975):185–190; Rosalyn L. Barclay and Mel L. Barclay, "Aspects of the Normal Psychology of Pregnancy: The Mid Trimester," *ibid.*, 125, No. 2 (May 15, 1976):210.

2. American College of Obstetricians and Gynecologists, District II (New York State), "Position Paper on Out-of-Hospital Maternity Care, Adopted January, 1976," *International Childbirth Education Association News* 15, No. 1 (1976):2–3.

3. David Stewart and Lee Stewart, eds., *Safe Alternatives in Childbirth* (Chapel Hill, N.C.: NAPSAC, 1976).

4. Lewis E. Mehl, M.D., *et al.*, "Home Birth Versus Hospital Birth: Comparisons of Outcomes of Matched Populations," paper presented at 104th annual meeting, American Public Health Association, Miami Beach, Florida, October 20, 1976.

5. William R. Rosengren and Spencer DeVault, "The Sociology of Time and Space in an Obstetrical Hospital," in Eliot Friedson, ed., *The Hospital in Modern Society* (New York: Free Press, 1963), pp. 266–292.

6. The death rate for nonwhite infants under one year of age is 26.2 per 1,000 live births and for white infants 15.2. The mortality rate for neonates (under one month) is 17.9 for nonwhites and 11.8 for whites per 1,000 live births. The maternal death rate is figured on a basis of 100,000 births. The rate for Negro and other nonwhites is 34.6; for whites it is 10.6. United States Department of Commerce,

Bureau of Census, *Statistical Abstract of the United States, 1975,* page 63. The figures are for 1973.

7. David M. Burkons and J. Robert Willson, "Is the Obstetrician-Gynecologist a Specialist or Primary Physician to Women?" *American Journal of Obstetrics and Gynecology* 121, No. 6 (March 15, 1975):810.

Bibliography

The following bibliography offers a selection of works that illuminate various aspects of childbirth.

Histories of Birth and Obstetrics

Two generally reliable popular histories of obstetrics and gynecology in the Western world are Harvey Graham, *Eternal Eve: A History of Gynaecology and Obstetrics* (Garden City, N.Y.: Doubleday, 1951), and Palmer Findlay, *Priests of Lucina: The Story of Obstetrics* (Boston, 1939). Among the more scholarly histories are those by Irving S. Cutter and Henry R. Viets, *A Short History of Midwifery* (Philadelphia: Saunders, 1964), and Theodore Cianfrani, *A Short History of Obstetrics* (Springfield, Ill.: Charles C. Thomas, 1960). Herbert Thoms has written several concise and excellent books, including *Chapters in American Obstetrics* (Springfield, Ill.: Thomas, 1933), *Classical Contributions to Obstetrics and Gynecology* (Springfield, Ill.: Thomas, 1935), and *Our Obstetric Heritage* (Hamden, Conn.: Shoestring Press, 1960). Walter Radcliffe, *Milestones in Midwifery* (Bristol, Eng., 1967), discusses the English and French beginnings of obstetrics. James Hobson Aveling, *English Midwives, Their History and Prospects* (London, 1872), presents a detailed inspection of English midwifery. Harold Speert has catalogued major advances in obstetrical science in *Obstetric and Gynecologic Milestones: Essays in Eponymy* (New York: Macmillan, 1958) and has gathered graphic illustrations of historical practices in *Iconographia Gyniatrica: A Pictorial History of Gynecology and Obstetrics* (Philadelphia: F. A. Davis, 1973).

Popular Manuals of Advice

The earliest birth manual in English was *The Byrth of Mankind, otherwyse named the womans booke* (sic), translated from the *Frauen Rosegarten* of Eucharius Roesslin and published in London in 1540 by Thomas Raynalde and reprinted in numerous editions until 1626. It was a "protestant" document in the sense of being virtually free of magical suggestion. Nicholas Culpeper's *Directory for Midwives* (London, 1653 to 1777) included sympathetic magic and astrology among the aids to birth. *Aristotle's Compleat Midwife,* "made English by W.S., M.D." (London, 1684–1831), included many of Culpeper's magical prescriptions as well as palmistry. This sex-and-marriage manual enjoyed wide circulation in America after the first New England edition of 1809, and the entire volume was often known as *Aristotle's Masterpiece.*

These manuals included the belief that conception occurred immediately after menses. See, for example, Thomas Bull, *Hints to Mothers* (New York, 1842), p. 123. This view persisted concurrently with the scientific view that conception occurred in the middle of the menstrual cycle. See *London Medical Gazette,* July, 1849.

There were many popular manuals for prospective mothers written by doctors during the Victorian period. One of the most representative and widely circulated was Frederick Hollick, *Matron's Manual of Midwifery* (Boston, 1848). Later in the century several manuals with a somewhat feminist emphasis were written by women physicians. The most notable was Alice B. Stockham's *Tokology: A Book for Every Woman* (Chicago, 1885). Other manuals promoted methods of escaping pain; these included M. L. Holbrook, *Parturition Without Pain: A Code of Directions for Escaping the Primal Curse* (New York, 1891). Both Holbrook and Stockham endorsed family limitation.

Religion and Magic

Thomas Rogers Forbes, *The Midwife and the Witch* (New Haven: Yale University Press, 1966), gives a picture of the often bizarre cultural aspects of birth in seventeenth-century England; these practices were not typical in America. His account must be set in a broader contextual understanding, however; Keith Thomas, *Religion and the Decline of Magic* (London: Oxford University Press, 1972), is a magisterial account of religious belief and magical practices with many references to birth in seventeenth-century England.

The idea of "marking the child" had a long reign in America. See George H. Naphys, *The Physical Life of Woman* (Philadelphia, 1880), p. 169; O. S. Fowler, *Maternity* (New York, 1868), pp. 90–99. For twentieth-century survivals of folklore see Eliot Wigginton

(ed.), *Foxfire 2* (Garden City, New York: Doubleday, 1973), and
Marie Campbell, *Folks Do Get Born* (New York, 1946).

The Puritan religious attitude toward birth is best expressed in
Cotton Mather's sermon, *Elizabeth in Her Holy Retirement* (Boston,
1710), which also appears as "Retired Elizabeth" in *The Angel of
Bethesda,* Gordon Jones, ed. (Barre, Vt.: Antiquarian Society,
1972). One expression of a twentieth-century Protestant view is
Helen Wessel, *Natural Childbirth and the Christian Family* (New
York, 1963), which advocated the Dick-Read method.

Demography, Vital Statistics

The reasons for the incompleteness of vital statistics before the
twentieth century is the subject of James H. Cassedy, *Demography
in Early America: Beginnings of the Statistical Mind, 1600–1800*
(Cambridge, Mass.: Harvard University Press, 1969). See also his
article, "The Registration Area and American Vital Statistics: Development of a Health Research Resource, 1835–1915," *Bulletin of
the History of Medicine (BHM)* 39 (May–June, 1965):221–232. Also
very useful is John B. Blake, "The Early History of Vital Statistics
in Massachusetts," *BHM* 29 (January–February, 1955):46–98. Historians of colonial demography are mentioned in the opening
chapter. A basic source on the development of modern birth registration is Robert H. Bremner, *Children and Youth in America: A
Documentary History, Vol. II, 1866–1932* and *Vol. III, 1933–1973*
(Cambridge, Mass.: Harvard University Press, 1970–1974). These
volumes include primary sources on public health funding for
maternal and infant health and on the establishment of the Children's Bureau. For a recent discussion of federal involvement, see
Joan Elizabeth Mulligan, "Three Federal Interventions on Behalf
of Childbearing Women: The Sheppard–Towner Act, Emergency
Maternity and Infant Care, and the Maternal and Child Health
and Mental Retardation Planning Amendments of 1963" (Ph.D.
dissertation, University of Michigan), Spring 1976.

For a study of trends in maternal and infant mortality since
World War II, see Sam Shapiro, Edward R. Schlesinger, and
Robert E. L. Nesbitt, *Infant, Perinatal, Maternal and Childhood
Mortality in the United States* (Cambridge, Mass.: Harvard Univer-
sity Press, 1968).

Professionalism in Medicine and Birth Attendance

Jane Donegan, "Midwifery in America, 1760–1860: A Study in Medicine and Morality" (Ph.D. Dissertation, Syracuse University, 1972), provides the best account of attitudes toward and conflicts between male and female attendants at birth. John Blake, "Women and Medicine in Ante-Bellum America," *BHM* 39 (March–April, 1965), provides a wider view of the social and medical context of conflict. Joseph F. Kett, *The Formation of the American Medical Profession: The Role of Institutions, 1780–1860* (New Haven: Yale University Press, 1968), is a scholarly account of professional development. Further information about women practitioners and medicine, and about the medical sectarians, appears in Richard H. Shryock, *Medicine and Society in America, 1660–1860* (Ithaca, N. Y.: Cornell University Press, 1962); Rosemary Stevens, *American Medicine and the Public Interest* (New Haven: Yale University Press, 1971); and William G. Rothstein, *American Physicians in the Nineteenth Century: From Sects to Science* (Baltimore: Johns Hopkins Press, 1970). For a discussion of organized medicine in the twentieth century, see Daniel S. Hirshfield, *The Lost Reform* (Cambridge, Mass.: Harvard University Press, 1970). An excellent history of an early maternity hospital is Harold Speert, *The Sloane Hospital Chronicle* (Philadelphia, F. A. Davis, 1963). Frederick C. Irving, *Safe Deliverance* (Boston, 1943), is a history of the Boston Lying-in Hospital in the nineteenth century.

The diaries and autobiographies of birth attendants shed light on the medical practices of the times. The best example of a midwife's diary in print is found in Charles Eventon Nash, *The History of Augusta, Including the Diary of Mrs. Martha Moore Ballard (1785–1812)* (Augusta, Me., 1904), pp. 229–464. J. Marion Sims, *The Story of My Life* (New York, 1888), is the autobiography of an eminent gynecologist who shared the prevalent nineteenth-century attitudes toward women. S. Josephine Baker, *Fighting for Life* (New York, 1939), is the autobiography of a famous New York public health physician and her work in improving standards of maternity and infant care in the slums. Also of interest is Mary Breckinridge's autobiography, *Wide Neighborhoods: A Story of the Frontier Nursing Service* (New York, 1952), which relates in personal form the beginnings of nurse-midwifery.

Some works on the medical education of women in the

nineteenth century include Elizabeth Blackwell, "Address on the Medical Education of Women" (New York, 1856); Harriot Kezia Hunt, *Glances and Glimpses* (Boston, 1856), which is the autobiography of a woman practitioner who was refused by Harvard; Frederick Waite, *History of the New England Female Medical College, 1848-1874* (Boston, 1950); Gulielma Fell Alsop, *History of the Woman's Medical College, Philadelphia, 1850-1950* (Philadelphia, 1950); and Esther Pohl Lovejoy, *Women Doctors of the World* (New York: Macmillan, 1957). The most recent history of women's exclusion from the American medical profession is Mary Roth Walsh, *"Doctors Wanted; No Women Need Apply": Sexual Barriers in the Medical Profession, 1835-1975* (New Haven: Yale University Press, 1977).

The best summary of the relation between the medical profession and twentieth-century immigrant and rural midwives is Frances E. Kobrin, "The American Midwife Controversy: A Crisis in Professionalization," *BHM* 40 (1966):350-363.

Medical Attitudes Toward Women

A comprehensive historical account of nineteenth-century medical attitudes is Carroll Smith–Rosenberg and Charles Rosenberg, "The Female Animal: Medical and Biological Views of Woman and Her Role in Nineteenth-Century America," *Journal of American History* 60 (September, 1973):332-356. For a description of treatments of women's illnesses, with a psychoanalytic interpretation, see Ann Douglas Wood, "'The Fashionable Diseases': Women's Complaints and Their Treatment in Nineteenth-Century America," and the response by Regina Morantz, "The Lady and Her Physician," both in Mary Hartman and Lois W. Banner, *Clio's Consciousness Raised* (New York: Harper & Row, 1974). For a classic description of cultural attitudes toward women, see Barbara Welter, "The Cult of True Womanhood, 1820–1860," *American Quarterly* 18, No. 2 (1966):151–174. A famous obstetrical lecture reflecting these views was Charles D. Meigs, "Lecture on the Distinctive Characteristics of the Female," in *Females and Their Diseases: A Series of Letters to His Class* (Philadelphia, 1848). Other instances of the influence of these views about women upon medical literature are found in Anonymous [Walter Channing or John Ware], *Remarks on the Employment of Females as Practitioners in Midwifery* (Boston, 1820), an antimidwife tract, and in Edward H.

Clarke, *Sex in Education: A Fair Chance for Girls* (Boston, 1873), a treatise on the deleterious effects of brain-work upon the female constitution. Azel Ames, *Sex in Industry* (Boston, 1874), is a corollary report on the dangers of work for potential mothers. A summary of medical attitudes toward women is found in John S. Haller and Robin M. Haller, *The Physician and Sexuality in Victorian America* (Urbana: University of Illinois Press, 1974).

Barbara Ehrenreich and Deirdre English have written concise and polemical histories of women's health, *Complaints and Disorders: The Sexual Politics of Sickness*, and of women healers throughout Western history, *Witches, Midwives and Nurses* (both Old Westbury, N.Y.: Feminist Press, 1973), arguing that men's control of medicine has played a key role in the oppression of women.

A very interesting sociological exmination of twentieth-century medical views is Diane Scully and Pauline Bart, "A Funny Thing Happened on the Way to the Orifice: Women in Gynecology Textbooks," *American Journal of Sociology*, January, 1973. See also Joan P. Emerson, "Behavior in Private Places: Sustaining Definitions of Realities in Gynecological Examinations," *Recent Sociology No. 2: Patterns of Communicative Behavior*, Hans Peter Dreitzel, ed. (New York, 1970).

Birth Control

The most important histories relating to birth control are David M. Kennedy, *Birth Control in America: The Career of Margaret Sanger* (New Haven: Yale University Press, 1970), and James W. Reed, *Private Vice to Public Virtue: The Birth Control Movement and American Society, 1830–1975* (New York: Basic Books, forthcoming).

Recent Comparative Studies of Childbirth

Doris Haire, *The Cultural Warping of Childbirth* (Hillside, N.J.: International Childbirth Education Association, 1972), provides important information about birth practices in other industrial and nonindustrial countries. Suzanne Arms, *Immaculate Deception: A New Look at Women and Childbirth in America* (Boston: Houghton-Mifflin, 1975), bases its critique of American birth practices on comparisons with England, Denmark, and the Netherlands. The

Josiah Macy, Jr., Foundation has published the proceedings of a conference of midwives from all over the world, *Macy Conference on the Training and Responsibilities of the Midwife* (New York, 1967), and of a conference of American midwives, *The Midwife in the United States* (New York, 1968). The atlas with the most comparative statistical information on the location of birth and birth attendant was produced by the Joint Study Group of the International Federation of Gynaecology and Obstetrics and the International Confederation of Midwives, entitled *Maternity Care in the World: International Survey of Midwifery Practice and Training* (New York: Pergamon Press, 1966).

Anthropological comparisons, including a summary of the information in the Human Relations Area Files, may be found in Margaret Mead and Niles Newton, "Cultural Patterning of Perinatal Behavior," in Stephen A. Richardson and Alan Guttmacher, eds., *Childbearing: Its Social and Psychological Aspects* (Baltimore: Williams & Wilkins, 1967), pp. 142–244.

Nancy Stoller Shaw, *Forced Labor: Maternity Care in the United States* (New York: Pergamon Press, 1974), is the best sociological study of hospital maternity practice during the late 1960s. See also William R. Rosengren and Spencer DeVault, "The Sociology of Time and Space in an Obstetrical Hospital," in Eliot Friedson (ed.), *The Hospital in Modern Society* (New York: Free Press, 1963).

Literature supporting home birth has become more extensive in recent years. Perhaps the most representative work is David Stewart and Lee Stewart, eds., *Safe Alternatives in Childbirth* (Chapel Hill, N.C.: National Association of Parents and Professionals for Safe Alternatives in Childbirth, 1976). The article by Lewis E. Mehl, M.D., on "Statistical Outcomes of Homebirths in the United States: Current Status," is of particular interest, as is his paper, "Home Birth Versus Hospital Birth: Comparisons of Outcomes of Matched Populations," presented at the American Public Health Association, 104th Annual Meeting, Miami Beach, Florida, October 20, 1976.

Finally, there are two recent books that criticize, from different points of view, the current emphasis upon disease care rather than health care. These are Victor R. Fuchs, *Who Shall Live? Health, Economics, and Social Change* (New York: Basic Books, 1975), and Ivan Illich, *Medical Nemesis* (New York: Pantheon Books, 1976).

Index